Sacred Languages of the World

Sacred Languages of the World

An Introduction

Brian P. Bennett

WILEY

This edition first published 2018

Registered Offices
John Wiley & Sons Ltd, The Atrium, Southern Gate, Chichester, West Sussex, PO19 8SQ, UK

Editorial Office
9600 Garsington Road, Oxford, OX4 2DQ, UK

For details of our global editorial offices, customer services, and more information about Wiley products visit us at www.wiley.com.

Wiley also publishes its books in a variety of electronic formats and by print-on-demand. Some content that appears in standard print versions of this book may not be available in other formats.

Library of Congress Cataloging-in-Publication Data

Names: Bennett, Brian P, author.
Title: Sacred languages of the world : an introduction / Brian P. Bennett.
Description: 1 | Hoboken, NJ : Wiley, 2017. | Includes index.
Identifiers: LCCN 2017010480 (print) | LCCN 2017031228 (ebook) |
ISBN 9781118970751 (pdf) | ISBN 9781118970768 (epub) |
ISBN 9781118970782 (hardback) | ISBN 9781118970775 (paper)
Subjects: LCSH: Language and languages–Religious aspects–History. |
Language and languages–Social aspects–History. | Sociolinguistics. |
Comparative linguistics. | BISAC: RELIGION / Comparative Religion.
Classification: LCC P53.76 (ebook) | LCC P53.76 .B36 2017 (print) |
DDC 401/.47–dc23
LC record available at https://lccn.loc.gov/2017010480

Cover Image: (Hebrew Alphabet) Blue Circle by Tsilli Pines
Cover Design: Wiley

Set in 10/12.5pt Galliard by SPi Global, Pondicherry, India
Printed and bound in Malaysia by Vivar Printing Sdn Bhd
10 9 8 7 6 5 4 3 2 1

Contents

Preface

What are the most important languages in the world? The answer depends in part on one's location:

> The relative importance of … languages currently alternates during the course of each day. When the sun is over the western Pacific, the national language of China is the most in use, but when the sun is over the Atlantic and China sleeps, English takes the lead. The world's second most spoken language also alternates daily, between Hindi + Urdu and Spanish respectively. (Dalby 2001, 24)

Yet other languages, ancient consecrated codes, which can still be seen and heard across the globe, also merit consideration. Five times a day, millions of Muslims stop what they are doing, face Mecca, and recite their prayers in Classical Arabic, the language of the Qur'an. Buddhist monks in the Theravada tradition rise at the crack of dawn and begin a chanting session in Pali, said to be the language of Gautama Buddha himself, who lived 2500 years ago. *Scriptores* in Vatican City work on translating the pope's words into Latin. Russian Orthodox priests from Moscow to Bellingshausen Station in Antarctica celebrate the liturgy in Church Slavonic. Ultra-Orthodox Jews utter blessings in Hebrew throughout the day, while at the other end of the ideological spectrum so-called Jubus (Jewish Buddhists) meditate using Hebraic mantras. Coptic Christians in Egypt and the diaspora sing hymns in a language that can be traced back some five millennia to the time of the pharaohs. In gyms and studios across America, practitioners try to master Sanskrit names for yoga poses at the same time as enthusiasts in India trumpet Sanskrit as a symbol of the nation's spiritual and technological prowess. When the sun rises the next day, it happens all over again.

Around the world, in temples, monasteries, synagogues, and mosques – but also in tattoo studios and concert halls – people interact with these allegedly dead languages in a variety of ways and for a host of different reasons. These are not the major languages that confidently bestride the globe, though some of them did so in their heyday. Rather, these are conserved languages, precious symbolic resources, utilized for scriptures, rituals, chants, and amulets. Ancient? Yes. Dead? No. In fact, many devotees would insist that *these* are truly the most significant languages in the world.

This book offers a kind of guided tour of these sacred languages and locales. Drawing upon the academic disciplines of comparative religion and sociolinguistics, it is neither a narrow treatise in linguistics nor a comprehensive global history (see, for example, Ostler 2005). We are interested in the "outside," not the "inside," of sacred languages. That is to say, instead of focusing on the nuts and bolts of the language (grammar, morphology, phonology, etc.), we will be looking at languages as a social and religious phenomenon. Though sacred languages are typically used for worship and scripture, this is not the place to find a rundown of all the rituals and canons of Judaism, Islam, Buddhism, and so on, as there are plenty of handbooks and websites that provide such information. Instead, we are interested in the following questions:

Why do some religions conserve these ancient languages? What mythic conceptions exalt them above regular vernaculars?

How are sacred languages used? And if adherents do not actually understand what they read or chant, what is the point?

Since no one grows up speaking Latin or Pali or the rest, how do people actually go about learning a sacred language?

Why is it that sacred languages seem uniquely qualified to foster a sense of collective identity – yet also be so divisive?

Finally, what place do these hallowed languages have at a time of rapid cultural change, globalization, and fundamentalism?

Despite the fact that sacred languages are still vital to different branches of Judaism, Hinduism, Islam, Buddhism, Christianity, and Zoroastrianism, the phenomenon is not particularly well understood. Excellent histories penned by experts are available for individual languages – Arabic, Hebrew, Sanskrit, and especially Latin (e.g., Versteegh 2014; Spolsky 2014; Pollock 2006; Leonhardt 2013). But those admirable studies tend to focus on the ancient and medieval periods, giving the impression that the recent history of sacred languages is somehow less interesting or authentic. Moreover, they provide few details about the various and sundry ways that sacred languages figure in the lives of believers. By contrast, this book is comparative in scope and is intended for those unfamiliar with the global phenomenon of sacred languages. It concentrates on recent times, tracing the myths and mysteries that surround these ancient tongues, the diverse practices they are used for, the distinctive methods employed for teaching them, and the ways they can unite – and divide – international faith communities. This is a vast terrain. Our survey is far from complete. We will not be able to see everything and many important locations (e.g., Ecclesiastical Greek, Classical Tibetan) have been left off the itinerary altogether.

Instead of simply describing the sacred languages in serial fashion (Hebrew, Latin, Sanskrit, and so on), we take a more structural and thematic approach. With the exception of the first, each chapter starts with one sacred language to illustrate a particular aspect of the phenomenon, but is broadly comparative in approach, noting various points of similarity and difference between the specimens. This strategy makes it possible to learn something about the individual languages while at the same time to acquire a conceptual framework that can be applied to other examples and help guide further research and investigation. Chapter 1 discusses what makes a sacred language, and considers alternative classifications, such as dead or classical. Chapter 2 looks at Arabic – to many, the sacred language par excellence – as a way to sketch the emergence of sacred languages in world history and locate their current position in the "linguasphere," the network of languages that encircles the planet. In Chapter 3 we lay out our conceptual framework for sacred languages and introduce Ecclesiastical Latin as a test case. This framework starts with four main factors or components: beliefs, practices, institutions, and communities. Based on the example of Latin, we also argue that sacred languages should be considered fixed or conserved, not dead or extinct. The next four chapters zoom in to explore in more detail the four components, while also adding further distinctions and sub-types. The case of Pali, a Buddhist language, illustrates the myths and beliefs that accompany sacred languages. Following that, Hebrew showcases the surprising range of practices – not only religious, but political and artistic – that a single sacred language can be deployed for. Coptic leads off our discussion of why and how people learn these ancient idioms. Next the example of Church Slavonic demonstrates the fact that sacred languages can provide an essential fizz to social chemistry, but can also be combustible. Chapter 8 zooms back out to consider the role of sacred languages in relation to fundamentalism and globalization: Sanskrit provides a telling instance of these opposing trends. In the Conclusion we distill the key features of sacred languages in the contemporary world and ponder their fate in cyberspace.

Since it can be difficult for non-specialists to observe or get information about how sacred languages are actually used by contemporary religious practitioners, each chapter includes a vignette of a particular language "in action," from well-known locales like London, Rome, Moscow, Jerusalem, and Hong Kong, to less familiar ones such as Fort Ross, California, and North Tonawanda, New York. These tableaux provide entry points for discussing different facets of the phenomenon, as well as helping to convey something of the ongoing global significance of sacred languages.

Michael Pye reminds us that, "any attempts to view religions in their plurality, in a conspectual frame of reference, involve the intellectual act of comparison" (2013, 350). Each sacred language discussed in this book has its own complex backstory and is embedded in specific places, people, practices, polemics, and paraphernalia. While remaining cognizant of history and cultural context, a comparative approach involves isolating and foregrounding certain aspects for consideration, while leaving everything else in the background. Such an artificial procedure necessarily involves a difference of perspective – even a certain tension – between the "committed insider and the observing comparativist" (Paden 2009, 236). It is important for all parties to remember that comparison is never a matter of identity: Sanskrit, Hebrew, Latin, and the others are not the "same" – nor are they totally dissimilar. The very format of a book seems to compel a black-or-white linearity that can be harmful to the comparative enterprise. It would be preferable if we could somehow present the information by means of a volvelle or kaleidoscope, each click of which would bring into focus a pattern of chromatic similarities and differences. Comparison is fraught with difficulties, yet there is no way to achieve a conspectual view of things – no way to understand the world – without it (Smith 2004).

***

This book is an excursion into the world of sacred languages. However, before embarking, we must recognize that certain widely accepted ideas may hinder our journey. A 2009 article in *Newsweek* magazine entitled "We Are All Hindus Now" claimed that many Americans have quietly, without really knowing it, absorbed a number of tenets of Hinduism, including belief in reincarnation and a tolerant all-are-equal religious universalism. When it comes to sacred languages, though, the headline would be: "We Are All Protestants Now." The Protestant critique of sacred languages, which was originally aimed at the use of Latin by the Catholic Church, has been absorbed widely as if by osmosis. We now live in a vernacular age. To many, the notion of praying or reading scriptures in an archaic, unintelligible language seems utterly baffling. The Protestant ethos has been felt even in doctrinal controversies outside the orbit of Protestantism, including debates within Judaism with respect to Hebrew, within Russian Orthodoxy about Church Slavonic, within Zoroastrianism regarding Avestan, and within Catholicism during the contestation over Latin that culminated at Vatican II (some four centuries after the Protestant Reformation).

This originally theological position has been reinforced by the stirring motto of the Internet age: "information wants to be free." By now the notion that information should be free-flowing, readily intelligible, and available to all seems incontrovertible. Yet sacred languages would appear to represent the opposite: fixed, formal, and difficult of access, often taking years of diligent study as the price of entry. As a result, the dominant Protestant/Internet ideology can make it hard to understand a phenomenon that directly and indirectly touches the lives of hundreds of millions of people around the globe.

Similes may help us get around this mental roadblock. Throughout the book we will compare sacred languages to precious metals, vehicles, clothes, divas, and computer codes. Latin, Sanskrit, Hebrew, and the other languages discussed in this book, may also be likened to wine. Water is essential for most things: quenching thirst, washing clothes, watering gardens. No one can deny that. Yet water is not so great for offering a toast or celebrating a victory. Many would say that wine or champagne is far preferable for such occasions, while it makes little sense to bathe with Dom Pérignon. For some religious adherents, a vernacular language is water – functional, transparent – whereas a sacred language is wine: less practical, but it gladdens the heart (Karelin 2008). (Critics would counter that it merely confuses the brain.) The religious communities discussed in this book in effect say: one language is not suitable for every occasion. Water and wine both have a place and purpose. *Sancta sancte* – "sacred matters should be treated in a sacred manner." It is this elemental religious impulse that helps explain why communities around the world continue to value these centuries-old consecrated languages.

References

Dalby, David. 2001. "The Linguasphere: Kaleidoscope of the World's Languages." *English Today* 65, vol. 17 (1): 22–26.

Karelin, Rafail Archimandrate. 2008. Appendix to *Samye pervye shagi v khrame: Sovety nachinaiushchemu khristiianinu*. Moscow: n.p.

Leonhardt, Jürgen. 2013. *Latin: Story of a World Language*. Translated by Kenneth Kronenberg. Cambridge, MA: The Belknap Press of Harvard University Press.

Ostler, Nicholas. 2005. *Empires of the Word: A Language History of the World*. New York: HarperCollins.

Paden, William E. 2009. "Comparative Religion." In *The Routledge Companion to the Study of Religion*, second edition, edited by John R. Hinnells, 225–242. New York: Routledge.

Pollock, Sheldon. 2006. *The Language of the Gods in the World of Men: Sanskrit, Culture, and Power in Premodern India*. Berkeley: University of California Press.

Pye, Michael. 2013. *Strategies in the Study of Religions*. Vol. 2: *Exploring Religions in Motion*. Berlin and Boston: De Gruyter.

Smith, Jonathan Z. 2004. *Relating Religion: Essays in the Study of Religion*. Chicago: University of Chicago Press.

Spolsky, Bernard. 2014. *The Languages of the Jews: A Sociolinguistic History*. Cambridge: Cambridge University Press.

Versteegh, Kees. 2014. *The Arabic Language*. Second edition. Edinburgh: Edinburgh University Press.

Acknowledgments

This book is intended as a conspectus for students and the general reader. It synthesizes my own research on Church Slavonic with that of experts on other sacred languages, and attempts to fit together ideas drawn from comparative religion and from sociolinguistics. I hope that scholars in these different disciplines will find something of value here and will forgive me for believing that the end (providing an accessible introduction to an important but daunting topic) justifies the means (traversing areas of specialization where I really do not belong).

A number of individuals helped me at various points of what turned out to be a circuitous intellectual journey. Many years ago I had the privilege of studying several of the languages discussed in this book with a series of brilliant teachers: Latin with George Dunkel (then at Princeton University); Pali with Lance Cousins and Arabic with Rex Smith (both then at Manchester University); Old Church Slavonic with Victor Friedman (University of Chicago) and Church Slavonic with Fr. Paul Lazor (St. Vladimir's Orthodox Theological Seminary). More recently, a number of scholars and clerics answered my email queries or allowed me to observe them in action: Aleksandr Andreev, Sharon Avni, Fr. Jason Barone (and the instructors at the Veterum Sapientia program), Steven Collins, Kate Crosby, Ven. K. Dhammasami, Fr. Mark Iskander, Grigory Kazakov, Pyi Kyaw, Alexei Krindatch, Justin McDaniel, Christian Muench, Elena Nelson, Ven. S. Nyanasamilankara, Tope Omoniyi, Rabbi Gary Pokras, Imam Syed Khalilullah Qadri, the late Martin Riesebrodt, Andrey Rosowsky, and Fisseha Tadesse. I could not have written this book without their assistance. To Msgr. Daniel Gallagher, who took time out of his busy schedule to meet with me during a whirlwind visit to the Vatican: *gratias*. I feel fortunate to have crossed paths with Joshua Fishman (d. 2015) when this project was in a formative stage. None of these individuals can be blamed if I was too obtuse to follow their directions and went astray.

As this book was going to press, I learned of the death of Tope Omoniyi – a tragic loss for the field of sociolinguistics. As I think back to some of the stopovers along my journey (conferences in Berlin, New York, Hong Kong, London, and Murcia where I first tried out some of the ideas developed in this book), I will always remember with gratitude Tope's scholarly guidance and generous welcoming spirit.

I would like to express my sincere thanks to Tsilli Pines for generously allowing me to use her beautiful artwork for the cover, and to René Drouyer, Peter Gottschalk, and Ori Ronen, as well as Ethiopianapps, the Saratoga Hindu Temple and Community Center, and the Coptic Orthodox Diocese of the Southern United States, for kindly granting me permission to reproduce their images.

I am truly indebted to Rebecca Harkin of Wiley Blackwell. She saw something of value in the original prospectus and then waited patiently through several major delays for the final product to appear. Niagara University afforded me the time, travel funds, and teaching conditions needed for work on the project. A special word of appreciation goes to the staff at the NU library for handling my requests for materials in a Babel of tongues.

Finally, I wish to thank my children Camille and Jacob for their love and encouragement; and my wife Donna Delahoussaye, who, with patience and personal sacrifice, has accompanied me on the long and winding road that led to this book – it is dedicated to her.

Chapter 1

What Exactly Is a Sacred Language?

The Buddha spoke Pali. Tattooed on the body, the truth inherent in the Pali script can shield one from knives and bullets.

Listening to the Arabic-language Qur'an, one hears the very words of Allah.

The Devil loathes the Church Slavonic language.

The cosmos was created through the Hebrew alphabet. The twenty-two letters continue to pulsate with divine light and energy.

Divine Providence chose the Roman Empire – and with it, the Latin language – to spread the Gospel.

Coptic dates back to the time of the pharaohs. Jesus himself learned the language during his childhood sojourn in Egypt.

Sanskrit is the most logical language. The "language of the gods" is the perfect instrument for computer programming.

Sacred languages are like, but also unlike, everyday vernacular languages. Although both types of language have nouns, verbs, adjectives, and all the other ingredients needed to express thought, they differ in a number of crucial ways.

First, sacred languages are mythologized, being connected to divine personages and events. According to the Theravada Buddhist tradition, the Buddha spoke Pali. Russian Orthodox devotees say that the Church Slavonic language was inspired by the Holy Spirit – hence the Devil fears it.

Sacred Languages of the World: An Introduction, First Edition. Brian P. Bennett.

In Hindu discourse Sanskrit is often called the language of the gods, while the image of Yahweh creating the universe through the Hebrew alphabet is a familiar one in Jewish mysticism. A number of sacred languages are associated with divine revelation as embodied in canonical texts: the Torah, the Qur'an, the Vedas, the Tipitika. The supreme value of the message rubs off on the medium, such that the language becomes endowed with its own sanctity. In some traditions, the very alphabet in which the language is written is credited with miraculous powers. Thus, unlike their more earthly counterparts, sacred languages are those that appear to be endowed with a kind of halo, a supernatural aura, a higher calling. They are said to play a role in the drama of salvation history.

Second, sacred languages are not used for ordinary communication – to chat around the dinner table, tease in the schoolyard, give orders in the factory, or bicker in the market. Some people, especially clerics, are in fact able to converse in languages like Latin, Sanskrit, or Ge'ez (e.g., Endangered Language Alliance Toronto 2013). In general, though, sacred languages are reserved for special religious practices involving a predetermined content: chanting a mantra, performing a ritual, reciting a passage from scripture, wearing a protective amulet. These practices and paraphernalia are usually found in specially consecrated places, including mosques, churches, synagogues, and temples – these are the "natural habitats" of sacred languages.

This fact that sacred languages are not typically used for everyday conversation leads to another key difference between them and vernacular tongues: namely, the matter of comprehension. We assume that language is about interpersonal communication and conveying ideas to one another. However, religious practitioners may have memorized entire books in their sacred language, yet be unable to explain a single sentence. Indeed, it sometimes seems that, for believers, the lack of understandability heightens the mystery and allure of these ancient tongues. A different mode of literacy is at work here. Instead of intelligibility, sacred languages are often prized for other values which they are said to embody, such as antiquity, beauty, purity, solemnity, or magical efficacy. Indeed, it is often the *idea* of the sacred language, the symbolism as opposed to some specific content, that is determinative. Referring to the Catholic Mass, the scholar of comparative religion Wendy Doniger writes:

> if Latin is no longer a useful form of communication for most congregations, it still has the function of communion. That is, the Mass, in contrast with the sermon (which communicates, or at least tries to communicate,

> to convey new thoughts or information), has the function of communion; people participate in it not to learn something new but to relive, together, the words that they already know, words about themselves as a community (communion). Where communication is effective, communion is evocative. Where communication seeks to influence the future, communion draws upon the past. (2007)

Relying on a sacred medium like Latin or Hebrew often means valuing the symbolic and the spiritually evocative – the "look and feel" of the language – over the more directly informational side of things.

Third, sacred languages are not mother tongues. Although there are occasional reports of a child being raised to speak a sacred language (e.g., Kiraz 2007, xxvii), these are rare cases indeed. As a general rule, children do not grow up speaking Pali or Coptic around the house with their relatives. (The monumental exception of Hebrew will be discussed in Chapter 5.) These are secondary, bookish languages added on to one's linguistic toolkit later in life. (In the nomenclature of sociolinguistics, they are categorized as L2 as opposed to L1.) If anything, they might be considered "father tongues," since they are often (though not always or necessarily) associated with male clerics such as Christian priests and Buddhist monks. Sacred languages are usually not transmitted organically within the family, but through a kind of artificial dissemination involving monasteries, seminaries, yeshivas, pathshalas, and similar institutions. Spanish, Korean, Evenki, and other mother tongues could survive from generation to generation without schools if they had to; that is not the case with sacred languages.

Fourth, sacred languages seem to have the remarkable ability to connect believers scattered to the four corners of the earth. For centuries Latin linked Roman Catholics across oceans and continents. Many Jews would say that it is Hebrew that unites "an English speaking teacher in New York, a Russian speaking scientist in Moscow, an Amharic speaking farmer in Ethiopia, and a Yiddish speaking Hasidic rabbi in Israel" (Avni 2011, 55). The rich sonorities of the Church Slavonic language can be experienced in onion-domed sanctuaries from Russia to California. Sacred languages wield an impressive symbolic power. Indeed, the identification between the language and the religious community may be so close and intense that the script comes to function as a kind of logo that "brands" the faith for both insiders and outsiders.

Yet, although sacred languages contribute in powerful ways to religious solidarity, at the same time, they also have their detractors. The tension between communion and communication can become a flashpoint, sometimes leading to bitter polemics that divide a community, as has happened in Judaism over the question of Hebrew, Zoroastrianism over Avestan, and – perhaps most famously – Catholicism over Latin. Of course, passionate debates have from time to time engulfed French and Irish and Tamil and many other vernaculars. But because the stakes are so high with sacred languages, being connected not only to communal identity but soteriology (a program of salvation), such disputes can become quite polarizing, with charges of heresy and sacrilege hurled about. In sum, though they can contribute to social chemistry, sacred languages can also be combustible, sparking conflicts or even schisms among believers.

Sacred languages, then, do not differ in formal ways from other languages: they consist of words, sentences, and so on. Instead, they differ in their overall social meaning and location, being fixed, mythicized, textual languages, used for a range of projects and practices, transmitted institutionally, and cherished – but also at times contested – by certain religious communities.

Sacred Choices

Religion involves the culturally patterned interaction between a social group and its postulated superhuman powers (cf. Spiro 1966). A religious topography therefore involves actual places, such as churches, shrines, mosques, and synagogues with street addresses, but also encompasses imagined realms – heaven, hell, paradise, nirvana, the etheric plane, and so forth. This unseen spiritual dimension may be imagined as above and beyond our earthly concerns and conceptions, or considered to be within the material world, inspiriting people, places, plants, and animals. It may be visualized as populated by superhuman agents: deities, spirits, ghosts, angels, demons, *jinn*, bodhisattvas, ascended masters. Alternatively, it may be conceived in terms of impersonal forces: karma, universal consciousness, the Source. Whether transcendent, immanent, personal, or impersonal (or some combination thereof), the superhuman order is thought to frame human life. Religious believers talk and act as if it really exists: "a religious world is one where gods function as environmental realities" (Paden 2013, 94). The religious premise is that it is both possible and desirable for people to interact with the superhuman dimension in order to overcome human limitations.

Religious systems offer "big" rewards (paradise, heaven, nirvana) as well as "small" ones (freedom from harm, personal wellbeing, success in romance or commerce). Since the spiritual realm is invisible, it must be represented by stories, symbols, icons, dances, fragrances, and other tangible means. Practitioners relate to the supposed divine realm through such practices as praying, chanting the name of a god, offering sacrifices, performing a ritual dance, following an ethical code, fasting, or going on pilgrimage. In those religious traditions that have them – not all do – sacred languages are considered a prestigious linguistic resource for both revealing and reaching the superhuman realm.

All religions teach that certain times, places, actions, and objects (and not others) constitute the ways and means of interacting with the imagined spiritual zone:

> Almost the first thing which the student – or indeed the casual observer – of religious affairs notices, is that "believers" subject the times and places, the objects and personalities of the waking world to a definite scale of values. A house may be full of books; but one book is somehow different from all the others, being both handled and read in a special way. A village is full of buildings; but before entering one of them people make special preparations, while once inside, their normal behavior changes.... The days of the week are differently treated; on Fridays for some, Saturdays for others and Sundays for a third group.... (Sharpe 1983, 49)

While every religious system necessarily requires the use of language, some religions honor one language as the premier (perhaps the only) vehicle for communicating with and about the divine, a language that supersedes all others on the linguistic scale of values. As it turns out, sacred languages usually go with sacred books, buildings, and days of the week; they are parallel and intersecting religious phenomena. Thus, Muslims pray in Classical Arabic, which is linked to the Qur'an, to mosques, and to the fivefold daily prayer, especially the Friday noontime gathering. Similarly, the nexus of synagogue, Sabbath, Torah, and Hebrew is central to the religious experience of many Jews.

Of course, needless to say, if a religion has a sacred language, that does not mean its practitioners only use or speak the sacred language – far from it. Just as gold is too soft on its own and has to be hardened by the addition of alloying elements like copper, nickel, or palladium, sacred languages are always mixed with everyday spoken vernaculars, such as Burmese, Tigre, Serbian, French, or Urdu. If we could somehow calculate a word-count for all the books and speeches and utterances produced within a religion, the results would be overwhelmingly in the vernacular. The importance of sacred language tends to be more qualitative than quantitative. For example, if one attends a Latin Mass in an Anglophone country, the foyer will be full of English-language materials (bulletins, periodicals, etc.); people will greet each other and catch up on the week's events in English; there will be bilingual Latin–English missals available to help churchgoers follow along (though some bring their own); during the ritual itself, people will whisper to each other, or hush their children, in English; and afterwards, the priest will chat with parishioners in English. Similar scenarios take place *mutatis mutandis* with Pali, Hebrew, Coptic, and Avestan. Vernaculars always set the stage for sacred languages, which come on like divas after all the work has been done.

The category of sacred language should be distinguished from the much broader category of *religious language*, which would include a whole range of genres and occurrences, including hymns, oracles, euphemisms, incantations, sermons, channeling, and speaking in tongues (Sawyer and Simpson 2001). It should also be differentiated from the narrower category of *liturgical language*. It is true that sacred languages like Latin and Coptic are used for liturgies, but in some cases mother tongues are as well. Since the reforms of Vatican II, for example, English, Polish, Vietnamese, and many other languages have been authorized for use in the Catholic Mass. Various Christian communities rooted in the Middle East (Orthodox, Coptic, Melchite, Maronite, etc.) use Arabic in their worship services, but do not treat the language as divine, the way that Muslims do. Sacred languages thus overlap with, but are a distinct phenomenon compared to, religious language on one side and liturgical language on the other.

Sociolinguists often speak of *varieties* because it helps sidestep the intractable problem of differentiating a language from a dialect. Sacred languages are "named varieties": Latin, Sanskrit, Hebrew, and so on. Now, some sociolinguists assert that the whole notion of languages as discrete, bounded entities ("Russian," "French," etc.) is illusory (Jørgensen et al. 2011). Languages, they contend, are less like self-contained canisters than hazy clouds, nebulously blending into one another: it is hard to tell where one stops and another starts. Be that as it may, sacred languages are perceived and treated by religious adherents as separate, self-standing languages and not just a fancier or more archaic version of their everyday spoken dialect. For example, some Anglophone Christians recite this version of the so-called Our Father or Lord's Prayer:

Our Father which art in heaven,
Hallowed be thy name.
Thy kingdom come.
Thy will be done in earth,
as it is in heaven.
Give us this day our daily bread.
And forgive us our trespasses,
as we forgive those
who trespass against us.
And lead us not into temptation,
but deliver us from evil:
For thine is the kingdom,
and the power, and the glory,
forever and ever.
Amen.

Several archaic features impart an elevated ambiance to this text, but we would not say that it represents a sacred language per se, since it is still recognizably English. The words *which art*, *thy*, and *thine* do not constitute a separate, nameable language. Now, it is not always easy to know where to draw the line between religious language and a sacred language. After all, many forms of religious language display a desire for mystery and transcendence – elevating above ordinary speech by means of stylized diction or esoteric terms. But a good rule of thumb is this: to count as a sacred language, it must (among other things) be named, perceived, and taught as such. Believers usually recognize that Latin is related to Italian, Sanskrit to Hindi, and Church Slavonic to Russian, but they nonetheless discuss and teach Latin, Sanskrit, and Church Slavonic as independent fully fledged languages. There are no seminary or Sunday school courses devoted to "English with a Few Archaic Features." Thus, this version of the Lord's Prayer is a specimen of religious language, not a sacred language.

Although sacred languages are sometimes said to be *dead*, it is more accurate and helpful to think of them as *fixed* or *conserved*. According to the sociolinguist Joshua Fishman, "Languages of direct sanctity live on in their holy texts and, as such, are not subject to the winds of change and of influence (or interference) from other languages in the way that spoken languages are" (2006, 257–258). Their overall grammatical structure was codified hundreds or even thousands of years ago and has changed very little since then, though new words and even entire texts continue to be produced (Leonhardt 2013). James Sawyer's summary of how this fixing/conserving comes about is worth quoting:

> Respect for the original sources, especially when these are believed to have been composed by a much revered prophet or teacher, if not by the actual deity himself or herself, is a major factor in many cases.... Religious conservatism is another important factor related to this concern for getting back to the original. A fierce reluctance to accept innovation is common to many religious groups, despite pressures from many directions to evolve or move with the times. It is partly due to a desire to maintain continuity with the past, or even, somehow, an attempt to bring the past into the present during the experience of worship.... There is also the fact that language often has a dynamic of its own: words, phrases, even sounds hallowed by centuries of use in the highly charged context of religious ritual, can have a hold on worshippers which makes it difficult for them even to contemplate changes in language. (Sawyer 1999, 25–26)

(By the way, we should not necessarily think of sacred languages as spoken vernaculars that became frozen or fossilized over time as a result of piety. This notion does not fit all cases. For example, though its originators drew upon different Slavic varieties spoken in the ninth century, Church Slavonic was from the start a kind of virtual language found only in sacred books.)

Thus, the languages discussed in this book are best considered fixed, not dead. There is a real difference between the cases of (for example) Sanskrit and Sumerian, or Ecclesiastical Latin and Etruscan. No community uses Sumerian or Etruscan any more; those languages are museum artifacts, housed under glass and studied by a small circle of linguists, archaeologists, and numismatists (cf. Hagège 2009). But some Hindus still read, write, compose, and even converse or broadcast the news in Sanskrit. Every year the Catholic Church mints new Latin words and publishes original Latin texts. Coptic Orthodox Christians continue to offer hymns in Coptic, a language that can be traced back some five millennia, while Zoroastrians maintain Avestan, another language of great antiquity. Unlike Etruscan or Sumerian, the sacred languages treated here still occupy niches in the world's religious and cultural landscape (Haarmann 2002, 9).

Sacred languages are sometimes referred to as classical languages, which is reasonable, insofar as they are old and venerable and recognized as culturally influential. However, a classical language often provides a literary model to be emulated, which is only really the case now with Classical

Arabic. American Catholics do not strive to speak in an obviously Latinate way; Thai Buddhists do not usually labor to compose an email in Pali-esque prose. Moreover, the designation "classical" evokes images of leather-bound tomes perused in ivy-clad towers; it fails to capture the mythical, magical, mystical properties usually ascribed to sacred languages. The term *religious classical* seems like a good compromise, though it has not caught on beyond the field of sociolinguistics (e.g., Fishman 2006). The best label, though not perfect, is *sacred*.

Who Says It's a Sacred Language?

The term *sacred language* is open to misunderstanding. Believers and scholars, committed insiders and observing comparativists, may refer to this or that language as sacred, but they usually mean different things by it. Religious adherents typically claim that their language – Avestan or Classical Arabic or Church Slavonic – is sacred in an ontological sense: it truly emanates from or connects with the unseen spiritual order in a way that is unlike other languages. For their part, scholarly outsiders would say that there is no inherently sacred language; it is believers who construe this or that language as sacred. In other words, *sacred language* is a social as opposed to a metaphysical fact (Williams 2008, 126). Whatever one makes of different theological claims about Hebrew, Sanskrit, and so on, what can be said, and empirically verified, is that certain religious communities have in the past and still do treat certain languages as sacrosanct, just as they mark off and solemnize certain books, places, or days of the week as special, inviolate, and holy. A conspectual frame of reference reinforces this point. As Paden says, "One person's 'holiest day of the year' is just another working day for someone else.... Who among the Irish think that the Ganges River is holy?" (1994, x). Our starting point in this journey, then, is that sacredness is in the eye of the believer.

Sacred is the past participle of the Middle English verb *sacren* (from the Latin *sacrare*), meaning to consecrate. The word has a transitive, behavioral sense to it: something *has been consecrated* (Paden 1999, 95n6). Sacred languages, then, are those that have been designated by religious communities for sacred purposes. They have been elevated above ordinary vernaculars through myths, ritual practices, and dedicated institutions. We could say – and perhaps should say, for the sake of correctness and clarity – that these are *sacralized* or *sanctified* or *consecrated* languages. (For stylistic variety we will use all of these terms in addition to *sacred*.) Approaching things in this way, utilizing verbal forms, enables us to grasp the fact that sacredness is in part an observable social process, a process, moreover, that can be disrupted or reversed.

Sacrality works in circular fashion. Consider gold. The gleaming yellow metal has long inspired fascination and mythmaking. Humans have extolled it above other, lowlier metals, like nickel and chrome. It is reserved for extraordinary objects or occasions. As it turns out, gold is widely used in religious cultus, as in the strips of gold leaf applied to Buddha statues in Thailand or the gilded cupolas of an Orthodox church. Such ritualistic uses further enhance the prestige of gold ... which in turn makes gold suitable for ritualistic use. And so on, in iterative fashion. However, this recurring loop can be short-circuited. When an 18-karat toilet was installed in the Guggenheim Museum in Manhattan, this was clearly a provocative artistic statement, meant to upend the feelings, ideas, and behaviors customarily associated with the precious metal (see, e.g., *New York Times*, April 19, 2016). Of course, it will probably take much more than that to disabuse people of their emotional attachment to gold, but the stunt reveals that there is in fact a spell (a kind of social spell) to be broken.

Sacred languages may be thought of as semiotic gold. Within their communities, they are endowed with a mystical allure and are drawn upon for a wide range of religious practices, places, and paraphernalia. They are studied with reverence and care and are defended from threats of blasphemy or sacrilege. For example, some Church Slavonic teaching manuals refuse to use the grammatical charts, tables, and diagrams one normally finds in a Western language textbook – the idea being that such things desacralize the holy living word (e.g., Goriacheva et al. 2013). One index of this special treatment is the fact that sacred languages are often expressed through cantillation (chanting or solemn reading) and calligraphy (beautiful writing), two forms of symbolic heightening that ordinary vernaculars may not be deemed worthy of. Using sacred languages for rituals, scriptures, chants, and inscriptions further emphasizes their sacredness. This is the hidden circuitry of religion: sacred languages are sacred, in part at least, because they are handled sacredly (*sancta sancte*). But this seemingly closed system can also be short-circuited, either from within the community (as happened to Latin at Vatican II) or from without (as happened to Church Slavonic during the Soviet era). In these cases, the supposed sacredness of the language was questioned or violently debunked.

One wrinkle is the fact that adherents themselves, especially Christians, are not always of one mind about the sacred nature of a particular language. Christianity is not really a "religion of the book" in the same sense as

Judaism or Islam. It does not have one sacred language comparable to Hebrew or Arabic. Indeed, some Christians believe that the notion of a sacred language is inimical to pure Christianity, insisting that Jesus addressed his followers in colloquial terms, that the experience of Pentecost (described in the Acts of the Apostles) validated the world's Babel of tongues, that the Church has always engaged in translation projects, and so on. Indeed, many would agree with the following distinction:

> Islam rests on a text, which is God's very own Word, and emphasizes the importance of one idiom, Arabic, which is both divine and human. It is the language of the Qur'an, considered uncreated, inimitable, and the seal of prophecy.… On the other hand, Christianity, based on the person of Christ and not so much on a text, has scriptures in two idioms Hebrew and Greek, none of them that of Christ. It should not privilege any language and thereby emphasizes its universal appeal for speakers of any and every idiom. (Druart 2007, 2)

The key word in the above quotation is "should": the author may wish that Christianity should not privilege any language, but the fact of the matter is, over the course of its history, different Christian communities have indeed exalted – in varying ways and to varying degrees – certain languages closely affiliated with their own ecclesiastical traditions, including Latin, Church Slavonic, Coptic, and Ge'ez (Tornow 2009, 69–70), though all have also been challenged at times. What this exaltation entails, we will see in the course of this book. But, again, these are observable social and historical facts, and so, for a study such as this, which is concerned with observables (as opposed to metaphysics), it suffices.

Historical Relics?

Sacred languages are important filaments in world history. Hundreds or even thousands of years old, they link generations of believers across time and provide a vital connection to the religion's origins. Missionaries and migrants have disseminated sacred languages like Arabic, Pali, and Church Slavonic across oceans and continents, profoundly shaping the linguasphere, the network of languages that encircles the earth. Vast repositories of human wisdom are safeguarded in ancient tongues like Pali and Ge'ez. These rich and intricate languages have helped thinkers plumb the depths of the human condition. In the premodern era, sacred languages such as

Sanskrit and Latin were used not only in the religious sphere, but became influential vehicles of literature and learning, used for poetry, philosophy, law, medicine, astronomy, and mathematics. They continue to provide intellectual infrastructure for different world religions. The vocabulary of Jewish life, for example – *Adonai*, *Elohim*, *Torah*, *Kaddish*, *Kosher*, *Mitsvah*, *Shalom*, *Tallit*, *Minyan* – remains indebted to the "holy tongue" of Hebrew (Green 1999). Sacred languages have long functioned as lexifiers, furnishing the lexical building blocks for modern-day vernaculars. The national languages of South and Southeast Asia are studded with Sanskrit and Pali words, while elements of Church Slavonic enhance Russian, Bulgarian, and Serbian, and Ge'ez is a resource for scientific terminology in contemporary Amharic. (It should be noted that the opposite can also be observed: that is, regional languages can influence sacred ones.) Some governments and political parties have supported sacred languages, hoping to benefit from their symbolic cachet, while poets, composers, and typographers have drawn upon the visual and sonic properties of sacred languages for their respective creations.

But that is not the whole story. Cultivating a sacred language over against workaday vernaculars has profound linguistic, religious, and social consequences, not all of which may be judged positively. For one thing, while sacred languages can indeed foster trans-regional ties among believers, they may do so at the expense of local languages. Sacred languages have an imperialist track record (Williams 2008). For example, when Buddhist monks backed the use of Pali, this hindered the development of a native Sinhala literature in Sri Lanka (Deegalle 2006). Maintaining a sacred language has often been elitist and exclusionary, an instrument of obfuscation separating the literate from the illiterate. One critic claims that Sanskrit represents "institutional violence and the preservation of hierarchy" within Indian society (Sawhney 2009, 5). A well-known philologist contends that the adherence to Church Slavonic, while leading to beautiful expressions in liturgy and literature, isolated premodern Russia and led to its intellectual impoverishment (Thomson 1999). It has been suggested that the supreme sanctity bestowed upon Classical Arabic in the Muslim world has slowed the introduction of printing, mass education, democracy, and other attributes of modernity (Diner 2009). The artist and critic John Berger once said, "Mystifications protect power. Mysteries protect the sacred" (1991, 218). It would appear that sacred languages have done both.

Whatever we make of such sweeping historical judgments, has not the march of progress done away with all of that anyway? Are not sacred languages relics of the past? Are we not all basically Protestants now? The sociologist Bryan S. Turner (2011) suggests that the world is on the cusp of a new era in human history, moving from the age of revelation to the age of information. In the premodern epoch, the ineffable message of divine revelation was encoded in a language known only to clerical elites (rabbis, monks, priests, mullahs) who maintained a privileged position as guardians and interpreters. A wide gulf separated the clergy from the laity, the learned from the unlearned. But in the modern era, which is characterized by democracy and widespread literacy – and the near universal access to information via the Internet – the old arrangement is no longer tenable:

> In a democratic environment, the very idea that some truths are ineffable contradicts the ethos of modern society in which everybody claims a right to understand. Democracy tends to promote plain speech. The elite's control of ineffable knowledge is compromised and the whole idea of hierarchically organised wisdom evaporates. (195)

Clerical groups no longer have a monopoly on knowledge. The pyramidal arrangement, with a small coterie of religious intellectuals in a commanding position atop the masses, has given way to a broad-based marketplace of ideas. As Turner sees it, sacred languages cannot survive in this new topography. The replacement of Latin by vernaculars in the Catholic Church is a case in point.

While it is true that Latin, Pali, Church Slavonic, and the others do not occupy the place they did in the premodern world, they are still part of the daily life of millions of Muslims, Jews, Hindus, Zoroastrians, Christians, and Buddhists. The following table shows some of the major world religions, their estimated number of members, and their associated sacred language.

Religion	*Number of members*	*Sacred language*
Islam	1.6 billion	Classical Arabic
Roman Catholic Christianity	1.1 billion	Latin
Hinduism	1 billion	Sanskrit
Russian Orthodox Christianity	165 million	Church Slavonic
Theravada Buddhism	140 million	Pali
Ethiopian Orthodox Christianity	40 million	Ge'ez
Judaism	14 million	Hebrew
Coptic Orthodox Christianity	12 million	Coptic
Zoroastrianism	200,000	Avestan

Source: Pew Research Center 2012; World Council of Churches 2016.

Of course, by no means do all adherents know their tradition's sacred language. Nonetheless, even if just 1 percent is involved, that still comes out to be millions of people who are influenced in some measure, directly or indirectly, by these sacralized varieties. The case of Latin being displaced within Roman Catholic Christianity is certainly noteworthy, but not necessarily representative of the overall situation.

There is no doubt that Sanskrit, Church Slavonic, Latin, and other sacred languages have been buffeted by the forces of modernity. For one thing, they have been eclipsed by the rise of national varieties such as French, Hindi, Serbian, and Indonesian: *these* are now the languages of literature and learning – and, often, liturgy too, for that matter. Sanctified languages have also been affected by the creep of secularization – that is, the retreat of religion from science, art, law, medicine, education, and other domains. Their real estate, so to speak, has shrunk considerably. But secularization is not happening evenly and ineluctably across the planet; in fact, a number of conflicting trends are observable. Sacred languages, suggests Fishman, "do not come and go the way quotidian vernaculars do. They wax and wane and have a seemingly phoenix-like capacity to arise again out of their own ashes" (2006, 258). History is full of surprising twists and turns, and some recent developments suggest that ancient sacred languages may be shifting with the times. These trends include religious revivals, neotraditionalist movements, technological innovations, and globalizing spiritualities. Let us briefly consider an example for each development.

Religious revivals

Church Slavonic, the consecrated language of the Russian Orthodox Church and other Eastern Christian communities, has made a noteworthy comeback after decades of Communism. Soviet ideology was hostile to religion and had no use for a language like Church Slavonic. But then the USSR fell apart in 1991 and people became interested in the hitherto forbidden fruit of religion. Many new churches and monasteries have been constructed. Since Church Slavonic is the solemn liturgical language of the Russian Orthodox Church, this religious revival has entailed a linguistic revitalization as well, a fact well illustrated by the profusion of new akathists being composed. An akathist is a hymn composed to honor a saint or martyr. Since the demise of the USSR, the canonization of the so-called "new martyrs" – those faithful Christians who perished under

Figure 1.1 The Jesus Prayer in Church Slavonic ("Lord, Jesus Christ, Son of God, have mercy upon me, a sinner"). Prayer card, 1990s, Russia.

the Bolsheviks – has been a remarkable affair. Between 1721 and 1896, the Russian Orthodox Church only canonized (i.e., elevated to sainthood) five individuals. But over a thousand new saints have been recognized since the year 2000. This means new liturgical services and hymns written in Church Slavonic by clergy and laity alike (Semenkov 2009). In fact, the number of akathists written since 1990 is comparable to the past three centuries combined (Liudogovskii 2004, 56). In sum, the language of Church Slavonic has been given a new vitality. (See Figure 1.1.)

Neotraditionalist movements

It should come as no surprise that believers on the conservative end of the ideological spectrum typically favor maintaining their sacred language. Often thousands of years old, linking generations of believers, safely preserving the deposit of faith and integral to ritual performance, sacred languages seem to be the very embodiment of religious tradition. Neotraditionalists (preferable to the overused term, fundamentalists) deliberately attempt to reassert the religious tradition over against what they see as harmful modern innovations. They look back to a supposed golden age for solace and inspiration. It is noteworthy how often a sacred language seems to symbolize that age. For example, there are neotraditionalist groups in India that claim Sanskrit used to be the lingua franca (common language) of all Indians and not just an elite priestly idiom. Seeking to promote Sanskrit as a spoken language, they offer immersion camps and other educational programs designed to teach people how to say things like

- Hello! How are you?
- Where do you work?
- I was merely joking, friend.
- When will this bus leave?
- The examination has been postponed.
- Next month we will buy a washing machine.

This is a grassroots effort by Hindu neotraditionalists who hope to expand knowledge of Sanskrit from home to village to nation. Restoring the former glory of Sanskrit is seen as the pathway to a successful future for India.

Technological innovations

Sacred languages, which are thousands of years old, are being given a boost by mobile computer and communication technologies. Projection screens are now used in some churches and synagogues, providing real-time vernacular translations of, say, Coptic or Hebrew prayers being said during the worship service. This is one technique for balancing the imperatives of communion and communication – a way for the group to have its linguistic cake and eat it too, as it were. Other platforms provide novel ways of disseminating ancient languages. For example, Benedict XVI was the first pontiff to use Twitter, which includes a Latin version among the various other languages. The practice continued under Pope Francis and grew into something of a sensation:

Ubi quaestus deficientia, ibi dignitatis humanae neglegentia.	Where there is no work, there is no dignity.
In sacramento Eucharistiae reperimus Deum se donantem.	In the Sacrament of the Eucharist we find God who gives himself.

(Pope Francis 2015a, 2015b)

The current Latin Twitter account (Papa Franciscus@Pontifx_In) has over seven hundred thousand followers. Though it is hard to know what effect this is having on the vitality of Latin within Catholicism – the English-language feed has more than ten million followers – it does at least seem to suggest that devotees might utilize new technologies to preserve and promulgate their sacred languages.

Globalizing spiritualities

Along with the more high-profile religious revivals and neotraditionalist movements, another, subtler trend is observable: namely, the growth of spiritualities that draw upon the global religious market in a do-it-yourself, mix-and-match kind of way. People are increasingly charting their own religious trajectory, often with the help of the Internet. These are fluid spiritualities that operate outside the walls of established religions, and tend to be highly individualistic, commercialized, and therapeutic in character (Turner 2011). The popularity of Kabbalah, a tradition of Jewish mystical thought and practice, is a good example of this. The celebrity-friendly Kabbalah Centre (often labeled a "cult" by its detractors) has retrieved this aspect of Jewish heritage and championed it in new, populist forms. The organization promotes the idea that the Hebrew alphabet is the hidden code or DNA of the cosmos, so that tapping into that alphabetic power can generate real benefits in one's personal and professional life. The group's online store sells a number of products (books, CDs, posters, etc.) related to Hebrew letters and the deity's names, which the customer need not be able to read to benefit from:

> In The 72 Names of God, you'll find a remedy for just about every challenge that's likely to come up in the course of a lifetime. Simply by properly meditating on the appropriate Name, you will be able to:
>
> * Bring more money into your life whenever you need it.
> * Ignite sexual energy and passion unlike anything you've experienced before.
> * Eliminate guilt forever and undo the damage it has caused you.
> * Recharge physical energy and heal illnesses – your own, and others'.
> * Radiate beauty to everyone who sees you.
> * Stop attracting the wrong people into your life.
> * Meet your true soul mate.
>
> And so much more!
>
> (Kabbalah Centre 2016)

This Kabbalistic "spiritual technology" is marketed to seekers who may or may not be Jewish. Busy professionals living in a fast-paced, globalized world can tap into the alleged spiritual power of the Hebrew alphabet without actually learning how to read it (Altglas 2014).

What the future holds for the world's sacred languages is, of course, impossible to divine. Who would have predicted that, starting in the nineteenth century, the "holy tongue" of Hebrew would be transformed into a full-fledged spoken language, known now as Modern Hebrew or Israeli? Or that, roughly a century later, the seemingly impregnable position of Latin across the Catholic world would crumble? In any event, this book is not an exercise in futurology; rather, it offers a comparative account of some of the beliefs, practices, teaching methods, social groups, and ideological debates pertaining to the world's major sacred languages in the late twentieth and early twenty-first centuries.

References

Altglas, Véronique. 2014. *From Yoga to Kabbalah: Religious Exoticism and the Logics of Bricolage.* Oxford and New York: Oxford University Press.

Avni, Sharon. 2011. "Toward an Understanding of Hebrew Language Education: Ideologies, Emotions, and Identity." *International Journal of the Sociology of Language* 208: 53–70. DOI: 10.1515/ijsl.2011.012

Berger, John. 1991. *Keeping a Rendezvous.* New York: Vintage International.

Deegalle, Mahinda. 2006. *Popularizing Buddhism: Preaching as Performance in Sri Lanka.* Albany, NY: State University of New York Press.

Diner, Dan. 2009. *Lost in the Sacred: Why the Muslim World Stood Still.* Translated by Steven Rendall. Princeton and Oxford: Princeton University Press.

Doniger, Wendy, 2007. "Super-Titles for the Kingdom of Heaven." *OnFaith*, July 12. Accessed August 8, 2007. http://www.faithstreet.com/onfaith/2007/07/12/supertitles-for-the-kingdom-of/8549

Druart, Thérèse-Anne. 2007. "One Divine and Human Language or Many Human Languages." *Journal of Religion and Society* 9: 1–13.

Endangered Language Alliance Toronto. 2013. "Ge'ez Conversation." Accessed July 19, 2016. https://www.youtube.com/watch?v=BMNtOldl1go

Fishman, Joshua A. 2006. *Language Loyalty, Language Planning and Language Revitalization: Recent Writings and Reflections from Joshua A. Fishman.* Edited by Nancy H. Hornberger and Martin Pütz. Clevedon, Buffalo, and Toronto: Multilingual Matters.

Francis, Pope. 2015a. Twitter post. June 9, 2015. https://twitter.com/pontifex_ln/status/608199128141565952

Francis, Pope. 2015b. Twitter post. June 11, 2015. https://twitter.com/pontifex_ln/status/608909286408769536

Goriacheva, I. A., I. A. Kornilaeva, and S. M. Shestakova. 2013. *Azbuka tserkovnoslavianskaia. Metodicheskoe posobie dlia uchiteliia.* Moscow: Izdatel'skii Dom "Dimitrii i Evdokiia."

Green, Arthur. 1999. *These are the Words: A Vocabulary of Jewish Spiritual Life.* Woodstock, VT: Jewish Lights Publishing.

Haarmann, Harald. 2002. *Lexikon der untergegangenen Sprachen.* Munich: C. H. Beck.

Hagège, Claude. 2009. *On the Death and Life of Languages.* Translated by Jody Gladding. New Haven, CT: Yale University Press.

Jørgensen, J. N. et al. 2011. "Polylanguaging in Superdiversity." *Diversities* 13 (2): 23–37. Accessed August 11, 2016. http://www.unesco.org/new/en/social-and-human-sciences/resources/periodicals/diversities/past-issues/vol-13-no-2-2011/polylanguaging-in-superdiversity/

Kabbalah Centre, The. 2016. Accessed July 19, 2016. http://store.kabbalah.com/topics/meditation-tools/72-names-god-set-cd-0

Kiraz, George Anton. 2007. *The New Syriac Primer: An Introduction to the Syriac Language with a CD.* Piscataway, NJ: Georgias Press.

Leonhardt, Jürgen. 2013. *Latin: Story of a World Language.* Translated by Kenneth Kronenberg. Cambridge, MA: The Belknap Press of Harvard University Press.

Liudogovskii, F. B. 2004. "Tserkovnoslavianskii akafist kak sovremennyi gimnograficheskii zhanr: struktura, adresatsiia, funktsionirovanie." *Slavianovedenie* 2: 56–67.

Paden, William E. 1994 (1988). *Religious Worlds: The Comparative Study of Religion.* With a new preface. Boston: Beacon Press.

Paden, William E. 1999. "Reconceiving the Category of the Sacred." In *Comparative Studies in History of Religions: Their Aim, Scope, and Validity,* edited by Erik Reenberg Sand and Jørgen Podemann Sørensen, 93–108. Copenhagen: Museum Tusculanum Press, University of Copenhagen.

Paden, William E. 2013. "Tracks and Themes in a Shifting Landscape: Reflections on 50 Years of the Study of Religion." *Religion* 43 (1): 89–101.

Pew Research Center. 2012. "The Global Religious Landscape: A Report on the Size and Distribution of the World's Major Religious Groups as of 2010." Accessed February 8, 2017. http://www.pewforum.org/2012/12/18/global-religious-landscape-exec/

Sawhney, Simona. 2009. *The Modernity of Sanskrit.* Minneapolis: University of Minnesota Press.

Sawyer, John F. A. 1999. *Sacred Languages and Sacred Texts.* London and New York: Routledge.

Sawyer, J. F. A., and J. M. Y. Simpson. 2001. *Concise Encyclopedia of Language and Religion.* Amsterdam and New York: Elsevier.

Semenkov, V. E. 2009. "Iazyki bogosluzheniia v sekuliarnom kontekste sovremennoi kul'tury." *Etnograficheskoe obozreniie* 1: 27–38.
Sharpe, Eric. 1983. *Understanding Religion*. New York: St. Martin's Press.
Spiro, Melford E. 1966. "Religion: Problems of Definition and Explanation." In *Anthropological Approaches to the Study of Religion*, edited by Michael Banton. London: Tavistock.
Thomson, Francis. 1999. *The Reception of Byzantine Culture in Mediaeval Russia*. Aldershot and Brookfield, VT: Ashgate.
Tornow, Siegfried. 2009. *Abendland und Morgenland im Spiegel ihrer Sprachen: Ein kulturhistorischer Vergleich*. Wiesbaden: Harrassowitz.
Turner, Bryan S. 2011. *Religion and Modern Society: Citizenship, Secularisation and the State*. Cambridge and New York: Cambridge University Press.
Williams, Alan. 2008. "The Continuum of 'Sacred Language' From High to Low Speech in the Middle Iranian (Pahlavi) Zoroastrian Tradition." In *Religion, Language, and Power*, edited by Nile Green and Mary Searle-Chatterjee, 123–142. New York and London: Routledge.
World Council of Churches. 2016. Accessed August 18, 2016. https://www.oikoumene.org/en/

Further Reading

Austin, Peter K., ed. 2008. *One Thousand Languages: Living, Endangered, and Lost*. Berkeley and Los Angeles: University of California Press. A user-friendly overview of the world's languages, with plentiful maps and illustrations; however, extinct languages like Etruscan are lumped together with fixed ones such as Latin and Sanskrit.
Fishman, Joshua A. 2006. "'Holy Languages' in the Context of Societal Bilingualism." In *Language Loyalty, Language Planning and Language Revitalization: Recent Writings and Reflections from Joshua A. Fishman*, edited by Nancy H. Hornberger and Martin Pütz, 251–259. Clevedon, Buffalo, and Toronto: Multilingual Matters. Despite Fishman's compressed writing style, contains keen insights about the phenomenon of sacred languages.
Sawyer, J. F. A., and J. M. Y. Simpson. 2001. *Concise Encyclopedia of Language and Religion*. Amsterdam and New York: Elsevier. An essential compendium on a wide range of relevant issues and materials.

Chapter 2

Sacred Languages, Past and Present

With its numerous skyscrapers and hilly terrain, Hong Kong is a place of striking verticality. Perhaps nothing symbolizes this better than the outdoor escalators that help residents negotiate some of the inclines. Hong Kong is also "a binary metropolis of East and West … a cocktail of East Asian, Chinese, and Western values, commodities, social mores" (O'Connor 2012, 12, 21), and it almost seems as if the convergence of these two cultures forces the city upward – the result of a kind of civilizational plate tectonics. The creative juncture of East and West is reflected in the meeting and melding of two of the world's dominant languages and scripts. Standard Written Chinese (Mandarin or Putonghua) is used for high-level purposes – education, journalism, governance, and the like. English, the prestigious parlance of international communication, is primarily associated with tourism, trade, and travel. Meanwhile, the majority of citizens speak Cantonese on a daily basis. Chinese and English are blended both in everyday speech and in the signage found throughout the urban landscape, from billboards to restaurant menus. The Roman alphabet and the Chinese writing system are two global powerhouses. But they are more than just neutral communication technologies. A script symbolizes ethos, history, society, values, literature, and much more – the totality of which may be called a *scriptworld*. As David Damrosch, who coined the term, says,

> Alphabets and other scripts continue to this day to serve as key indices of cultural identity, often as battlegrounds of independence or interdependence.… local cultures make important decisions when they position themselves in relation to global scripts – or when they have scripts thrust on them. (2007, 195, 218)

Sacred Languages of the World: An Introduction, First Edition. Brian P. Bennett.

The binary nature of Hong Kong is expressed in its bilingual and biscriptal life. A simple street sign, with its Chinese characters and Roman letters, speaks volumes about the historical encounter of two civilizations or scriptworlds.

We do not normally think of Islam in conjunction with Hong Kong – the words "seem mismatched, a random juxtaposition of un-related terms" (O'Connor 2012, 3). In fact, Hong Kong is home to almost a quarter of a million Muslims. Some are Chinese Muslims or *Hui*, others are from South Asia, primarily Pakistan, while the largest subgroup (about 150,000) consists of Indonesian domestic workers. Tucked in the middle of the Wanchai neighborhood is the Ammar Masjid and Osman Ramju Sadick Islamic Centre – not quite a skyscraper, but tall for a mosque nonetheless. Completed in 1981, there is a traditional prayer space that can accommodate up to 700 for the Friday prayer, a library, a kindergarten, and a cafeteria serving halal food. The mosque is primarily associated with Chinese adherents but is also a hub for general Muslim community affairs, outreach, publications, and proselytism.

The façade of the Ammar Masjid and Osman Ramju Sadick Islamic Centre is rather typical for Hong Kong insofar as it combines writing representing two dominant scriptworlds: the Chinese and the English, East and West, vertical and horizontal. But one also sees something else there: a metallic plaque in a curvaceous Arabic script announcing the name of the mosque. The trilingual and triscriptal (Chinese, English, Arabic) signage continues inside, the walls being adorned with ornate calligraphic inscriptions in Arabic, as is typical of the Islamic approach to sacred space. (See Figure 2.1.)

Why is this Arabic sign noteworthy? We might say: it is just a sign – there is no need to make too much of it. Yet, signs point to practices, and practices point to people. Space is always "semiotized" – that is to say, marked by words and symbols indicating affiliation, membership, or exclusion. They tell us who can come in, who belongs, who is discouraged or prohibited from entering. This is true for a place of worship, a business, a classroom, or a café. Signs also reflect the flows and sedimentations of history (Blommaert 2013). For the presence of English writing across the Hong Kong landscape did not just happen; it is a legacy of British colonialism. Similarly, the ornate Arabic sign designates the space as Muslim. Its appearance on the mosque reflects the extraordinary spread of the Islamic faith across the planet: Mecca, the spiritual home of Islam, is located some 4700 miles away, in a very different region and in the heart of the Arabic

Figure 2.1 Mosque with English, Chinese, and Arabic signage, Hong Kong.

scriptworld. Whether believers are Chinese, Pakistani, or Indonesian – or American or British or any other nationality – the sacred Arabic language and script play a vital role in connecting them as members of the *ummah*, the global Muslim community.

Using Classical Arabic as our main example, but with comparative glances at other cases, this chapter looks at the origins of sacred languages in world history and their current place in the linguasphere, the network of languages that encircles Earth.

The Global Language System

It is very hard to know how many languages there are in the world, in part because there is no surefire scientific way of differentiating languages from dialects. Is the language spoken in the United States a dialect of English or is it sufficiently different to count as a language on its own, "American"? Who gets to say? For this reason, sociolinguists often prefer to speak of "varieties." Languages are like clouds that blend into one another – delineating and enumerating them is an elusive task (De Swaan 2001, 3). Moreover, what counts as a separate language is often a matter of extra-linguistic factors (social prejudices, government policies, etc.). As the old saying goes, a language is a dialect with an army and a navy. With all of these caveats in mind, scholars usually put the number of languages at 6000–7000, and that suffices for our purposes.

Linguists are fond of saying that all languages are equally capable of expressing the full range of human thought and emotion. One language is inherently no better than any others in terms of logicality or expressivity. That may be true, but from a sociolinguistic standpoint, not all languages are equal. Just as Hong Kong is a vertiginous city with many different levels, the world as a whole is not linguistically flat. Some languages and alphabets stand taller than – and overshadow – others. The most common way of ranking languages is by the number of speakers. This criterion makes Chinese the most important language in the world. Yet there is no denying the importance of English, which dominates in the areas of trade, aviation, entertainment, science, and education, among others. So which is more important?

A number of scholars have tried to devise ways to gauge the relative height or importance of the world's languages. For example, the linguist Louis-Jean Calvet has developed a "barometer" (*Baromètre Calvet des langues du monde*) that combines a variety of criteria to produce a score for languages with more than 500,000 speakers (smaller ones are not considered). This instrument allows us to assess and compare the importance of different languages on the world stage. The factors are as follows:

- the number of speakers
- the number of countries in which the language has official status
- the number of articles in Wikipedia written in the language
- the number of literature Nobel Prizes in the language
- entropy, or the degree to which the language is used in different countries (e.g., Amharic, which is largely confined to Ethiopia, has a score of 0.019 compared to the much more widespread Spanish, with a tally of 2.509)
- vehicularity, or the extent to which the language functions as a lingua franca (i.e., a contact language used by speakers of different mother tongues)
- the birth rate of countries where the language is spoken

- the ranking of countries where the language is spoken in terms of the United Nations' human development index (HDI)
- the rate of diffusion of the language across the Internet
- the number of translations in the language (based on UNESCO's *Index Translationum*)

Calvet acknowledges that other criteria could be considered, including:

- whether or not it is an official language of international organizations
- the number of scientific publications in the language
- the rate of telephone (fixed and mobile) dissemination in the countries in which the language is spoken
- the number of students studying the language as a foreign language

By using these metrics, each language can be given a score. English tops the list, followed by Spanish, French, German, and Russian. Mandarin is in tenth place. Turkish is ranked number 12 and Finnish 16. Urdu, Thai, Estonian, and Afrikaans are ranked 39–42. Amharic is 62, Xhosa 191, and Balinese 427. Karen Pao, a language with a half million speakers in Burma (Myanmar), is last on the list at number 563 (Calvet 2012).

Calvet's *Baromètre* website is set up so that the different factors can be manipulated depending on the interests of the researcher, for example putting greater emphasis on electronic and telephonic diffusion. But none of these criteria work well for sacred languages, which are non-spoken varieties conserved for things like prayers, scriptures, amulets, and yogic meditations. Latin and Sanskrit are recognized in the political sphere, by Vatican City and India, respectfully, but this is more of an honorary title; running a country is not their primary task. In the nineteenth and twentieth centuries, Classical Hebrew was rebuilt as an all-purpose vernacular – Modern Hebrew (also known as Israeli or Ivrit), which has official status in Israel and is ranked 21 according to Calvet's barometer. However, though the two are obviously related, this is not the same thing as the historic "holy tongue." Calvet's *Baromètre* treats the different dialects or varieties of Arabic as independent languages: Gulf (108), Chad (115), Moroccan (129), Egyptian (134), Jordanian (150), and so on. Again, these are not Classical Arabic, which has no native speakers per se but is the idiom of Muslim prayer and literature. Pali, Coptic, Ge'ez, Church Slavonic, and other sacred languages are part of the lifeworld of millions of adherents, but likewise have no barometric ranking.

The point we are trying to make is that sacred languages cannot be measured according to Calvet's criteria. A different set of factors is needed to assess their significance, for example:

- the scale of mythologization of the language (the extent to which the language is connected with superhuman personages and events)
- the ubiquity of prayers and rituals performed in the languages
- the number of scriptural texts composed in the language
- the degree of clericalization associated with the language (the extent to which it is the intellectual property of priests, monks, rabbis, pandits, or other religious leaders)
- the extent to which the language is expressed through cantillation and calligraphy
- the diffusion of amulets and tattoos bearing the sacred language

In theory, it would be possible to create a separate sacred language barometer, though there is no such instrument as yet.

David Dalby's concept of the linguasphere provides another wide-angled view of the world's language situation. He writes, "Just as 'bio-sphere' denotes the terrestrial mantle of living organisms, so the term 'linguasphere' denotes the mantle of communication gradually extended around the planet by humankind." It is an "organic continuum, a global medium for human communication and the circulation of ideas," encompassing all the languages that have emerged and evolved within all human societies throughout history (2001, 22). To represent this complex planetary system, Dalby devised an elaborate coding system encompassing so-called inner languages, outer languages, arterial languages, zones, sectors, phylosectors (Afro-Asian, Austronesian, Indo-European, etc.), and geosectors (Africa, Eurasia, North-America, etc.). An arterial language, for instance, is one that is spoken by at least 1 percent of Earth's population. This category includes Mandarin Chinese, English, Hindi + Urdu (grouped together because they are two closely related varieties), Spanish, Russian, Arabic, Bengali, Portuguese, and Malay (Dalby 2012).

The Linguasphere Register does not necessarily offer a way of determining the relative "height" or influence of these different languages, so in that sense it is not as useful as Calvet's *Baromètre*. However, Dalby does include sacred languages in his incredible map of the complex web of languages that encircle the world, though he prefers the designation *classical*.

He notes that most of the world's major arterial languages are related to, or are influenced by, just five classical languages: Classical Chinese, Sanskrit + Pali (two closely related varieties), Church Slavonic, Classical Arabic, and Latin (2001, 24). Embodied in written texts propagated by world religions and political empires, these languages have exercised an outsized impact on the linguasphere. But they are not just historical artifacts "inherited from earlier centuries"; they are "still read as literary or liturgical languages (and which thus still form part of the modern linguasphere)" (Dalby 2012, 299, 295). As far as specific languages are concerned, Dalby provides the following annotations:

- Coptic is "surviving as liturgical language of Coptic Church" (84)
- Ge'ez is "still in liturgical and poetic use" (93)
- Latin is "extinct as a natural spoken language, but still cultivated on a small scale, especially within the Catholic church, as an international written and spoken vehicular" (407)
- Church Slavonic "survives as liturgical language of the Eastern Orthodox Church" (440)
- Avestan is "preserved as a liturgical language by Zoroastrian (Parsee) communities" (455)
- Pali is "studied and read within Buddhist communities" (469)
- Sanskrit is "studied and read (and sometimes spoken) within Hindu communities" (469)

Setting aside for now the specifics regarding each language, the word "still" offers both good news and bad news. On the one hand, it informs us that the language is not extinct and continues to be part of the linguasphere, "humankind's greatest and most complex creation" (2001, 24). On the other hand, terms such as "still," "preserved," and "survives" suggest a decline from an earlier, more fulsome period of usage. Indeed, the reach and influence of sacred languages has certainly dwindled over time, and it is not yet clear if recent developments (including neotraditionalist movements and technological innovations) will alter the situation.

Of course, because they are not all the same, we must look at the status of different sacred languages on a case-by-case basis. They have followed different, at times converging and conflicting, pathways to the present day. Classical Arabic, as we shall see, is in a better position than several other sacred tongues. Dalby (2001, 24) suggests that the most important language in the world changes in the course of a day, shifting, as the sun rises and sets, from Chinese to English. There are some 1.6 billion Muslims in the world. The Islamic *ummah* spans the globe, mostly hugging the equator, from Mecca to Jakarta. Five times each day, as hundreds of millions of Muslims stop what they are doing, turn toward Mecca, and recite their prayers, Classical Arabic becomes one of the most impactful languages on Earth. According to Andrey Rosowsky, "Its importance and role as a liturgical language means that as a written language it rivals Mandarin, with 1 billion speakers, as the most widely known language in the world" (2008, 208).

In what follows we will look at sacred languages across time and space, retracing the twinned birth of world religions and sacred languages in human history, the rise and fall of what sociolinguists call diglossia, and the place of Classical Arabic and other sanctified languages in the modern-day linguasphere. Just as ancient churches and mosques are nowadays often surrounded by office towers, shopping malls, and apartment complexes, sacred languages may have lost ground but continue to occupy important niches in the cultural landscape. To appreciate their current position (and predicament), we need to see where they have come from.

A Very Short History of the World

Where did sacred languages come from and how did they enter the linguasphere? There are different ways to periodize world history. In addition to the familiar ancient–medieval–modern model, for example, some speak of a transition from the age of revelation to the age of information (Turner 2011). Every such schema is simply a conceptual device for handling a hugely complicated topic. In what follows, we will outline a five-part paradigm: ancient, axial, premodern, modern, postmodern (see Gellner 1995). Superimposed on this periodization we might imagine a trajectory that looks something like a bell curve: sacred languages started small with the emergence of the world religions in the transition from the ancient to the axial age, then bulged out in the premodern era before being reduced in scope under the forces of modernity. Conflicting trends are evident in the postmodern period and it is not yet clear which way the trajectory will continue. We will offer a brief synopsis of the key religious and linguistic features of each time period.

Ancient

The Roman phrase *pax deorum* ("peace of the gods") is a fitting motto for the ancient era of religious history as a whole, not just the ancient Romans. This "peace" or covenant was "a mutually beneficial state of peace between Rome and its deities, with the gods safeguarding Rome's public welfare … and the Romans providing the gods their desired worship and cult" (Johnson 2012). Peaceful relations with the divine were thought to be achieved and maintained primarily through ritual, especially sacrifices performed in civic temple complexes. Similar notions motivated the religions of other ancient civilizations. Though there were sacred languages in the ancient period (e.g., Sumerian), the phenomenon in general is associated with the post-ancient mode of religion.

Axial

This period is seen as one of the great turning points in human history, marked (among other things) by the emergence of the so-called world religions as well as vast multiethnic empires, the two often going hand in hand. Determining what counts as a world religion is a notoriously tricky endeavor. Some scholars emphasize number of members, while others point to the presence of certain telltale phenomena like soteriology (a message of salvation) or missionary work. Some scholars have suggested alternative terms. For the comparativist Michael Pye, size has nothing to do with how these religions should be classified. He thinks the key issue is, rather, their basic orientation to the human condition. Accordingly, he distinguishes "primal" from "critical" religions (2013, 54). In a similar vein, Richard Gombrich refers to "communal religion" versus "soteriology" (1988, 25–28). Some scholars, including Pye and Gombrich, would generally place Judaism and Hinduism in the former category (primal, communal) as opposed to the latter (critical, soteriological). Those faiths have both dabbled in missionary work, but not to the same extent as Christianity or Buddhism. It should be noted that a number of scholars in religious studies reject altogether the very idea of *world religions*, considering it a deeply flawed Western category that obscures more than it illuminates (e.g., Smith 2004, 167–171).

The sociologist Stephen Sharot acknowledges this critique but believes the notion of *world religion* does apply to an observable slice of reality and therefore retains its analytical usefulness. He suggests that transcendence, in several different senses, is the defining feature of the world religions.

First, unlike the religions of the ancient riverine civilizations, these religions offer a transcendental vision. The unseen superhuman dimension that is central to any religion is no longer imagined to be a kind of mirror image of this world (the way that Roman gods were in many ways like magnified human beings, some beautiful, some rather oafish, and so on), but is now said to be radically different, other, superior – hence newfound conceptions of Brahman or Yahweh. Second, religion is not just about sanctification, receiving blessings and boons and reinforcing (and, when necessary, repairing) the status quo by means of ad hoc sacrifices and appeals to deities (as in the *pax deorum*). This new breed of religion offers a soteriology, that is to say, a thoroughgoing critique of human existence (which is said to be ruined by sin, ignorance, evil, idolatry) and a correspondingly totalistic solution that is "out of this world," normally achieved after death (heaven, paradise, nirvana). Third, this salvific message is considered to be valid for everyone: it transcends social and political boundaries. Membership in these new religious formations is theoretically by conversion – being won over by the message – not simply a matter of birth and societal obligation. The world religions are universalist in aspiration, if not in reality (Sharot 2001, 7–10).

Thus, the topography of religion – and with it, the linguasphere – shifted in the transition from the ancient to the axial age. We see this on four interconnected levels (Lincoln 2012), each of which is pertinent to the phenomenon of sacred languages:

Beliefs There is a movement in the post-ancient period from inspired utterances, for example the oracle at Delphi in ancient Greece, to canonical books like the Islamic Qur'an or Buddhist Tipitika, which in turn give rise to enormous volumes of scriptural commentary and theological speculation. Since they are the words that transmit the revelatory Word, languages like Arabic and Pali become themselves mythologized. These holy languages are treated with special care and enhanced through chanting and calligraphy. The very scripts in which they are written may be said to possess cosmic meaning and magical potency.

Practices The focus of religion morphs from ritual sacrifice performed in temples, as we see in ancient Rome or Jerusalem, to such practices as yoga, meditation, alms-giving, and dietary regulations. Sacred languages like Arabic and Sanskrit figure into a range of bookish practices, from the recitation of mantras to the intensive study of scriptures to the wearing of textual amulets.

Institutions Ancient priesthoods were part of civic or political hierarchies in one location, for instance the "Eternal City" of ancient Rome. In the axial period, however, organizations like the Buddhist *sangha* (monastic order) and the Catholic priesthood represent more autonomous, international purveyors of scriptures and salvation. They become custodians of sacred languages like Pali and Latin, which may function as a lingua franca (common language) among clerics who live in different countries and speak different mother tongues.

Communities In the ancient period, religion was blended into life, being coterminous with polity and ethnicity. Adherents "spoke the same language, shared the same norms, celebrated the same festivals, and worshipped at the same altars, seeking favor of the same gods for the group of which they were all a part" (Lincoln 2012, 79). But now, as result of missionary work and migration (sometimes, as in the case of Judaism and Zoroastrianism, due to persecution), we see the emergence of geographically dispersed communities linked by religious texts and symbols, as well as international codes like Latin, Pali, Hebrew, and Arabic. At the same time, issues of doctrine, heresy, and schism – which would have been unknown to the ancient Romans or Babylonians – begin to loom large. Religions like Christianity and Buddhism fractured from sectarianism even as they expanded across borders.

Needless to say, this epochal transformation from the ancient to the axial is not something that happened immediately or uniformly around the world. There are many connections and continuities between the two modes of religion. In some places, bloody sacrifices are still made to this day in statue-filled temples. In others, the archaic legacy has been spiritualized, with churches and synagogues occasionally designated as "temples," and the Catholic Mass understood as a sacrifice. More substantially, because they have to attend to people's daily needs, axial-age faiths such as Christianity and Buddhism eventually become much like the communal/primal religions they supposedly replaced (Pye 2013, 59–60). Like their ancient forebears, the so-called world religions may reinforce the status quo and dispense small rewards of protection, healing, or military success in addition to the big prize of ultimate salvation or liberation. Similarly, over the centuries, membership in Islam or Buddhism or Christianity has largely become a matter of birth and societal obligation, not conversion. Though ostensibly universal in scope, world religions often play a major part in ethnic or national identities. For many, being

Thai is synonymous with being Buddhist; for centuries, Irish identity was indubitably Catholic. Yet, bearing all of these caveats and qualifications in mind, overall we can observe a broad typological difference between religiosity in the ancient and post-ancient worlds. Every religion has its "hot spots" or "magnets" (Paden 2016, 127) that attract and focus the energies of its members. In this fundamental historical transition, these start to gravitate from sacrifices to scriptures, temples to texts, libations to libraries.

Premodern

As the so-called world religions grew and solidified during the premodern era (sometimes dubbed the "Age of Faith" in history textbooks), sacred languages found themselves in a situation known as diglossia. This involves a rather stable arrangement between two language varieties which sociolinguists typically designate H for high and L for low. The two varieties may be genetically related languages (e.g., Latin and French) or not (e.g., Pali and Thai). Diglossia involves a kind of division of labor between the two languages, with each performing different communicative tasks. The H variety is used for liturgy, literature, and learning, not informal communication. It is nobody's first language, but is transmitted by formal educational means (seminaries, madrasas, etc.). The L variety is employed for everyday conversations at home, among friends and neighbors, and in the marketplace. The H language has high societal prestige and is used for serious purposes, whereas the L variety tends to be viewed as primitive and lacking in *gravitas* – the verbal equivalent of wine and water. Typically, the H language is written while the L is oral. The advent of writing does not automatically lead to diglossia, but it creates a "particularly hospitable environment" for it (Hudson 2002, 24). Another factor in the emergence of diglossia is the appearance of organized religious intellectuals – the Christian priesthood, the Buddhist monastic order, the Jewish rabbinate, and so on – who have the time, opportunity, and resources to learn the sacred language and become adept in reading and performing the texts written in it. In sum, the appearance of the world religions, with their particular constellation of beliefs, practices, and institutions, was conducive to the emergence of diglossia in many places around the world.

The phenomenon of diglossia is now quite foreign to many people. One way to get a very basic sense of it is to consider the numerous doublets in

English that mean more or less the same thing but come from either Anglo-Saxon or Latin. The former tend to be shorter and sound rougher, while the latter are longer and have a more elevated (or pompous) ring to them. For example:

leave	relinquish
ask	inquire
boon	advantage
belly	abdomen
cold	frigid
deer	venison
drink	imbibe
fill up	replenish
western	occidental
green	verdant

(cf. Ferguson 1959, 334)

In a situation of true diglossia, religious rituals as well as lectures and literature and other forms of serious discourse would always draw upon words from the right-hand column, whereas conversations at home and on the street would use words from the left. This diglossic way of sorting things out would be a predictable pattern of communication for all members of the community.

A number of sacred languages experienced a "bulge" period, like the fat part of a bell curve, in the premodern era. Being prestigious, the language was extended beyond the religious sphere into more and more domains. For example, the Christian corpus of Latin texts is something like 10,000 times that of the Classical ("pagan") one. The famous works of ancient Roman authors like Vergil or Cicero are but tiny dots in a vast Latinate galaxy. The overwhelming majority of Latin texts come from the era of Christendom, including works on government, diplomacy, science, theology, law, medicine, and theater. According to Jürgen Leonhardt:

> If we assume that the sum total of Latin texts from antiquity may be snugly accommodated in five hundred volumes running an estimated five hundred pages each, we would need about ten thousand times that number, that is, at least five million additional volumes of the same size, to house the total output in Latin texts. (2013, 2)

That is quite a bulge. Similarly, Sanskrit morphed from being a language originally restricted to liturgical hymns and formulae into a vehicle for poetry and statecraft. At its zenith Pali was used by Buddhist communities in South and Southeast Asia not only for scriptural texts, but for history, cosmology, medicine, literature, and jurisprudence. We might say that, as the religion expands and assumes the attributes of a civilization ("Islamic civilization," "Buddhist civilization," and so on), the sacred language is extended, gaining real estate, taking on more tasks and topics. But the forces of modernity reverse this trend and curtail further expansion – this is the downward slope of our imaginary bell curve.

Modern

The pattern of religion and the size and configuration of the linguasphere changed dramatically once again in the modern era, though not uniformly and not all at once, of course. The Renaissance, the Protestant Reformation, and the Enlightenment; the growth of secularization (the reduction of religious thought and influence), nationalism, democracy; the spread of mass education and commercial printing – all of these forces chipped away at the prevailing diglossic division-of-labor arrangement and challenged the vaunted position of sacred languages. In this stage of history,

> the vernaculars that had sprouted from the great classical [sacred] languages were coming into their own: they were crafted into standard versions by poets, writers and scholars, increasingly used in trade, science, law, administration and, in the West, also in religion at princely courts. (De Swaan 2001, 9)

Previously L (low) languages like French and Russian achieved a dignity of their own vis-à-vis their H (high) counterparts of Latin and Church Slavonic, though not at the same speed (French came of age before Russian did). During the modern era, the major European languages – Spanish, French, Portuguese, English, Dutch, Russian – were then exported around the world in massive colonial endeavors. The ideology that each nation should have its own homegrown vernacular was also exported. As a general rule, modernity shrunk the bulge: sacred languages lost out to their vernacular rivals in domain after domain (education, literature, etc.), being largely confined to the cultic sphere – and even there, vernacular languages started to make inroads (e.g., Fellman 1993). That is why we say that sacred languages are "still" in use as liturgical tongues, or that they "survive" or "persist." The combined forces of modernity have eroded their scope and status, though not entirely.

Postmodern

Not everyone agrees that there is such a thing as a postmodern era, some preferring the label late modern. Ernest Gellner, a brilliant but at times curmudgeonly scholar, derided this epoch as the "Californian" period of world history, the motto of which should be "anything goes," for "a kind of total permissiveness in belief prevails" (1995, 280). Indeed, a number of conflicting trends are observable. In the "center," the so-called world religions (Buddhism, Islam, Christianity, etc.) still hold sway across much of the planet, and their sacred languages, though reduced in scope from their premodern heyday, continue to be used and cherished. On the "right" side of the spectrum, different fundamentalist versions of these religions promote sacred languages with renewed vigor, while on the "left," we can see various forms of easy-access commercialized spirituality, some of which involve sacred languages (e.g., Sanskrit with yoga, Hebrew with Kabbalah).

As noted above, diglossia was one of the hallmarks of the premodern era, but thanks to the forces of modernity, this pattern no longer prevails throughout most of the world. The domains of Latin, Ge'ez, Pali, and other sacred languages have been severely reduced – they were put on a diet and lost their "bulge" and are no longer much used for the writing of history, astronomy, poetry, and other learned subjects. National vernaculars have taken over those roles. The case of Classical Arabic, however, is quite different. The closest thing to a full-fledged version of diglossia in the world today is found in the Arabic-speaking countries of the *ummah* (the majority of Muslims speak other languages as their first language). The linguistic situation is captured well by Kees Versteegh:

> Perhaps the best analogue to the situation in the Arabic-speaking countries would be that of a hypothetical modern France, where all newspapers and books are written in Latin, and in churches the only language used by the priests is Latin. On the other hand, people talking in a café use French, people at home or among friends use French. In school, the official language of the classroom is Latin, but during the breaks between classes students use French among themselves, and so do the teachers … In Arabic-speaking countries, the actual situation is very much like the hypothetical situation sketched here for France. (2014, 241)

This is a simplified picture, of course. In reality, there are many intermediate forms between the H and L varieties of Arabic (Bassiouney 2009). The key thing for our purposes, though, is the fact that the precious linguistic resource of Classical Arabic is set above all vernacular versions, with which it interacts in a diglossic division of labor.

Niloofar Haeri's book, *Sacred Language, Ordinary People* (2003), provides a sustained look at the place of Classical Arabic in one Muslim society, Egypt. The contrast there is between Classical Arabic and Egyptian Arabic. Classical Arabic is the language of the Qur'an and Islamic rituals, but a kind of updated version, sometimes called Modern Standard Arabic, is used in the government bureaucracy, the media, literature, and education. Egyptian Arabic is used in conversation, in film, theater, and some poetry. The difference between Classical and Egyptian Arabic varieties is perhaps comparable to the gap between Shakespeare and modern-day English: "a version of English crystallized at a particular moment in history, and the spoken language of today, 400 years later. For most first-language English speakers, much of what Shakespeare has written is incomprehensible on first hearing without the aid of the text" (Rosowsky 2008, 7).

There are clear and significant differences between Classical and Egyptian Arabic in terms of their sounds, vocabulary, and syntax. Classical Arabic has a case system of nominative, accusative, and genitive that is absent from the vernacular. For example:

Classical *al-kitaabu jamiilun* "the book is beautiful" (nominative case endings)
Egyptian *il-kitaab gamiil* (no cases)

Furthermore, in Classical Arabic the word order is verb–subject–object (linguists abbreviate this as VSO), whereas in Egyptian Arabic it is subject–verb–object (SVO):

Classical *ate the boy the food* (VSO)
Egyptian *the boy ate the food* (SVO)

(Haeri 2003, 4–5, Table 1.1)

Classical Arabic is no one's mother tongue. And in fact, most people do not use Classical Arabic for work, unless they are in a profession relating to the government or media. It is part and parcel of their religious life, though this requires instruction: "For Egyptians and for other Muslims, the correct pronunciation of the prayers, their meanings, the different postures of the body, the number of prayer cycles and their repetitions all must be formally taught" (34). Classical Arabic has a pronounced oral dimension, consisting of prayers uttered on a daily basis or for life-cycle occasions (birth, marriage, sickness, death) and scriptural recitations heard in person or via television or cassette tapes. If it is read by Egyptian Muslims, it is not read in the same way as a news story; rather, it is often pondered, appreciated, ruminated upon. Such pious practices do not really prepare Egyptians to read and write in Classical Arabic, or take exams in the language. (Imagine having to write a term paper or deliver an oral report in Shakespearean English.) Therefore, people approach such tasks with a certain amount of trepidation, fearing to make a mistake, especially with the case system (which, as noted above, is absent from the spoken vernacular).

The case of Classical Arabic is rather distinctive in the postmodern era, because a basic diglossic pattern can still be found in Egypt and other Arabic-speaking Muslim countries. The history of Classical Arabic is not a simple line, though. The importation of Islam into ancient Egypt muscled out Coptic as a spoken language, reducing it to a liturgical idiom (and Arabic would eventually penetrate the liturgy as well). Elsewhere, however, Classical Arabic came in more as a language of liturgy, influencing local languages in a multitude of ways, but not overwriting them. Thus, in places like Hong Kong and indeed throughout much of the Islamic world, Classical Arabic is used for liturgical and thaumaturgical (miraculous or magical) purposes, not for lectures and literature. Most Muslims are not native Arabic speakers. They may only know selected pieces of the sacred language – the *shahada* (creed), some prayers, perhaps some chapters of the Qur'an, formulaic salutions, and so on. Pious expressions like *inshallah* (God willing) and *alhamdulillah* (praise be to God) may pepper their speech.

So we should not expect believers to be "fluent" in Classical Arabic. Instead, we should recognize that, in certain places and during certain moments of the day, Muslims will see, hear, recognize, and possibly recite or exclaim snippets of their sacred language. Nor should we should think that a language like Latin or Pali or Coptic has to be used in all areas of life or be consigned to the dustbin of history. It is not a zero-sum linguistic game. Even in the case of Classical Arabic, the sacred language functions as a precious resource drawn on for some pursuits and projects, but not for others. Words or verses in Classical Arabic can create a "solemn atmosphere," being associated with piety, authority, and formality, while the vernacular language suggests family, intimacy, and, informality (Versteegh 2014, 251). Fundamentalists may lard their speeches with chunks of Classical Arabic, hoping that the prestigious aura that comes with the language will suffuse them as well (Kermani 2015). Other believers use the sacred language in a much more restricted way, for prayers, amulets, pious expressions, wall decorations, and scriptural recitations. This is in addition to the varieties they speak at home or at the market. Not every language is suitable for every purpose.

Bits and Pieces

We often talk about languages as if they are whole entities that one either knows or does not know. In reality, people do not command an entire language. Even native speakers of French (or Russian or English or Thai) do not know and control all the stylistic levels and technical vocabularies that make up the totality of that language. Every language is always known in piecemeal or truncated fashion. People pick up bits and pieces of diverse languages through formal means (school, self-study books, smartphone apps) and informal ones (friendships, movies, work, travel). We can speak about certain topics in certain ways, but not all topics in all ways (Blommaert and Backus 2011).

Instead of thinking in all-or-nothing terms about languages, we should approach the matter in terms of linguistic resources and competencies. Languages are like resources, pieces of which one can add to one's linguistic repertoire or toolkit. According to Blommaert and Backus (2011), in addition to one's mother tongue(s), there are a variety of ways to learn a language and a range of competencies to be achieved:

- language(s) learned at school
- temporary language learning; for example, travelers learning a few words or phrases for greeting, booking a hotel room, or ordering a meal
- single-word learning in languages one does not otherwise know: sayonara, shalom, ciao, aloha, salud!, bon appétit, merde, asshole, cojones!
- learning to recognize the sound or appearance of certain languages, for example, Chinese, Cyrillic, Korean, Hebrew, and so on

- learning bits of languages with certain topics or techniques; for instance, English words are often embedded in courses of study having to do with computers and information technology (e.g., seminars at work, instructional videos)
- learning snippets of a language through a hobby or recreation; one might learn some French or Italian by studying French or Italian cooking, or pick up bits of Chinese or Japanese by engaging with Feng Shui or Karate

Mastering bigger or smaller chunks of different languages in a range of contexts and situations – this is how most people deal with languages. It is the way of the world. It is particularly important to recognize this because, when it comes to sacred languages, we are often dealing with a highly restricted linguistic competence. Depending on the person, the tradition, and a number of other variables, competence may be simply the ability to recognize, decode, memorize, or utter certain words or phrases at the appropriate time and place: for example, the weekly greeting of *Shabbat shalom* [Sabbath greetings] in Hebrew or the Easter exclamation of *Khristos voskrese!* [Christ hath risen!] in Church Slavonic.

Everyone has a linguistic repertoire or toolkit. The contents are unevenly distributed and reflect the person's particular biography, the places of their birth, school, work, travel, recreation, worship, and so on. Moreover, this repertoire is constantly shifting. Someone who spoke a language as a child with her grandparents might travel back to the "old country" for a refresher course, thereby enhancing her repertoire. Another person might learn a language like Latin or Greek in school, but lose proficiency in it over the years. Thus, repertoires are always partial and dynamic (Blommaert and Backus 2011). In sum:

> Language users employ whatever linguistic features are at their disposal to achieve their communicative aims as best they can, regardless of how well they know the involved languages; this entails that the language users may know – and use – the fact that some of the features are perceived by some speakers as not belonging together. (Jørgensen et al. 2011, 34)

We have to approach language in this way if we are to properly understand and appreciate the place of sacred languages in the contemporary linguasphere. Sometimes people know the sacred language very well, as can be the case with (predominantly male) clerics like priests, imams, monks, and debteras (in the Ethiopian Church). They are the experts and have had the time and opportunity to study the language in depth over many years. Even if sacred language learning is widespread in the tradition, as is the case with Hebrew in Judaism or Arabic in Islam, clerics typically exhibit a greater expertise than ordinary religionists. But this is not to say that they themselves understand everything. Many Theravada Buddhist monks have memorized long texts in Pali, but may not be able to explain them. There are Islamic madrasa teachers who instruct youth in Qur'anic recitation, even though they themselves might have great trouble translating the Arabic text. We have to be aware that what counts as competence in a sacred language may be quite different than what is expected in terms of vernacular languages.

Like religions, languages are not uniform and unchanging entities. Terms of "Latin" (or "Hebrew" or "Pali") are deceptive shorthand labels for immense linguistic traditions stretching over thousands of years, encompassing a wide range of styles, genres, and specialized vocabularies. For example, Ecclesiastical Latin encompasses liturgical, theological, juridical, inscriptional, and other sub-varieties. Certain texts might easily trip off the tongue, while others pose challenges even to experts. To recite the lines of the Angelus prayer is one thing, to read a passage (let alone a complete tome) of Augustine is quite another. A Catholic group that promotes the study of Latin encourages its members with these words: "It is enough that they value the language highly as the Church's own and, insofar as it is possible without inconvenience, that they desire to learn at least some things in the language, such as certain texts of the Holy Mass and certain liturgical chants" (Familia Sancti Hieronymi 1989). That kind of modest scope is actually quite typical of sacred languages in general. Thai monks might be able to recite the most common *paritta* (protective) chants, but struggle mightily with *Abidhamma* (advanced philosophical) literature. People also forget sacred languages. Jews may not remember what they had to learn for their Bar Mitzvah; Buddhists may forget what they memorized when they were in the robes (it is possible in some Theravada countries to join the monastic order on a short-term basis). Restricted literacy is the order of the day.

The Arabic Scriptworld

Writing has played a key role in the propagation of the so-called world religions, profoundly transforming the linguasphere in the process. Dalby puts it this way: The linguasphere started approximately 50,000 years ago, with the inception of human speech. About 5000 years ago, the invention of writing had profound effects in codifying, preserving, and transmitting a select group of languages – the vast majority of others remaining purely oral phenomena. Then, the development of printing some 500 years ago "has generally accelerated the flow of words among individual languages" (2001, 22). Now, with the dawn of electronic communication – what Dalby dubs the neolinguasphere (2012, 104) – the global dissemination of languages of all kinds is occurring in unpredictable ways.

As already noted above, one of the hallmarks of religion in the axial period is a shift in the nature of religion, from civic temples to canonical texts like the Bible, Qur'an, and Tipitika. Given an assist by alphabetic writing, which is a nimbler writing technology than the ancient systems of hieroglyphics or cuneiform, the world religions were able to spread across much of the planet. As Sharot notes, "Sacred writings provide a common measuring stick of truth, a common reference point for the performance of ritual, and a common foundation for identity across all social and political boundaries" (2001, 16).

Scripts are closely connected with the so-called world religions. As the faith spreads by means of migration or missionary work, it carries along its sacred texts – and the script in which they are composed. Associated with divine revelation and salvation history, the script exudes a "charisma" that influences speakers of local languages, who may decide to dress up their own language in the vesture of the important writing system (Aytürk 2010). For instance, the Hebrew script has been adapted for Yiddish, Judeo-Arabic, Ladino, and other domestic Jewish languages. Russian, Bulgarian, and Serbian, as well as numerous non-Slavic varieties across Eurasia, are written in different forms of Cyrillic, all of which are ultimately derived from the Church Slavonic version. Christian countries that have been influenced by Catholic or Protestant Christianity employ the Latin alphabet. The case of Sanskrit is somewhat anomalous. Historically, it was written in different regional scripts, though now it is primarily associated with Devanagari, which carries over to vernacular languages like Hindi, Marathi, and Nepali. The end result is that, "The distribution of major types of writing systems in the world correlates more closely with the distribution of the world's major religions than with genetic or typological classifications of languages" (Ferguson 1982, 95). In other words, a map of the world's scripts matches up well with a map of the world's scriptures. Each alphabet or writing system seems to embody a different civilizational style, ethos, mentality, and religious tradition – a different scriptworld.

Converting from one script to another is rarely just a practical decision. The word "conversion" seems apt, because scripts are not just neutral instruments; they signal identity and allegiance. They seem to embody a group's history and ethos. Using the Arabic script may facilitate trade and travel between communities, but it also expresses a bond with fellow Muslims.

Classical Arabic is in many ways a sonic phenomenon – the sound of Qur'anic recitation is of utmost importance in the lived religious experience of Muslims. But the sanctity and authority of the holy book, written in the Arabic alphabet, means that the script itself has been vested with a kind of holy cachet. Before the modern era, "the Arabic alphabet reigned supreme, providing a seamless zone of alphabetic unity among the Muslim elite, stretching from Morocco to India and Java" (Aytürk 2010, 101). With the spread of Islam, scores of unrelated languages adopted the Arabic writing system as a prestigious semiotic resource: Persian, Pashto, Baluchi, Kurdish, Kashmiri, Sindhi, Uyghur, Moplah, Malagasy, Sulu, and Urdu. (See Figure 2.2.) Roughly a third of the world's languages are spoken in Africa. Arabic served there as a "super-regional" script, preceding the introduction of Latin by some 500 years and encompassing about eighty

Figure 2.2 Qur'an with interlinear Urdu translation. Courtesy of Peter Gottschalk.

different languages (Mumin 2014). In the wake of European colonization, there has been a kind of bifurcation and competition between two script-worlds: Arabic and Islam on one side versus Latin and Christianity/the "West" on the other.

When a local community in Africa or South Asia or elsewhere adopted the Arabic script for its own local language, this required a certain logistical and ideological transformation. There are many technical issues in changing scripts, not the least of which is a possible switch in directionality (left to right, right to left). Letters may have to be modified to convey sounds not found in Arabic. The script has to be adapted to the language, rather like a suit being tailored – tucked in a little here, let out a little there. Some may eventually come to feel that this foreign garb is constricting. For example, for centuries the Turkish language was written with a modified Arabic script. However,

> the Arabic alphabet, adopted for religious reasons, functioned as a straightjacket that smothered the Turkish phonetic repertoire. Turkish is distinguished, for instance, by its wide range of vowels – eight in modern Turkish: *a*, *e*, *ı*, *i*, *o*, *ö*, *u*, *ü* – but those had to be expressed with only three characters from the Arabic grapheme inventory, making it quite difficult to read a text accurately. (Aytürk 2010, 112)

For example, the same word could be read as *ulu* (great), *avlu* (courtyard), or *ölü* (dead).

In addition to the technical issues of switching from one alphabet to another, there is also an ideological or even mythological dimension. Scripts have all kinds of historical, literary, cultural, and artistic associations. They are emblems of identity and, for believers, may symbolize the unfolding of salvation history. (Imagine switching from writing English with the Latin alphabet to doing so in Arabic or Cyrillic or Devanagari – there would certainly be some emotional resistance, at least at first.) But there are also possible advantages to alphabetic conversion. If one writes (say) Tamil, Malay, or Javanese with a modified Arabic script, then all of a sudden, it becomes possible to retain actual Arabic words from the Qur'an in one's writing (Ricci 2011, 174). A single alphabet or writing system facilitates the integration of dispersed believers. In that way, one's local community can become part of a trans-regional intellectual and spiritual exchange. Moreover, using the Arabic script bestows a kind of prestige on one's native tongue, now appearing dressed up in this cosmopolitan garb.

In different ways, then, to use the Arabic script is to be connected to the mythic origins of the faith, to the holy center of Mecca, to the heaven-sent Qur'an, and to the *ummah*, a multiethnic community of fellow Muslims.

We should note that history also records numerous attempts to move away from a sacred script. Some Muslim communities have switched from using Arabic to the Latin alphabet for writing their native tongue, including Indonesian (Malay), Hausa, Somali, Sudanese, and Swahili. This does not necessarily signal a conversion to Christianity, but an attraction to aspects of the West and the trappings of modernity. In other cases, languages have been transferred from Arabic to Devanagari (e.g., Punjabi, Kashmiri) or Cyrillic (e.g., Chechen, Kabardian). Perhaps the most famous case involved the reforms of Kemal Atatürk, the first president of Turkey, who not only legislated a switch from the Arabic to the Roman alphabet for writing the Turkish language, but also changed the traditional calendar, clock, and clothing – a bold attempt to relocate a country to a different scriptworld (see Lewis 1999).

***

The purpose of this chapter has been to provide a highly simplified and schematic map of sacred languages, past and present, outlining their appearance in history and their current place in the linguasphere. The emergence of the so-called world religions (or "critical religions" or "soteriologies") was one of the turning points in history and had enormous global ramifications. For centuries or even millennia, sacralized languages like Latin, Hebrew, Pali, and Sanskrit have been the linguistic means to codify and convey messages of broad spiritual appeal; they have been the focal points of intense study, exegesis, devotion, and mystical speculation; they have served as linking languages for far-flung religious clergies and communities. The transcendental message of Islam, codified in the Qur'an, led to the diffusion of the Classical Arabic language and its charismatic script across large swaths of the planet. In Arabic-speaking countries like Egypt, the prestige of Classical Arabic continues to serve H (high) functions in the linguistic division of labor. Elsewhere, as in Hong Kong, the sacred language operates in a more restricted sphere in the form of salutations, prayers, pious exclamations, and decorative inscriptions.

Like the iconic slim-line double-decker trams that traverse parts of Hong Kong, sacred languages follow a fixed, narrow path in the midst of a bustling multilingual world. They are unmistakable symbols of history and identity, but also more than that: though limited in range, sacred languages are still functioning vehicles of communication, conveying human thoughts and emotions across the linguasphere.

References

Aytürk, İlker. 2010. "Script Charisma in Hebrew and Turkish: A Comparative Framework for Explaining Success and Failure of Romanization." *Journal of World History* 21 (1): 97–130.

Bassiouney, Reem. 2009. *Arabic Sociolinguistics: Topics in Diglossia, Gender, Identity, and Politics*. Washington, DC: Georgetown University Press.

Blommaert, Jan. 2013. *Ethnography, Superdiversity and Linguistic Landscapes: Chronicles of Complexity*. Bristol and Buffalo: Multilingual Matters.

Blommaert, Jan, and Ad Backus. 2011. "Repertoires Revisited: 'Knowing Language' in Superdiversity." *Working Papers in Urban Language and Literacies*, Paper 67: 2–26.

Calvet, Louis-Jean. 2012. *Baromètre Calvet des langues du monde*. Accessed June 28, 2016. http://wikilf.culture.fr/barometre2012/

Dalby, David. 2001. "The Linguasphere: Kaleidoscope of the World's Languages." *English Today* 65, vol. 17 (1): 22–26.

Dalby, David. 2012 (1999/2000). *The Linguasphere Register of the World's Languages and Speech Communities*. Accessed May 15, 2016. http://www.linguasphere.info/lcontao/bienvenue-welcome.html

Damrosch, David. 2007. "Scriptworlds: Writing Systems and the Formation of World Literature." *Modern Language Quarterly* 68 (2): 195–219.

De Swaan, Abram. 2001. *Words of the World: The Global Language System*. Cambridge: Polity.

Familia Sancti Hieronymi. 1989. Constitution, Amendment I. Accessed July 24, 2016. http://hieronymus.us.com/Constitutio/FSH-Anglice.htm

Fellman, Jack. 1993. "The Birth of an African Literary Language: The Case of Amharic." *Research in African Literatures* 24 (3): 123–125. http://www.jstor.org/stable/3820120

Ferguson, Charles A. 1959. "Diglossia." *Word* 15 (2): 325–340. DOI: 10.1080/00437956.1959.11659702

Ferguson, Charles A. 1982. "Religious Factors in Language Spread." In *Language Spread: Studies in Diffusion and Social Change*, edited by Robert L. Cooper, 95–106. Bloomington: Indiana University Press; Washington, DC: Center for Applied Linguistics.

Gellner, Ernest. 1995. "Fundamentalism as a Comprehensive System: Soviet Marxism and Islamic Fundamentalism Compared." In *Fundamentalisms*

Comprehended, edited by Martin E. Marty and R. Scott Appleby, 277–288. Chicago: University of Chicago Press.

Gombrich, Richard F. 1988. *Theravāda Buddhism: A Social History from Ancient Benares to Modern Colombo.* London and New York: Routledge and Kegan Paul.

Haeri, Niloofar. 2003. *Sacred Language, Ordinary People: Dilemmas of Culture and Politics in Egypt.* New York: Palgrave Macmillan.

Hudson, Alan. 2002. "Outline of a Theory of Diglossia." *International Journal of the Sociology of Language* 157: 1–48.

Johnson, Michael. 2012. "*Pax deorum.*" In *The Encyclopedia of Ancient History.* Accessed July 19, 2016. DOI: 10.1002/9781444338386.wbeah17327

Jørgensen, J. N. et al. 2011. "Polylanguaging in Superdiversity." *Diversities* 13 (2): 23–37. Accessed August 11, 2016. http://www.unesco.org/new/en/social-and-human-sciences/resources/periodicals/diversities/past-issues/vol-13-no-2-2011/polylanguaging-in-superdiversity/

Kermani, Navid. 2015. *God is Beautiful: The Aesthetic Experience of the Quran.* Translated by Tony Crawford. Cambridge: Polity.

Leonhardt, Jürgen. 2013. *Latin: Story of a World Language.* Translated by Kenneth Kronenberg. Cambridge, MA: The Belknap Press of Harvard University Press.

Lewis, Geoffrey. 1999. *The Turkish Language Reform: A Catastrophic Success.* Oxford and New York: Oxford University Press.

Lincoln, Bruce. 2012. "Ancient and Post-Ancient Religion." In *Gods and Demons, Priests and Scholars: Critical Explorations in the History of Religions.* Chicago and London: University of Chicago Press.

Mumin, Meikal. 2014. "The Arabic Script in Africa: Understudied Literacy." In *The Arabic Script in Africa: Studies in the Use of a Writing System*, edited by Meikal Mumin and Kees Versteegh, 41–76. Leiden and Boston: Brill.

O'Connor, Paul. 2012. *Islam in Hong Kong: Muslims and Everyday Life in China's World City.* Hong Kong: Hong Kong University Press.

Paden, William E. 2016. *New Patterns for Comparative Religion: Passages to an Evolutionary Perspective.* London and New York: Bloomsbury Academic.

Pye, Michael. 2013. *Strategies in the Study of Religions.* Vol. 2: *Exploring Religions in Motion.* Berlin and Boston: De Gruyter.

Ricci, Ronit. 2011. *Islam Translated: Literature, Conversion, and the Arabic Cosmopolis of South and Southeast Asia.* Chicago and London: University of Chicago Press.

Rosowsky, Andrey. 2008. *Heavenly Readings: Liturgical Literacy in a Multilingual Context.* Bristol and Buffalo: Multilingual Matters.

Sharot, Stephen. 2001. *A Comparative Sociology of World Religions: Virtuosos, Priests, and Popular Religion.* New York and London: New York University Press.

Smith, Jonathan Z. 2004. *Relating Religion: Essays in the Study of Religion.* Chicago: University of Chicago Press.

Turner, Bryan S. 2011. *Religion and Modern Society: Citizenship, Secularisation and the State.* Cambridge and New York: Cambridge University Press.
Versteegh, Kees. 2014. *The Arabic Language.* Second edition. Edinburgh: Edinburgh University Press.

Further Reading

Ernst, Carl W. 2013. "The Global Significance of Arabic Language and Literature." *Religion Compass* 7 (6): 191–200. DOI: 10.1111/rec3.12049. A short but helpful demonstration of the impact of Arabic not only on Islam, but on Christianity and the wider world.
Haeri, Niloofar. 2003. *Sacred Language, Ordinary People: Dilemmas of Culture and Politics in Egypt.* New York: Palgrave Macmillan. A brilliant study that examines the sociopolitical standing of a sacred language in one modern-day society.
Healey, John F., and G. Rex Smith. 2009. *A Brief Introduction to the Arabic Alphabet: Its Origins and Various Forms.* London, San Francisco, and Beirut: Saqi. A helpful primer written by experts.
Qutbuddin, Tahera. 2007. "Arabic in India: A Survey and Classification of Its Uses, Compared With Persian." *Journal of the American Oriental Society* 127 (3): 315–338. An illuminating account of the various roles and functions of Classical Arabic in a major non-Arabic-speaking country.
Ricci, Ronit. 2011. *Islam Translated: Literature, Conversion, and the Arabic Cosmopolis of South and Southeast Asia.* Chicago and London: University of Chicago Press. An elegant historical study of the spread of Islam and Arabic outside the Middle East.

Chapter 3

Not Dead Yet: Latin as Test Case

Thousands of pilgrims and tourists gather in St. Peter's Square in Vatican City on a blazing Sunday in June. They talk, mingle, try to find a patch of shade, and take pictures of their family, friends, and themselves ("selfies"). Many have just come from Mass within the Basilica. The Mass is a symbolic reenactment of Jesus' Last Supper, involving prayers, hymns, and scriptural readings. This time it was celebrated in Latin, with readings in French, Spanish, and English. On other occasions it might involve a mixture of Latin, Italian, Portuguese, German, and Vietnamese.

Latin lettering adorns the interior of the sacred space. There are inscriptions for popes, saints, even doctrines: a dedication near the altar indicates where the Dogma of the Immaculate Conception was pronounced. Most impressive are the monumental inscriptions in black letters against a golden background running along the top of the interior. On the ring of the cupola is a key text from the so-called Petrine Commission, making the apostle Peter – and, according to Catholic teaching, his successor, the pope – the spiritual leader of Christians:

> TV ES PETRVS ET SVPER HANC PETRAM AEDIFICABO
> ECCLESIAM MEAM ET TIBI DABO CLAVES REGNI CAELORVM
>
> [Thou art Peter and upon this Rock I will build my church,
> and I will give unto thee the keys of the Kingdom of Heaven.]
> (Lansford 2009, 526–527)

Sacred Languages of the World: An Introduction, First Edition. Brian P. Bennett.

Stepping outside one cannot help but notice that a massive dedication figures prominently on the façade of the church:

IN HONOREM PRINCIPIS APOST PAVLVS V BVRGHESIVS
ROMANVS PONT MAX AN MDCXII PONT VII

[Paul the Fifth Borghese of Rome, Supreme Pontiff,
in honor of the Prince of the Apostles, in the year 1612, seventh of this office]
(Lansford 2009, 510–511)

In the middle of St. Peter's plaza is a large obelisk (see Figure 3.1). Originally from Egypt, it is said to have been dedicated to Caesar, then Christianized and moved at tremendous cost and labor from another location in Rome to its present setting. One of the inscriptions echoes the Catholic rite of exorcism:

ECCE CRVX DOMINI
FVGITE
PARTES ADVERSAE
VICIT LEO
DE TRIBV IVDA

[Lo, the Cross of the Lord!
Take flight,
hostile ranks;
the Lion of the Tribe of Judah
has conquered.]
(Lansford 2009, 508–509)

At noon Pope Francis appears, speaking high above the crowd from the Papal apartments in the Apostolic Palace. The pontiff's image is blown up on three large Panasonic jumbotron screens spaced throughout the piazza. The assembled crowds cheer. Francis speaks in Italian, welcoming "brothers and sisters" and noting that today is the Solemnity of the Body and Blood of Christ (according to the Latin expression, the feast of *Corpus Christi*). He continues in sermonic style:

> L'odierna festa evoca questo messaggio solidale e ci spinge ad accoglierne l'intimo invito alla conversione e al servizio, all'amore e al perdono. Ci stimola a diventare, con la vita, imitatori di ciò che celebriamo nella liturgia. (Libreria Editrice Vaticana 2015)

Figure 3.1 Vatican obelisk with Latin inscription, St. Peter's Square, Vatican City.

> [Today's feast evokes this message of solidarity and encourages us to embrace the intimate call to conversion and to service, to love, and to forgiveness. It encourages us to become, in our life, imitators of what we celebrate in the liturgy.] (Vatican Radio 2015)

Then, switching to the fixed code of Latin, the pope leads the crowd in the Angelus prayer:

> Angelus Domini nuntiavit Mariae.
> Et concepit de Spiritu Sancto.
>
> Ave, Maria,
> gratia plena,
> Dominus tecum;
> Benedicta tu in mulieribus
> Et benedictus fructus

ventris tui, Iesus.
Sancta Maria,
Mater Dei,
Ora pro nobis peccatoribus
Nunc
et in ora mortis nostrae.
Amen.

Ecce ancilla Domini.
Fiat mihi secundum verbum tuum.

Ave, Maria…

[The angel of the Lord declared unto Mary.
And she conceived by the Holy Spirit.

Hail Mary,
full of grace,
the Lord is with thee.
Blessed art thou among women,
and blessed is the fruit
of thy womb, Jesus.
Holy Mary,
Mother of God,
pray for us sinners,
Now
and at the hour of our death.
Amen.

Behold the handmaid of the Lord.
Be it done unto me according to your word.

Hail Mary…]

Some in the crowd recite the lines with diligence, others mouth half-remembered words, still others continue to chat, mill about, and take more photographs of themselves using selfie sticks hawked by enterprising street vendors. The formal prayer concluded, the pope switches back to the informal code of Italian. When he mentions his trip to Sarajevo, some in the crowd cheer.

> E ora saluto tutti voi, cari pellegrini provenienti dall'Italia e da diversi Paesi. Vedo bandiere di diversi Paesi. In particolare saluto i fedeli di Madrid, Brasilia e Curitiba; e quelli di Chiavari, Catania e Gottolengo (Brescia). A tutti auguro una buona domenica. Per favore, non dimenticate di pregare per me. Buon pranzo e arrivederci! (Libreria Editrice Vaticana 2015)
>
> [And now I greet all of you, dear pilgrims from Italy and other countries. I see flags of different countries. In particular I greet the faithful of Madrid, Brasilia and Curitiba [Brazil]; and those of Chiavari, Catania and Gottolengo ... I wish you all a good Sunday. Please do not forget to pray for me. Good lunch and goodbye!] (Vatican Radio 2015)

More cheers erupt as groups respond to the mention of their respective homelands.

This vignette reiterates what was established in the previous chapter: namely, that sacred languages are still part of the linguasphere. Latin may be an ancient tongue, but it continues to figure in the institutional and individual toolkits of Catholics. Of course, largely gone now is the premodern pattern of diglossia (wine and water), a kind of linguistic division of labor in which Latin would be used for "high" purposes (religion, literature, science) and vernaculars like Italian for "low" ones (conversation with neighbors, working in the fields). Nationalism, vernacularization, democratization, and the other forces of modernity have made their impact felt even in the bastion of Catholicism, especially at the landmark Second Vatican Council (Vatican II), the 1960s church gathering that ended up dislodging Latin from its pride of place. Nevertheless, a kind of residual diglossia is still observable within the Roman Catholic Church, with the old language being called upon for certain liturgical celebrations, official texts, and inscriptions, while colloquial tongues handle everyday tasks and interpersonal transactions. If we were to follow the tourists and pilgrims who were there for the recitation of the Angelus, we would hear them speaking Portuguese, Spanish, or Croatian with friends or family, while probably using bits of Italian or English when ordering a gelato or asking directions to the Colosseum.

Latin is a valuable test case because it occupies a curious position compared to other sacred languages, being at one and the same time central and peripheral to the faith. As we will see below, Latin continues to play a role part in Catholic texts, rituals, institutions, and communities, especially in the "center" (the Vatican). At the same time, for the vast majority of churchgoers in the "periphery" around the world, Latin is no longer the language of liturgy, let alone of learning and literature. Traditionalist Catholics continue to eagerly promote the sacred language, but statistically speaking they are rather marginal.

Though Latin is still spoken in some offices of Curia (the Catholic ecclesiastical bureaucracy), it is no one's mother tongue. Italian (which, of course, is closely related to Latin) is the real working language of the Vatican. Naturally, clerics who come from different parts of the world to work in the Vatican bring their own languages. The Vatican is a multilingual enterprise. Its website has pages in Latin, French, English, Italian, Portuguese, Spanish, German, Arabic, and Chinese. Vatican Radio broadcasts in roughly forty tongues, including Latvian, Malayalam, Russian, Korean, Czech, Modern Hebrew, Kiswahili, Vietnamese, Albanian, Arabic, Polish, and Esperanto. The linguasphere is indeed well represented in this tiny city-state in Rome. Latin remains an important part of this multilingual medley, though we need to remember that it is not an all-or-nothing proposition: deploying bits and pieces of a sacred language in specific contexts – that is similar to what we see around the world in other religious settings.

The purpose of this chapter is not to retell the remarkable story of Latin through the centuries, since there are a number of excellent books that do that (e.g., Ostler 2007; Leonhardt 2013). For one thing, we are only interested in the variety known as Ecclesiastical Latin, which is related to, but distinct from, the Classical Latin that is typically taught in schools and that dominates the narrative of most language history books. Furthermore, our account is conspectual rather than chronological. While drawing on historical information, Ecclesiastical Latin (henceforth Latin) is used here *exempli gratia* (by way of example) to delineate and illustrate the makings of a sacred language. And because it is often labeled a dead language, focusing on Latin will give us a chance to say a bit more about that important topic.

Framing Sacred Languages

In what follows we begin to outline our framework or template for understanding sacred languages and apply it to the case of Latin. This template will then guide the discussion and comparison of other sacred languages in the following chapters, where further typological distinctions will be introduced.

Every religion entails four interconnected factors or components: beliefs, practices, institutions, and communities (cf. Lincoln 2012). This fourfold matrix provides the starting point for our consideration of sacred languages.

Beliefs

Every religion involves a more or less coherent belief system (worldview, ideology) regarding such topics as the existence of an unseen sacred order, the number and nature of the gods, the problem of suffering, and the origin and destiny of humankind. This belief system may be expressed in part in authoritative texts like the Qur'an, Avesta, Bhagavad Gita, or Talmud. These books serve as reference points for the religious community and are usually quoted and "proof-texted" in sermons and conversations.

Though the official teachings of the Catholic Church are now available in numerous languages, they are enshrined first of all in Latin-language texts of varying sanctity and authority, including the Bible (*Nova Vulgata*, the New Vulgate edition), the Catechism (*Catechismus Catholicae Ecclesiae*), the Roman Missal (*Missale Romanum*), the Code of Canon Law (*Codex Iuris Canonici*), and the ever-growing collection of papal and curial (i.e., bureaucratic) documents. The Latin version of these texts is usually called the typical edition (*editio typica*, plural: *editiones typicae*), meaning the "reference text." According to Bernadette Lécureux (1998, 23), who wrote a book in defense of Latin around the time of Vatican II, if one wants to preserve a standard that is not prone to alterations, one generally uses a precious metal, which becomes the fixed standard of measurement. Within the Catholic religious system, an *editio typica* serves as a kind of textual and doctrinal gold standard, providing a template for multiple vernacular translations, much as a monetary gold standard helps guide and regulate local currencies. Thus, Latin to this day functions as a reference language for expressing the teachings of the Roman Catholic Church. However, although encyclicals and other publications are put out in Latin, they may be first drafted in a modern language like Italian and then translated backwards, as it were, into the ancient Roman tongue. A well-known example is the most recent edition of the Catechism, which actually started in French due to a lack of knowledge of Latin among the authors; only later was the Latin-language reference text published, to which national translations were then to be aligned

(Stasiuk 2006). But it is worth noting that the *editio typica* is almost a thousand pages long – a not insignificant amount of new Latin!

Language has a uniquely self-referential capacity: it can refer to itself. Words can be written about words. Not only are the beliefs of a given religion expressed in its canonical texts, there are also beliefs *about* sacred languages. Sacred languages are not unique in this regard. Every language has beliefs, sentiments, and judgments projected onto it. These have to do with, among other things, the alleged origins and qualities of the language. Languages are said to be ancient, beautiful, logical, difficult, harsh-sounding, and so on. For example, many people say that French sounds elegant and that English is the most powerful language on Earth. Whether such claims are true or even measurable is a different issue. The fact of the matter is, people have always judged their own language, implicitly or explicitly, against other languages on a scale of values. When these beliefs are repeated over and over in a variety of contexts, they achieve a kind of solidity and self-evidentness. Sociolinguists refer to this as language ideology, a term that may have a negative ring to it, but simply means a more or less coherent and consensual view of one language in relation to others. At the most basic level, a language ideology praises one language and denigrates the rest.

Like French or English, consecrated languages such as Arabic, Hebrew, Sanskrit, and Church Slavonic are praised for being aesthetically pleasing and historically significant. But more than that, they are *mythologized*. A thesaurus will list the following terms as synonyms for myth: illusion, superstition, fabrication, tall tale. But in the field of comparative religion, to say that something is mythologized (or mythicized) means it is connected to the superhuman personages and events which are considered true and foundational by a given community.

When we talk about Catholic beliefs about Latin – or any language ideology, for that matter – we must be clear if we mean official pronouncements or popular comments from the pew. Official statements are generally easier to track because they appear in print. Surveys, fieldwork, interviews, and other research methods are required to ascertain what ordinary churchgoers think about the matter. And, as is well known, many Catholics profess allegiance to church teachings but also go their own way on certain issues. So, when it comes to language ideology, we need to always ask: what is the source?

Over the past century or so, church leaders have made a number of statements about Latin in documents, from apostolic letters to papal allocutions.

Such texts are typically in Latin, and get their name from the first words of the text. They include *Inter Sollicitudines*, *Officiorum Omnium*, *Mediator Dei*, *Sacrificium Laudis*, *Dominicae Cenae*, and *Lingua Latina* (Gane 2009). Particularly important is *Veterum Sapientia*, an Apostolic Constitution promulgated by St. Pope John XXIII in 1962, on the eve of Vatican II. It continues to serve as a kind of Magna Carta for the pro-Latin faction within the Catholic Church. The document first references the once common Catholic idea that Divine Providence chose the Roman Empire (and thus, the Latin language) to propagate the Gospel (Resnick 1990). Then, drawing upon previous Catholic statements, it articulates three key attributes of Latin:

- universal: "Of its very nature Latin is most suitable for promoting every form of culture among peoples. It gives rise to no jealousies. It does not favor any one nation, but presents itself with equal impartiality to all and is equally acceptable to all."
- immutable: "Modern languages are liable to change, and no single one of them is superior to the others in authority. Thus if the truths of the Catholic Church were entrusted to an unspecified number of them, the meaning of these truths, varied as they are, would not be manifested to everyone with sufficient clarity and precision. There would, moreover, be no language which could serve as a common and constant norm by which to gauge the exact meaning of other renderings. But Latin is indeed such a language. It is set and unchanging."
- non-vernacular: "the Catholic Church has a dignity far surpassing that of every merely human society, for it was founded by Christ the Lord. It is altogether fitting, therefore, that the language it uses should be noble, majestic, and non-vernacular."

(Pope John XXIII 1962)

The themes of Latin as universal, unchanging, and majestic are repeated in varying combinations in the books, websites, and blogs of traditionalist Catholics. Tucked into this third point is another motif, a kind of 3b: "[Latin] is a general passport to the proper understanding of the Christian writers of antiquity and the documents of the Church's teaching. It is also a most effective bond, binding the Church of today with that of the past and of the future in wonderful continuity" (Pope John XXIII 1962).

We find similar sentiments expressed in other religious communities. The claim that a sacred language provides a connection over time (linking past and present) and space (uniting believers in different countries) is also said about Hebrew, Sanskrit, and Church Slavonic. This is a point of similarity. But we should also note what is *not* being claimed about Latin. Unlike Muslims with regard to Classical Arabic, Catholics do not claim that God uttered words of revelation in the Latin language. And in contradistinction to the widespread Theravada belief that the Buddha spoke Pali, the Catholic Church does not teach that Jesus conversed in Latin (despite the fanciful scene in the movie *The Passion of the Christ* when Jesus interacts with Pontius Pilate in Latin). A comparative approach is indispensable for noting salient differences between specimens.

Practices

Beliefs are obviously important, but religion is not just a matter of cogitation; it involves doing things. Sacred languages constitute a "golden" linguistic resource that members of the religion can draw upon for a range of activities. It is helpful to distinguish between practices (which are customs, rituals, and routines) and projects (which refer to more extensive intentional endeavors, like building a library or launching a missionary campaign). There are all sorts of practices and projects. Educational ones will be discussed in the section below (and Chapter 6) on institutions, while the arts will be treated more extensively in Chapter 8. Here, we focus on discursive and interventionist practices (Riesebrodt 2010).

It bears repeating that, just as gold is usually alloyed with copper or silver or some other metal, sacred languages do not operate in isolation in these practices. They are almost always accompanied by vernacular languages, which provide commentary, translation, instruction, and so on. We saw this at the start of the chapter, with the example of Pope Francis code-switching back and forth between the formal Latin and the informal Italian during the Sunday Angelus recitation.

Discursive practices are the kind of thing one could do at a desk. They involve reading, writing, and speaking the sacred language. There are still people in the Vatican who speak and compose in Latin on a daily basis. As mentioned in Chapter 1, there is now a papal Twitter account with hundreds of thousands of followers. New 140-character texts are generated every day, though these are minuscule compared to heftier tomes like the *Catechismus Catholicae Ecclesiae*.

The Vatican regularly coins new Latin words to address new realities. Coming in at just over 700 pages, the two-volume *Lexicon recentis latinitatis*

[Dictionary of Contemporary Latin] (Opus Fundatum "Latinitas" 2003; Pavanetto n.d.) has thousands of entries. A quick perusal makes it clear that one can still have a good time in Latin. There are terms for basketball (*follis canistrīque ludus*), casino (*aleatórium*), motel (*deversorium autocineticum*), merlot (*vinum rubrum Burdigalense*), yacht (*lembus lusorius*), snack bar (*thermopolium potorium et gustatorium*), and weekend (*hebdomadae exitus*). Neologisms for jet airplane (*aërināvis celérrima*), computer (*instrumentum computatórium*), and trademark (*ergastérii nota*) reflect some of the innovations of a globalized world, while racket (*illícita pecúniae exáctio*) and overdose (*nimia medicamenti stupefactivi sumptio*) reflect some of the attendant problems.

Another volume, the *LEXICON NOMINVM LOCORVM* or Dictionary of Place Names (Egger 1977) enables Latin writers to discuss places like Hong Kong (*Siamkiamum*), Easter Island (*Pasqua Isola*), Liechtenstein (*Lichtenstenum*), and the city of New Orleans (*Nova Aurelia*) located in the state of Louisiana (*Ludoviciana*), part of the United States of America (*Foederatae Civitates Americae Septentrionalis*). These lexicons were put out by the Catholic Church's official publishing house, Libreria Editrice Vaticana. Indeed, new Latin volumes are part of their catalogue every year.

Latin is still used by various sections of the Vatican bureaucracy, most frequently in the area of Canon Law, the legal system for regulating the life of the Church (Stasiuk 2006). Mention should also be made of the Latin Section in the Secretariat of State, which is responsible for anything related to the pope's work, including encyclicals, apostolic constitutions, bulls, letters of appointment, and diplomatic correspondence. The Latin Section consists of several *scriptores* (writers) who come from different countries and who use Latin as the office lingua franca. Much of their work is formulaic, like writing up a letter in Latin appointing an ambassador to the Holy See. Other tasks are more complicated and linguistically challenging, as with the production of encyclicals, which are major publishing events worldwide. Inscriptions are another responsibility of the Latin Section (Monsignor Daniel Gallagher, pers. comm.). For example, Pope Benedict XVI had a new gateway dedicated with the following inscription:

BENEDICTVS XVI P M
CIVITATIS VATICANAE OFFICIALIVM COMMODITATI
OSTIVM
APERIRI IVSSIT
A D MMVI PONT I

[Benedict the Sixteenth, Supreme Pontiff,
ordered an entry to be opened
for the convenience
of the employees of Vatican City,
in the year 2006, first of his office.]
(Lansford 2009, 536–537)

Discursive practices involve believers communicating with other believers. *Interventionist practices*, on the other hand, are typically done in a sanctified space, like a basilica, temple, mosque, or synagogue, and involve communicating with postulated superhuman powers. They may involve the big promises of a religion (nirvana, eternal life) or small ones (success on school exams, protection against car accidents). For convenience we can array them in a fourfold typology:

Liturgical practices like prayer, chanting, and worship, often involving special, symbolic gestures (bowing, swaying, kneeling, prostrating, clapping hands), clothing (yarmulkes, vestments, headscarves, or going barefoot), and accoutrements (joss sticks, chalices, statues, candles, shofars, cymbals, umbrellas, foodstuffs) in a multisensory spectacle.

Thaumaturgical (magical, miraculous) acts like wearing an amulet or getting a tattoo in order to attract good fortune or repel evil influences.

Somatological disciplines such as yoga, meditation, and visualization. These regimens train the minds and bodies (*somata*) of practitioners in systematic ways, often with the goal of providing a sense of equipoise and wellbeing or even actualizing the divinity thought to dwell within the individual.

Behavioral practices involving the regulation of diet, hygiene, clothing, and recreation. Prohibitions against dancing or stipulations regarding *halal* or kosher food are examples of such conduct. This category also encompasses various moral codes – the Five Precepts of Buddhism, the Seven Corporal Works of Mercy of Catholicism, the Ten Commandments of Judaism. Sacred languages are least directly involved in this sector of religious life.

This schematism is, of course, artificial, for in reality the four modes may be interlinked and blur together. Nevertheless, like gridlines on a map, they help us find our way around the terrain and facilitate observation and comparison. For example, they allow us to articulate the fact that thaumaturgical and somatological practices are much more common with

Hebrew and Pali than (currently) for Latin and Coptic. Again, sacred languages are not all the same.

A further taxonomic distinction can be made in terms of where these various practices might be performed. As we saw in the case of the opening vignette, Latin was used for the Angelus prayer at a special time (noon on Sunday) and in a special place (the plaza in front of St. Peter's Basilica). All languages, including sacred ones, are defined by the places where they are spoken; they in turn help define those places. We speak differently, or may use entirely different languages, if we are in a kitchen, playground, store, or government office. When it comes to sacred languages, we might envision a topography consisting of three locations, which, for the sake of simplicity, we label *here*, *there*, and *anywhere* (adapted from Smith 2004).

Here is the domestic space. This is where children learn their mother tongue or native language (often referred to in sociolinguistics as L1). This is the variety used for playing, cooking, singing, teasing, fighting, and all the other things that family members do to and with each other. In terms of a cross-cultural survey, the home is not the primary domain of sacred languages.

There refers to specially consecrated buildings, like mosques, shrines, synagogues, and temples. This is the niche or "natural habitat" of sacred languages in society. Depending on the tradition, it is where liturgical, thaumaturgical, and/or somatological practices might take place. For example, chanting, tattooing, and meditating in Pali may all be done at a Thai Buddhist *wat* or temple. *There* usually entails *then*. In other words, sacred languages are typically used at stipulated times of the day, as in the fivefold daily performance of prayer for Muslims or the celebration of the Divine Liturgy in Church Slavonic on Sunday morning.

In sociolinguistics the term *linguistic landscape* refers to the visible display of language on signs, marquees, billboards, flyers, posters, and so on. One can determine quite a lot about the history and demographics of a community by surveying this aspect of the environment. Sacred spaces (*there*) are often marked off from the surrounding location by steeples, cupolas, friezes, and other architectural and design features. The sacred language may also adorn the façade, gates, and doorways of a sanctuary, distinguishing it from the immediate environment. Entering a church, synagogue, or mosque, one will not only hear the sacred language being sung, chanted, or recited, one will often see snippets of it in icons or inscriptions on the wall, and possibly on ritual vessels and vestments as well. The sacred writing is literally on the wall.

Anywhere refers to the public square, from schoolyards to cafés to sporting arenas to shopping malls. Sacred languages may be heard in the public realm in ritual processions or calls to prayer, or be seen on talismans and icons. Much depends on location, of course. It is quite normal for Classical Arabic to be broadcast on radio in Egypt, as it is for Slavonic in Russia or Sanskrit in India. Pali-language amulets and plaques, meant to ward off evil and bring good luck, show up in stores, banks, and tuk-tuks in Thailand. In this postmodern era of world history, sacred languages are increasingly crossing traditional boundaries and showing up in unexpected places, like concert halls, museums, and tattoo parlors.

Let us return now to the issue of Latin and Catholic interventionist practices. Somatological regimens such as yoga do not really belong to the Catholic repertoire, and thaumaturgical techniques, like wearing a Latin-language amulet, have largely vanished from the lifeworld of most Catholics. What remains is the liturgical; and this means, above all, the Mass, the central Catholic observance. The situation here with respect to Latin is somewhat complicated. The main ritual service book is called the *Missale Romanum*. This text was codified in 1570 by Pope Pius V after the Council of Trent (Tridentine is an adjective referring to Trent). It was promulgated anew by Pope John XXIII in 1962 – ironically, right before the start of the Second Vatican Council, which would open the door to increased use of the vernacular in the Mass. When people say "Latin Mass," this is what they usually have in mind. It is sometimes referred to as the Traditional Latin Mass (TLM), the Tridentine Mass, or the Extraordinary Form (Marx 2013). For enthusiasts, the 1962 typical edition of the *Missale Romanum* enjoys the status of a kind of talisman or palladium – a beautiful piece of gold from the golden age of Catholicism, right before the fall of Vatican II.

In the wake of the Second Vatican Council, a number of changes were made to the structure or order (*Ordo*) of the Mass. These changes were promulgated under Pope Paul VI in 1969–1970. As a consequence, the revised Mass is sometimes called – especially by its detractors – the *Novus Ordo* (New Order) Mass. Technically speaking, even the post-Vatican II Mass is also a Latin Mass, for two reasons: (1) the typical edition (reference text) is in Latin; current vernacular languages are derived from and guided by this "gold standard"; (2) the post-Vatican II (*Novus Ordo*) version can indeed be celebrated in Latin, though this is not very common overall.

The use of the Tridentine Latin Mass declined precipitously after Vatican II, but never went away completely. Traditionalists upset over Vatican II kept it up – sometimes challenging, or even breaking with, papal authority, to do so. A 2007 ruling by Pope Benedict XVI, in a document called *Summorum Pontificum*, paved the way for something of a return of the Tridentine version. He referred to the pre-Vatican II version as the "extraordinary" form (as well as the "older usage"), and the post-Vatican II one the "ordinary" form or usage, and said they were two valid expressions of the same Roman Rite (Benedict 2007). While traditionalists lauded this move, progressives worried about "turning back the clock" to pre-Vatican II times. Every day the Mass in both extraordinary and ordinary forms is celebrated throughout the Vatican's numerous chapels. The Latin Mass in its "ordinary" post-Vatican II form is particularly prominent in papal celebrations when there are pilgrims gathered from around the world. Multilingual booklets are available to help churchgoers understand the ceremony.

Away from Vatican headquarters, the Latin Mass is growing in popularity but is still rather peripheral in the overall scheme of things. According to one study, there are 433 locations in the United States where the Latin Mass is celebrated, though not every single Sunday; this is out of 18,201 parishes. This equates to a rough estimate of 50,000 adherents on a given weekend, which represents just 0.25 percent of total attendance at all Catholic Masses in the United States (Marx 2013, 64).

Since Vatican II the amount of Latin has likewise diminished across the linguistic landscape of the Catholic world. Naturally, Latin signs and inscriptions will be more noticeable in those parishes where the pre-Vatican II liturgy is regularly celebrated. Such spaces are usually filled with more representational statuary, votive candles, and pious decorations. Elsewhere throughout the Catholic linguistic landscape, however, bits and pieces of the sacred language are occasionally visible on vestments and liturgical furnishings (see Figure 3.2). But these have a residual feel – leftovers from another era.

Institutions

People often disparage "organized religion," yet it is impossible to maintain and perpetuate a religion without institutional structures of some kind. One of the hallmarks of the so-called world religions, as opposed to ancient religions, is a relatively autonomous clergy: the Christian priesthood,

Figure 3.2 Baptismal font with Latin inscription. St. Peter's Catholic Church, New Iberia, Louisiana.

Buddhist monastic order, Jewish rabbinate, and so on. Sacred languages like Latin, Pali, Hebrew, and Arabic are often in the hands of these custodians who oversee the beliefs and practices for the community. The language may function as a lingua franca (common language) among clerics and religious intellectuals from different countries. But there is quite a lot of variability here. In some traditions, like Islam, knowledge of the sacred language is comparatively widespread among ordinary believers, while in others, such as Theravada Buddhism, it is almost entirely restricted to monks and *mae chi* (female ascetics, similar to nuns).

Sacred languages are not mother tongues and, as such, must be transmitted by formal education, through institutions like seminaries, madrasas, and yeshivas, which are often clerical in nature. The goal of this education, which is usually conducted in the local vernacular (e.g., Thai, Yiddish, Russian, Malay, Amharic), is often quite targeted: the purpose may simply be to recite a scriptural text or perform a ritual in the sacred language. In-depth study of grammar may be reserved for more advanced students. Of course, a sacred language will not be studied alone, but as part of a broader religious curriculum. For example, a seminarian training to be a Catholic or Orthodox priest will also study the Bible, theology, canon law, church history, and possibly other languages like Hebrew and Greek.

Up until the Second Vatican Council in the 1960s, Latin was not only studied intensely but was even the language of instruction in some Catholic seminaries. Consider the following testimony:

> When I was a seminarian in the 1950s, Latin was the order of the day.... Once I embarked upon priesthood studies after the novitiate (three years of philosophy and four years of theology), all the major courses were taught in Latin. Our textbooks were written in Latin. We even took our exams, both oral and written, in Latin. Our prayer life was also expressed totally in Latin: the daily Mass and the Liturgy of the Hours. (Austin 2008)

The Code of Canon Law (article 249) stipulates that those training for the priesthood "should know Latin well" (*linguam latinam bene calleant*). However, in many Catholic seminaries and educational institutions Latin has shifted from being a required to a recommended subject. The Second Vatican Council opened the door to the vernacular and pulled the rug out from underneath Latin, so to speak. First, allowances were made for the liturgy to be celebrated in local languages like French and Polish. Then permission was granted for priests to recite their required cycle of daily prayers (the Breviary) in their mother tongue. There was, accordingly, less need to study Latin. As proficiency declined, there was less interest in the language, so proficiency declined even further. A downward spiral ensued (Stasiuk 2006). Over the years the Vatican has tried to shore up the study of Latin through things like the *Latinitas* Foundation and later the Pontifical Academy for Latin, both of which sponsored various publications and language competitions.

The place of Latin has slipped out of the curriculum across much of the Catholic world. At the same time, there are traditionalist organizations that are strongly dedicated to the pre-Vatican II Latin Mass. Such groups appear to be thriving. Perhaps the most successful is the Priestly Fraternity of Saint Peter or *Fraternitas Sacerdotalis Sancti Petri* (FSSP). A statement on their website (2016) explains their attachment to the traditional Latin Mass:

> Let us note too that the Tridentine rite, after the fashion of incense rising towards Heaven, elevates our souls to God, and, as it draws us from the

> realities of the senses to the eternal mysteries, permits us, already on earth, to unite our voices to those of the Blessed. This is the goal of all the gestures and of all the ceremonies. The orientation of the altar, the gestures of adoration, the sacred language, the mystery and the silence which surrounds the consecration: all these aspects manifest the sacrality of the Mass.

There are also non-clerical organizations like the Family of Saint Jerome, which promotes

> Diligent study and use of the Latin language, the living language of the Roman Catholic Church, in order to arrive at a sound command of the language in reading, thinking, speaking and writing.
>
> [Linguam Latinam vivam, Romanæ Ecclesiæ propriam, sedulo studio et cotidianis exercitiis ita discere satagant, ut tandem facile et expedite tum Latine scripta legere, quum et cogitare et loqui et scribere Latine valeant.]

To achieve that goal, the group proposes the following steps, which correspond well to what we are calling discursive and interventionist practices:

- to obtain contact with the living, spoken Latin language
- to read papal Encyclicals, the documents of Vatican II, the Latin Bible, the works of St. Thomas Aquinas, etc. in Latin
- to say one's daily prayers, like the Rosary, in Latin
- to regularly attend Mass celebrated in Latin

The group reminds members, who may be overwhelmed with all of this, that they "should never become discouraged in learning, knowing the proverb, 'Little droplets will gradually wear away a rock' (*GUTTA CAVAT LAPIDEM*)" (Familia Sancti Hieronymi 1989).

Communities

Sacred languages have a horizontal as well as a vertical orientation. They are used when communicating with alleged sacred powers, which are usually envisioned "above," or delving into the divinity that slumbers within. But there is also a horizontal dimension: sacred languages connect people. They are part of the fizz in the social chemistry of religious community.

As we saw in the previous chapter, the profile of religion gradually changed between the ancient and axial periods. Ancient religions were civic, centered on gods and goddesses housed in temple complexes, served by local priesthoods, the goal of which was maintaining a kind of *pax deorum* (peaceful relations with the gods). With the advent of the so-called world religions, there emerged geographically dispersed, international memberships linked by, among other things, canonical texts. Sacred languages like Pali, Hebrew, and Coptic function as lingua francas – also called vehicular languages – that help connect people who, whether as a result of missionary work or migration, live in different parts of the world and speak different mother tongues. To a greater or lesser extent, they are linking languages, uniting people from different cultures. The Pali language is one of the things that tethers the Theravada Buddhist communities of Sri Lanka and mainland Southeast Asia. Classical Arabic helps connect Muslims from Mecca to Hong Kong. The sacred language becomes a marker – and maker – of group identity. In some cases the sacred script functions as a kind of logo for the faith.

In a host of ways, both subtle and obvious, Latin still has a unifying function within Catholicism. As we saw in the opening anecdote, Latin-language liturgical practices like the Mass and the Angelus can bring together believers from Brazil, Croatia, Spain, and elsewhere. Papal encyclicals may not be widely read beyond their Latin titles, but still have a symbolic currency across the Catholic world. The Latin mottos of schools (*Christus Super Omnia*: Christ Above All; *Ad Majorem Dei Gloriam*: To the Greater Glory of God) far removed from the Vatican headquarters signal a Roman allegiance. (See Figure 3.3.)

However, although sacred languages can have a unifying influence, they can also be a source of controversy and division within the community. Unlike the ancient religions with their civic temples and festivals, axial-age religions like Buddhism and Christianity are formed in terms of a message (the Gospel, the Dharma) codified in canonical texts. The authority and prestige of the books help sanctify the language in which they are written. The message blends with the medium, the religious contents with the linguistic container. But the universalist aspirations of the clergy run into a linguistic obstacle. Not everyone speaks Arabic, or Pali, or Latin. How can the message of salvation be presented if converts do not understand the language? Moreover, since sacred languages are not

Figure 3.3 Priest's vestment with design that incorporates the Latin word for peace (*pax*).

mother tongues, but are reserved for religious purposes and cultivated by artificial means, they are prone to becoming misunderstood over time. Questions arise about whether translations can or should be used to bridge the comprehension gap.

What sociolinguists call *language ideological debates* may erupt in these situations. Some adherents may question the scale of values that puts the sacred language (and those who use it) above other languages (and their users). They make an appeal on behalf of other, usually vernacular languages, claiming they would serve the faith equally well or better. These debates seem to break out in unsettled times, when broader social, cultural, and political changes are underway. The sacred language may become a proxy for deeper tensions and grievances. That is to say, people may be debating the continued use of Hebrew or Church Slavonic in worship services, but they are also talking about broader issues like gender, the relationship between different faiths, assimilation, westernization, or secularization. These language debates can become quite bitter and threaten to tear the community apart. Claims of orthodoxy and charges of heresy are made. It can be hard for outsiders to understand what all the fuss is about. But for insiders, supremely important matters of faith and identity are at stake.

For centuries, Latin was something that Catholics in different countries shared. But that changed with Vatican II. Convened by Saint Pope John XXIII with the purpose of "updating" the Church and opening it to the world at large, the Council saw thousands of Catholic prelates gather in the Vatican for several years of difficult and wide-ranging debate. Shelves of books have been written about the causes and consequences of the Council. We are only interested in extracting some key points regarding the fate of Latin. Whatever the intent of the Council participants, the fact of the matter is that Vatican II is associated above all with the displacement of the sacred language. It is noteworthy that the linguistic reform has become *the* symbol of Council:

> Of all the changes in the church's life stemming from the Second Vatican Council, nothing else touched ordinary Catholic so immediately and tangibly as the changes in the liturgy. In the popular mind, these changes are often equated with the replacement of Latin by local languages. (Steinfels 2003, 167)

Since then, the question of Latin has often functioned as something of a litmus test for views about Catholicism and Vatican II – whether it was a blessing or a disaster, whether it represented a deadly rupture or life-giving revitalization of church tradition. There has been "a clear-cut face off between two sets of values and loyalties when dealing with the Catholic Church's liturgy" (Kiczek 2009, 38). This contestation is between the traditionalists and reformists, though there is actually a spectrum of views from right to left (Baldovin 2010).

In general, the Council shifted the mood and focus of the Catholic Mass from a vertical to a more horizontal orientation, from "a special, sacred, Sunday language to ordinary weekday tongues" (Steinfels 2003, 170). Though most Catholics seem to have accepted, or even cheered, this change in orientation, a small sub-community bewails what they see as the damaging results of the Council and have called for a "reform of the reform."

The question of Latin as a liturgical language was debated in the decades leading up to Vatican II, in various conferences, ecclesiastical gatherings, periodicals like *Amen* and *Worship*, and no doubt in mundane family conversations on the way to and from church. All of these things culminated in the great debate that unfolded at the Council itself. According to one study: "The vernacular question was the most discussed in the entire debate on the liturgy. Eighty-one speakers were heard on the subject and the opinions took up more than one hundred pages" (Pecklers 2003, 195). The end result of the debate was the 1963 Constitution on the Sacred Liturgy called *Sacrosanctum Concilium*, which was approved by a vote of 2147 to 4 (Pecklers 2009, 26). This would seem to be a decisive vote, but what the Constitution actually enjoins has been much debated. Those who are *pro* and those who are *contra* Latin both appeal to the text to justify their positions. The relevant section famously asserts the maintenance of Latin:

> 36.1. Particular law remaining in force, the use of the Latin language is to be preserved in the Latin rites.

Yet, in the next line, it opens the door to the vernacular:

> 36.2. But since the use of the mother tongue, whether in the Mass, the administration of the sacraments, or other parts of the liturgy, frequently may be of great advantage to the people, the limits of its employment may be extended. This will apply in the first place to the readings and directives, and to some of the prayers and chants.... (*Sacrosanctum Concilium* 1963)

But what started as an extension of limits for the vernacular became a wholesale abandonment of the ancient language. According to one conservative scholar:

> It would seem obvious from these articles of *Sacrosanctum concilium* that the Fathers of Vatican II did not envisage a general introduction of the vernacular, let alone a replacement of Latin with the mother tongue as the liturgical language of the Roman rite. (Lange 2012, 157)

The replacement of Latin happened *de facto*, not *de jure* (164). In other words, it was not what the law required; it happened more in the course of events.

It is important to understand that the issue of Latin became bound up with other notable changes to the Mass and the layout of the sacred space (*there*). These changes included: the orientation of the priest, who in the pre-Vatican II Mass predominantly faces *ad orientem* ("to the East," the symbol of light and the rising Son) and now faces *versus populum* (people often talk about how in the Tridentine Mass the priest had his "back to the people," though traditionalist Catholics find that expression both inaccurate and disparaging); the removal of the communion rail; the transfer of the tabernacle (where the communion bread is reserved) from the center point to the side of the sanctuary; the introduction of more biblical readings and the "sign of peace" handshake; the turn in some places from representational statuary and stained glass windows of Jesus, Mary, the saints, to more abstract artwork; the redesign of church architecture in a more modernist vein; and the replacement of Gregorian chant and organ with more contemporary musical styles and instruments. Again, a number of these innovations or developments were not decreed by the Council per se but occurred at the grassroots level. Be that as it may, traditionalist Catholics tend to see this daisy chain of events as connected to (of a piece with) the loss of Latin.

The question of Latin (and all that goes with it) continues to be a source of division within the Catholic Church. Though their numbers are small, devotees of the Latin Mass are a fervent and, at times, conspiracy-minded segment of the Catholic population. For them, the Catholic Mass is the apex of religious experience. It is a glimpse of heaven, a spiritual shelter. They cherish its "aura of timelessness in a world helplessly swept away by change" (Chupungco 2010, 7). For supporters of the pre-Vatican II Mass, the Latin language is clear and strong: there's nothing cutesy or syrupy about it. It possesses a simple grandeur (Lécureux 1998, 66–67). Parishioners who are drawn to the "Latin Mass" cherish the perceived sacrality and universality of the ancient language. They may resent what they view as the distracting chattiness and calisthenics (sit, stand, kneel, shake hands, etc.) of the *Novus Ordo* ritual. For this cohort of Catholics, communion is prized over communication, the vertical over the horizontal. According to one cleric who supports maintaining the Latin Mass:

> we can say that the most important thing in divine worship is not that we understand every word or concept. No. The most important consideration is that we stand in reverence and awe before God, that we adore, praise and thank him. (Arinze 2006)

Traditionalist Catholics also cherish the vehicular properties of Latin. Critics used to complain that, "The use of Latin had only managed to unify the whole Church in mystification because so few had mastered the ancient language" (McDannell 2011, 42). But Latin-Mass Catholics would counter that "a liturgical language common to us all reminds us that we belong to an institution greater than any nation, and one that binds the faithful all over the world" (Woods 2008, 68). They believe that the Latin language helps realize Jesus' wish for his disciples as expressed in the Gospel of John (17:21): "that they may be one" (*ut unum sint*, in the Latin translation). Traditionalists tie the declining numbers of priests and weakening Mass attendance to the abandonment of the Tridentine Latin Mass, though scholars dispute such causal connections (Marx 2013, 72).

Traditionalists also cherish the Latin Mass because, they say, it long sustained European civilization. Latin is extolled as the seedbed of Europe's greatest artistic, literary, and musical creations. The loss of the language is said to have been a blow to both church and culture. Popular books written in this vein have titles like *Where Have You Gone, Michelangelo?* (Day 1993). More profoundly, Catholic discourse seems to have shifted in tone from a recurring emphasis on matters of sin, holiness, and expiatory sacrifice, to talk of personal "brokenness," communal solidarity, and social justice. In sum, the question of using Latin has been bundled with broader theological, ritual, visual, musical, and architectural concerns.

A number of lay and clerical organizations, including Una Voce Federation, Coalition Ecclesia Dei, Fœderatio Internationalis Juventutem, and the Latin Mass Society, are dedicated to preserving and promoting the ancient language and the Mass celebrated according to the pre-Vatican II worship books. Some (though not all) of these groups have strained relations with the Vatican; a few extremist ones (like the Congregatio Mariae Reginae Immaculatae: The Religious Congregation of Mary Immaculate Queen of Heaven) are sedevacantist, meaning they believe the papal seat has been vacated due to heresy. One liberal critic likens such groups to "Japanese fighters holding out in their bunkers after V-J Day" (Wills 2016, 23). The war, he contends, is over. Indeed, most Catholics do seem to value the pastoral, ecumenical, and musical qualities of the post-Vatican II vernacular Mass.

And yet, Latin holds on. In a few parishes, a kind of *rapprochement* may be emerging between the supporters of the "extraordinary" and "ordinary" forms of the Roman Rite (Marx 2013). And some irenic voices suggest that both orientations – the mysterious and the ministerial, the vertical and the horizontal – are to be found within the Catholic tradition (Cassingena-Trévedy 2007).

Dead or Alive?

Latin and other sacred languages are sometimes said to be dead. It is interesting that organic or biological metaphors have become so widely applied to languages, and not only in the popular media. Languages are characterized as being vital, extinct, endangered, dormant, living, vulnerable, or moribund. In fact, scholars have developed sophisticated checklists for determining whether a language will live or die. The most influential of these is the Graded Intergenerational Disruption Scale (GIDS) developed by Joshua Fishman. There are other variants developed by UNESCO and the *Ethnologue* database (Lewis and Simons 2010). The problem, however, is the fact that these analytical frameworks are concerned with spoken languages. Sacred languages are a different breed. They are not mother tongues (L1 languages) and do not have native speakers. But this does not mean they are extinct. Now, there *are* sacred languages that are dead. For example, Sumerian is a museum artifact studied by historians and archaeologists. The sacred languages discussed in this book, by contrast, still occupy niches in the cultural landscape and play a role in the lives of religious practitioners. They continue to be used for prayer, worship, meditation, protective tattoos, educational curricula, musical compositions, and a host of other practices and projects.

Instead of dead or extinct, it is better to think of sacred languages as fixed or conserved. According to Leonhardt, "A fixed language is therefore not a language that is closed and can no longer develop but a language in which several core components remain unchangeable, while other parts continue to evolve as in any other normal language" (2013, 19). Sanskrit, for instance, was codified about 2500 years ago and the overall linguistic structure or skeleton has remained intact, with the exception primarily of new vocabulary. The codification of Church Slavonic took place more recently, about 250 years ago, and is usually said to have occurred with the printing of the so-called Elizabethan Bible. (Elizabeth was daughter of Peter the Great and Empress of Russia.) Both Sanskrit and Slavonic are still evolving, but at a far slower rate than spoken vernaculars. The sociolinguist Joshua Fishman put it this way: "The whole posture of religious classicals is tradition-and-stability ('eternity') oriented rather than progress-and-change oriented" (1991, 362).

What, then, about Latin? Is it a dead language? Some Catholics actually embrace this moniker: "Latin is the home of the classical Roman rite. This is the only language, precisely because it is a 'dead' language, that preserves perfectly and enduringly the content of the liturgy in its unchanged and unchangeable meaning" (Dobszay 2010, 79). But we have seen how Latin is still used within the Catholic Church, not only for rituals but for papal encyclicals and even pontifical messages on Twitter. If we substitute "fixed" or "conserved" for "dead" in the quotation above, the same point is conveyed.

The epic history of Latin is reflected in the thousands of inscriptions found on the buildings, monuments, bridges, and statues throughout the "Eternal City" of Rome. There are examples of Old Latin, Classical Latin (*c.* 90 BCE to 120 CE), Later Latin (120 to 500 CE), Medieval Latin (500 to 1400 CE), and Neo-Latin (1400 CE onward). The earliest inscription stems from the sixth century BCE; but there is also one for an elevator dedicated by the late St. Pope John Paul II (Lansford 2009, 493). Contrast this with the scores of Etruscan inscriptions housed in the National Etruscan Museum in Rome, which are definitely artifacts of an extinct civilization.

Latin is still being used, and even spoken, in Rome; Etruscan is not. The Latin utilized in the Vatican today – in liturgies, publications, and inscriptions – would be largely intelligible to the influential Jesuit preacher St. Peter Canisius (Neo-Latin), to the famous scholastic author St. Thomas Aquinas (Medieval Latin), and to St. Augustine whose voluminous writings were indispensable in the formation of the Christian faith

(Later Latin). Vikram Chandra asserts, "If you had a pandit in contemporary Varanasi write a letter in Sanskrit and time-machined it back 2,000 years, his ancestors would be able to read it with perfect ease" (2014, 94). That is the difference between a fixed and a dead language.

Yet – to add one more twist to the tale – it is still possible that a fixed language can be heading toward its demise. Indeed, a number of observers are convinced that, given the lethal effects of Vatican II, this is the fate of Latin:

> The language situation in the Church of the second half of the XX century is much like the extinction of languages of small nations in the assimilation of the past by larger nations ... authorities are calling for a revival of the traditional language and culture, but these calls resonate with only a relatively small number of enthusiasts.... Even the creation of special departments, publication of periodicals, competitions, active and creative lexicographical work cannot stop the irreversible necrosis of Latin. (Stasiuk 2006)

Latin is not dead – at least not yet.

References

Arinze, Cardinal Francis. 2006. "Language in Liturgy." Accessed July 25, 2016. http://www.piercedhearts.org/liturgy/language_in_liturgy_arinze.htm

Austin, Gerard. 2008. "The Reception of the Liturgical Reform of the Second Vatican Council." *Liturgical Ministry* 17: 49–57.

Baldovin, John F., SJ. 2010. *Reforming the Liturgy: A Response to Critics*. Collegeville, MN: Liturgical Press.

Benedict XVI. 2007. *Summorum Pontificum: On the Use of the Roman Liturgy Prior to the Reform of 1970*. Accessed July 25, 2016. http://w2.vatican.va/content/benedict-xvi/en/motu_proprio/documents/hf_ben-xvi_motu-proprio_20070707_summorum-pontificum.html

Cassingena-Trévedy, François. 2007. *Te Igitur. Le Missel de saint Pie V. Herméneutique et déontologie d'un attachement*. Preface by Grégory Solari. Geneva: Ad Solem.

Chandra, Vikram. 2014. *Geek Sublime: The Beauty of Code, the Code of Beauty*. Minneapolis, MN: Graywolf Press.

Chupungco, Ansar J., OSB. 2010. *What, Then, Is Liturgy? Musings and Memoir*. Foreword by Mark R. Francis, CSV, and Keith Pecklers, SJ. Collegeville, MN: Liturgical Press.

Day, Thomas. 1993. *Where Have You Gone, Michelangelo?* New York: Crossroad.

Dobszay, László. 2010. *The Restoration and Organic Development of the Roman Rite*. With an Introduction and edited by Laurence Paul Hemming. London and New York: T & T Clark.

Egger, Carolus. 1977. *LEXICON NOMINVM LOCORVM.* Vatican City: Officina Libraria Vaticana, Libreria Editrice Vaticana.

Familia Sancti Hieronymi. 1989. Constitution, Amendment I. Accessed July 24, 2016. http://hieronymus.us.com/Constitutio/FSH-Anglice.htm

Fishman, Joshua A. 1991. *Reversing Language Shift: Theoretical and Empirical Foundations of Assistance to Threatened Languages.* Clevedon and Philadelphia: Multilingual Matters.

Gane, Yorick Gomez. 2009. "*Pretiosus Thesaurus.*" *La lingua latina nella Chiesa oggi.* Vatican City: Libreria Editrice Vaticana.

John XXIII. 1962. *Veterum sapientia.* Adoremus Bulletin. Accessed February 10, 2016. http://www.adoremus.org/VeterumSapientia.html

Kiczek, Steven A. 2009. "Pope Benedict XVI's *Summorum Pontificum*: Reconciling Conflicting Values." *Journal of Religious and Theological Information* 8: 37–64.

Lange, Uwe Michael. 2012. *The Voice of the Church at Prayer: Reflections on Liturgy and Language.* San Francisco: Ignatius Press.

Lansford, Tyler. 2009. *The Latin Inscriptions of Rome: A Walking Guide.* Baltimore: Johns Hopkins University Press.

Lécureux, Bernadette. 1998 (1964). *Le Latin: Langue de l'Église.* New revised edition. Paris: Pierre Téqui.

Leonhardt, Jürgen. 2013. *Latin: Story of a World Language.* Translated by Kenneth Kronenberg. Cambridge, MA: The Belknap Press of Harvard University Press.

Lewis, M. Paul, and Gary F. Simons. 2010. "Assessing Endangerment: Expanding Fishman's GIDS." *Revue Roumaine de Linguistique* LV (2): 103–120.

Libreria Editrice Vaticana. 2015. Accessed July 25, 2016. https://w2.vatican.va/content/francesco/it/angelus/2015/documents/papa-francesco_angelus_20150607.html

Lincoln, Bruce. 2012. "Ancient and Post-Ancient Religion." In *Gods and Demons, Priests and Scholars: Critical Explorations in the History of Religions.* Chicago and London: University of Chicago Press.

Marx, Nathaniel. 2013. *Ritual in the Age of Authenticity: An Ethnography of Latin Mass Catholics.* PhD Dissertation, University of Notre Dame.

McDannell, Colleen. 2011. *The Spirit of Vatican II: A History of Catholic Reform in America.* New York: Basic Books.

Opus Fundatum "Latinitas." 2003. *Lexicon recentis latinitatis: Volumen 1. et 2.* Vatican City: Libraria Editoria Vaticana.

Ostler, Nicholas. 2007. *Ad Infinitum: A Biography of Latin.* New York: Walker.

Pavanetto, Cletus. n.d. "PARVVUM VERBORVM NOVATORVM LEXICVM." Opus Fundatum "Latinitas." Accessed May 28, 2014. http://www.vatican.va/roman_curia/institutions_connected/latinitas/documents/rc_latinitas_20040601_lexicon_it.html#1

Peckler s, Keith F., SJ. 2003. *Dynamic Equivalence: The Living Language of Christian Worship.* Collegeville, MN: The Liturgical Press.

Pecklers, Keith F., SJ. 2009. *The Genius of the Roman Rite: The Reception and Implementation of The New Missal.* London: Burns and Oates.

Priestly Fraternity of Saint Peter. 2016. "The Traditional Liturgy." Accessed July 25, 2016. http://www.fssp.org/en/liturgie1962.htm

Resnick, Irven M. 1990. "Lingua Dei, Lingua Hominis: Sacred Language and Medieval Texts." *Viator* 21: 51–74.

Riesebrodt, Martin. 2010. *The Promise of Salvation: A Theory of Religion.* Translated by Steven Rendall. Chicago and London: University of Chicago Press.

Sacrosanctum Concilium. 1963. Accessed June 25, 2016. http://www.vatican.va/archive/hist_councils/ii_vatican_council/documents/vat-ii_const_19631204_sacrosanctum-concilium_en.html

Smith, Jonathan Z. 2004. *Relating Religion: Essays in the Study of Religion.* Chicago and London: University of Chicago Press.

Stasiuk, Iu. 2006. "Latinskii iazyk v sovremennoi katolicheskoi tserkvi." Accessed November 28, 2015. http://www.binetti.ru/studia/stasiuk_5.shtml

Steinfels, Peter. 2003. *A People Adrift: The Crisis of the Roman Catholic Church in America.* New York: Simon and Schuster.

Vatican Radio. 2015. "Pope Francis: Seek Christ in Eucharist, in Neighbour." Accessed July 25, 2016. http://en.radiovaticana.va/news/2015/06/07/pope_francis_seek_christ_in_eucharist,_in_neighbour/1149834

Wills, Garry. 2016. *The Future of the Catholic Church with Pope Francis.* New York: Viking.

Woods, Jr., Thomas E. 2008. *Sacred Then and Sacred Now: The Return of the Old Latin Mass.* Fort Collins, CO: Roman Catholic Books.

Further Reading

Janson, Tore. 2004. *A Natural History of Latin: The Story of the World's Most Successful Language.* Translated and adapted into English by Merethe Damsgård Sørensen and Nigel Vincent. Oxford and New York: Oxford University Press. A congenial introduction to a potentially formidable topic, though without much attention to religion.

Lamberigts, Mathijs. 1997. "The Liturgy Debate." In *History of Vatican II.* Vol. 2: *The Formation of the Council's Identity, First Period and Intercession, October 1962 – September 1963*, edited by Giuseppe Alberigo, 107–166. English version edited by Joseph A. Komonchak. Maryknoll: Orbis; Leuven: Peeters. Offers a blow-by-blow account of the pivotal debate at Vatican II concerning Latin.

Mohrmann, Christine. 1957. *Liturgical Latin, Its Origins and Character: Three Lectures.* Washington, DC: The Catholic University of America Press. A classic explanation of the origin and rationale of Latin in Catholic worship.

Chapter 4

Beliefs about Sacred Languages

Saffron Days in L.A. is a collection of modern-day parables told by an amiable Buddhist monk from Sri Lanka who finds himself living in Southern California. Each tale presents a similar scenario: the monk, Bhante Piyananda, encounters an Angelino who has a predicament that can be resolved through Buddhism. The affable cleric provides advice on ethical dilemmas and marital disputes, and in dire cases performs a type of ritual intervention. Each encounter offers a teachable moment, a chance to show the real-world benefits of the Dharma (the Buddha's teaching about the nature of reality).

In one story we read about Todd, an individual with many problems: he lost his job, he has a sick wife, and his kids were taken away by a child welfare agency. Venerable Piyananda leads Todd to the shrine room of the local Buddhist temple, where he chants over him for an hour in Pali, the sacred language of Theravada Buddhism. Some props accompany the recitation: there is a pot of water with a white cloth over it and a string connecting the pot to a statue of Buddha. Ven. Piyananda and Todd hold the string. This procedure is replayed for seven days. On the seventh, Todd shows up "a clean-shaven, well-dressed young man, who looked completely different from the depressed, ashen-colored person of a week before." Todd brings his wife to the temple. She was allegedly possessed: "Her body was emaciated, and there were horrible odors in the room." The monk chants over her as well. Eventually, we are told, she is freed from her baleful condition and makes a full recovery (Piyananda 2001, 109–111).

Sacred Languages of the World: An Introduction, First Edition. Brian P. Bennett.

This vignette confirms what we have established thus far about sacred languages, but also adds to the picture. Bhante Walpola Piyananda belongs to the *sangha*, the Buddhist monastic order. Pali is not his mother tongue. Hailing from Sri Lanka, he speaks Sinhala, though obviously resorts to English to interact with Todd and the other residents of Los Angeles. The monk uses bits and pieces of Pali, especially the *paritta* chants, for a specific thaumaturgical (i.e., short-term, miraculous) purpose: healing Todd in body and mind. This is a small reward as opposed to the long-term goal of attaining nirvana, the big promise of Buddhism. The Pali chant functions as a kind of restorative: the conditions and constraints of world are still in place, but Todd and his wife are healed and given a fresh start. We see how this healing, with its ritual gestures and accoutrements, is done in a special location (*there*), a temple, the natural habitat of Pali. So far, so good.

But Ven. Piyananda's story also adds something new to our understanding of sacred languages. A *sutta* (Sanskrit *sutra*) is a sermon or discourse by the Buddha. The monk explains to Todd why the chants work:

> all *suttas* have intrinsic powers because the Buddha's teachings, as well as his *paritta* chantings, are assertions or affirmations of truth. At the end of the recital of each *sutta*, the chanters bless the listeners with the words, "*Etena saccha vacchena sothi te hotu sabbada*," which means, "By the power of the truth of these words, may you ever be well." (Piyananda 2001, 112)

In this view, it is not only the content of *suttas* per se that is vital. It is not just a matter of words conveying correct information – the *sound* of the Pali language is integral to the situation. As Ven. Piyananda explains,

> *Paritta* chanting is specifically for protecting ourselves from evil spirits, misfortune, sickness, and the negative influences of the planetary systems.... The rhythm of the chanting is important, and the vibrant sounds create a pleasant field of energy for the listeners as well as for the chanters. The monks chant the *suttas* with various intonations to produce vibrations that can calm the mental state of all participants. (109)

The Buddha's *suttas* are true, according to the Buddhist tradition. But understanding the content of the sermon is not only a matter of intellectual comprehension. The language is operating on a different level, that of vibrations repelling unseen spiritual forces and sound waves bringing about a state of inner calm, rather like a dog whistle that cannot be heard by humans but has an unmistakable effect on canines in the vicinity. This trans-human effect can occur regardless of whether or not the participants understand the informational level of the language: Todd clearly did not.

Within the Theravada Buddhist tradition, Pali is believed to be the language of the Buddha and the currency of eternal truth. But this entails a secondary and related belief: the sound and appearance of the language are inherently efficacious and can be tapped by adherents (especially, but not exclusively, clergy members) for specific benefits in the here-and-now (see McDaniel 2011).

In this chapter, we analyze some beliefs about sacred languages. Pali, a language closely related to (and influenced by) Sanskrit, will serve as our main case study. The belief system of a religion may be codified in a sacred language. But more than that, the language itself will be a focal point of religious beliefs. Sacred languages are mythologized, connected to spiritual agents and the unfolding of salvation history, however that is understood within the particular religion. This mythologization may extend beyond the informational level to the graphic and sonic dimensions – the look and sound of the language – which may be endowed with magical potency by believers. The discussion will focus on Pali but branch out to consider and compare other examples.

Powerful Beliefs

Religion involves a complex of beliefs, practices, institutions, and communities focused on a postulated spiritual realm for the purpose of overcoming human limitations. It is not the same thing as philosophy. There is an intellectual content, to be sure, but philosophers do not typically fast, meditate, sing hymns, light incense sticks, or parade icons through the streets. Religions posit the existence of superhuman powers, personal or impersonal in nature, which human welfare depends on. The religious premise is that it is both possible and desirable for people to relate their lives to this supramundane order via a network of sacred symbols. Just as a particular place (like Mecca) or action (like the Mass) may be viewed as the preeminent threshold between this world and the next, so too a sacred language may be held up as playing a definitive role in the interplay between the human and the superhuman. Religious believers may declare a special – perhaps exclusive – relationship between a named variety, like Pali or Arabic, and the divine.

As far as beliefs and sacred languages are concerned, there are two interrelated points. First, the belief system of a particular religious tradition may be expressed *in* the sacred language, from scriptural texts to papal encyclicals, law codes to liturgical hymns. The Qur'an is in Arabic and the typical edition of the Catholic Catechism is in Latin, though in each case paraphrases or translations also exist and are widely consulted by adherents. Similarly, Pali has been a linguistic resource called upon to hammer out the doctrines of Theravada Buddhism, the tradition that predominates in South and mainland Southeast Asia. Pali is the vehicle of Theravada learning and literature. It is the language of the voluminous Pali Canon or Tipitika (meaning "Three Baskets"), a massive corpus of scriptures that fills an entire bookshelf. There are also Pali-language chronicles, epistles, inscriptions, folktales, medical treatises, romances, and legal manuals (Crosby 2014, 87–88). The corpus of Theravada Buddhist thought in all its wide-ranging complexity is found in Pali, though texts are often combined with material in Thai, Sinhala, Burmese, and other vernaculars. New texts are still composed in Pali, necessitating (as with Latin) the creation of neologisms, though this discursive practice has diminished since the premodern "bulge" period. Even with this reduced output of new compositions, Pali is still vital to the expression of Theravada Buddhist belief, providing the building blocks of discourse on the Dharma, the Buddha's teaching. Interestingly enough, there has even been a modest increase in the use of Pali at academic/monastic conferences (see Chapter 7).

So, a consecrated language is the depository of a religion's myths, ethical guidelines, doctrines, and speculations. But there will also be beliefs *about* the sacred language itself. Believers have ideas about the origins, qualities, and proper uses of Arabic, Latin, Pali, and so forth. Of course, this is not just the case with sacred languages. All languages have certain notions, theories, and attitudes projected onto them. They are constantly being ranked on a scale of values, which is always a comparative venture. One language is held up as elegant in structure, mellifluous in sound, or capacious in vocabulary, while others are depreciated as unsophisticated, harsh-sounding, or defective. In sociolinguistics this is known as language ideology, meaning the more or less consistent and consensual set of beliefs, images, and assumptions that positions one language (and, by extension, its users) on a scale of values in relation to other languages (and, by extension, their users). These beliefs are typically built up over time, often imperceptibly, and are repeated in different venues: at school, in the media, and so on. Repeated enough, they may come to seem self-evident.

Of course French is beautiful, assume those who speak it. *It goes without saying* that English is the most important language in the world, according to Anglophones. Language ideologies may also depreciate the value of a language or languages. For some reason Indonesian (a variety of Malay) has attracted more than its fair share of unflattering attention. According to some it is a simplistic language with almost no grammar that can be learned in a few weeks. In the words of one critic, it is "a mere auxiliary language, only fit for communications of a simple and concrete kind." Others deride Indonesian as soulless, the "language of an alienated and bureaucratic intelligentsia ... turgid, humourless, awkward, mechanical and bereft of emotion or sensuality" (quoted in Sneddon 2003, 14, 18). We mention this example not to ratify these particular value judgments, but merely to demonstrate that language beliefs may be either positive or negative in character.

Iconization is also typically at work in rhetoric of this sort. This refers to the semiotic process whereby the values ascribed to the language are extended to the people who use it. The language becomes a kind of icon or reflection of the community. Clearly, social, racial, religious, and political factors play a role in shaping linguistic attitudes. If one's neighbor's language is derided as soulless or simplistic, then it is easy to dismiss or perhaps even invade them.

Language ideologies may be implicit or explicit, assumed or articulated. As we saw in the previous chapter, the Vatican has articulated ideas about Latin in *Veterum Sapientia* and a number of other documents of varying importance. But beliefs about language may also be conveyed through subtler means, like the way that people change their demeanor (or even their clothing) when they use the language; the way that the language is only heard in certain spaces and situations; or the way that books written in the language are handled with special care and attentiveness. In such cases, beliefs about language must be inferred from behaviors. During unsettled times, some may challenge the regnant ideology and question why a particular language is situated so high on the community's scale of values. Supporters and opponents may elaborate their arguments in conferences, editorials, and polemical tractates. This is what happened with Latin leading up to and at the Second Vatican Council in the 1960s.

On one level, sanctified languages are not that different from vernaculars. Speakers assume that their language is logical, easy to learn, and so on. But religious formulations tend to be rather extreme in this regard. For example, a small promotional book called *The Wonder that is Sanskrit* declares that "Sanskrit is rich in every way – rich in vocabulary, rich in literature, rich in thoughts and ideas, rich in meaning and values" (Sampad and Vijay 2002, 6). The text turns into a veritable thesaurus, hailing Sanskrit as wonderful, incredible, fecund, supple, compact, flexible, efficient, pithy, opulent, concise, suggestive, powerful, unambiguous, sweet, charming, precise, inspiring, perfect, and priceless. We can also see iconization at work here. If Sanskrit is the most perfect language in the world – supple, flexible, rich, fecund, and so on – then this reflects well on Indians. And indeed the authors of *The Wonder that is Sanskrit* make precisely this point: "It is but natural that a language will reflect the nature of the people who use it – mirror their culture, their outlook, their goals in life" (96).

One final point: language ideologies are not static, but are historical phenomena that can change over time. The book *The Wonder that is Sanskrit* makes the claim that "scholars of computational linguistics wholeheartedly accept Sanskrit as the best and most scientific language of the world" (148). Such a notion is obviously of recent vintage. But one isolated idea does not make a language ideology – there must be uptake among the community, though it does seem that this particular idea is gaining ground among Sanskrit enthusiasts.

Within their communities, sacred languages are the equivalent of linguistic gold. Unlike nickel, zinc, chromium, and other metals, gold has been mythologized across cultures and time periods. From the Golden Fleece to the Golden Calf, the Age of Gold to El Dorado, the gleaming yellow metal has been endowed with all kinds of mystical properties and has inspired countless legends and visions. No other metal has generated the same fascination and obsession:

> Gold is a rare, valuable metal, but the high regard in which it is held is not based on that alone. It is immortal in that it resists corrosion. In human consciousness it has thus been associated with those other symbols of the permanent, the eternal, and the supernatural.... Myths, sagas, and legends invoked the actions of the gods or mysterious powers to account for the existence of [gold] deposits. (Bachmann 2006, 17–18)

In a similar vein, sacred languages like Sanskrit or Arabic are not just praised for their beauty and nobility; they are mythologized as being connected to the spiritual realm and the unfolding of salvation history. Now, in popular speech and even in sociolinguistics, the word "myth" usually means something that is wrong or erroneous or misunderstood. But in comparative religion, myth is a neutral term. Mythologization refers to the way that something – a book, a place, a time – is connected to the gods and their mighty deeds. Myth eternalizes its object, lifting it out of its finite, purely earthly reality, and endows it with epic, larger-than-life characteristics. If a language is mythologized, then, it is elevated above the ordinary and associated with angels and seers and martyrs and prophets. It is useful to speak of mythologization, because this reminds us that we are dealing with a process that can change over time, including being reversed. For instance, during the Soviet era, Russian was hailed as the language of the eternal Lenin, the glorious Bolshevik Revolution, and a future communist paradise with a shiny space-age luster. The language achieved a kind of "lift off." Since the collapse of the USSR, however, Russian has fallen back to earth and is no longer vested with such cosmic capabilities. It has largely been demythologized.

Beliefs about sacred languages tend to involve four motifs:

- the revelatory: the sacred language is a vessel of divine revelation
- the interventionist: the sacred language is an effective instrument for communing with the superhuman realm
- the vehicular: the sacred language unites believers across time and space
- the cultural: the sacred language has enriched poetry, literature, science, art, music, or other aspects of culture

A sacred language ideology usually combines two or more of these themes. Naturally, beliefs about the language will be of a piece with the broader tapestry of a religion's doctrines regarding the human condition, the nature of divinity, and the problem of evil and suffering. It would not make sense, for instance, to claim that Pali is angelic when angels have no place in Buddhist cosmology. We should also note that these are religious beliefs/myths and, as such, are not open to empirical testing. We can observe and analyze a number of statements about Sanskrit, but cannot prove in a laboratory or classroom that it is the language of the gods. All we can prove is that some Hindus claim this.

Revelatory

Sacralized languages are connected directly or indirectly with divine revelation, with the disclosure of the superhuman to the human. This is usually not said about colloquial languages, which are thoroughly earthbound. It is helpful to distinguish between primary and secondary languages of revelation (cf. Lange 2012, 53). Primary revelatory languages are those that, according to devotees, are spoken by the deity or heard by prophets or seers. These revelations are then codified in holy scriptures. Arabic, Sanskrit, and Avestan are examples of this subtype, being the languages of the Qur'an, the Vedas, and the Avesta (the sacred book of Zoroastrianism), respectively. Here the language and the revelation comprise a kind of monocoque entity. This is an automotive term that refers to "a type of vehicular construction in which the body is combined with the chassis as a single unit" (Merriam-Webster). Transposed to the religious context, monocoque means that the sacred language is part and parcel of the content of revelation; the medium and the message are fused together and essentially inseparable. The Qur'an is only conceivable in Arabic. They are not two things, but one.

Saying that a language emanates from the divine realm places it on an unparalleled scale of values. In this conception the very structure of the language – its nouns, verbs, adjectives, etc. – are not just grammatical pieces but are charged with hierophanic power. Classical Arabic is the quintessential example in this regard. The Qur'an is perhaps the most self-referential of all scriptural texts, since in several places it insists on its own language. Sura 26:192–195 speaks of revelation coming in "a clear Arabic tongue" while 42:7 and 12:2 mention "an Arabic Qur'an" (Qutbuddin 2007, 316). Thus, Arabic is the language of Allah's final divine revelation that confirms yet supersedes previous forms (the Torah, the Gospel). It is considered the *ipsissima verba* of God, its beauty miraculous. Just hearing the golden words being recited can be an overwhelming experience for devotees. Islamic literature is full of stories of believers crying, and sometimes even dying, when they hear the empyrean sounds of the Arabic-language Qur'an. "It is a linguistic heaven on earth" (Kermani 2015, 129).

Claims are sometimes made about revelatory languages that their words express the essence of things. That is to say, the relationship between a word and a corresponding object is thought to be inherent and necessary, not arbitrary or random. The form and substance are one. *Canis familiaris* is the scientific Latin term for what is called *dog* in English, *chien* in French, and *собака* in Russian. But none of these terms bespeaks the essence of "dogness"; in other cultures, other words can be, and in fact are, used for canines. In sum, the relationship between the word and the referent (dog) is arbitrary. By contrast, in traditional Jewish thinking, Hebrew is the language of the creation of the world (and the world to come). The words capture the *realia* of the cosmos in an elemental and essential way. According to *The Wonder that is Sanskrit*, "the meaning of the fundamental Sanskrit roots is also not arbitrary but based on a deeper truth" (Sampad and Vijay 2002, 29). In this kind of religious ideology, the words of a sacred language correspond exactly and essentially to the various forms and facets of existence.

Such beliefs have consequences. If a community claims that its sacred text has been delivered from on high in a particular language, then that revelation must be transmitted precisely, either orally or in writing, with scrupulous care. These are celestial words, after all, not terrestrial ones, and are therefore not to be dealt with lightly. The more a language is mythologized, the more fraught the question of translation becomes. If the language came down from heaven, why shortchange it with some imperfect earthly tongue? If the language offers devotees an unerring description of reality, why bother with anything else? Who would dare to alter the words of God or of Universal Consciousness? Within the framework of this kind of language ideology, translation may be seen as (at best) cheating and (at worst) sacrilegious.

Other sacred languages, such as Latin and Ge'ez, are considered secondary transmitters of revelation. Fishman categories them as "holiness one step removed" (2006, 254). They are still mythologized but in more modest terms. Believers do not claim that God spoke in these tongues. It is acknowledged that they stem from ancient empires, not heavenly realms of glory. Nevertheless, they are not ordinary tongues and have been touched in some sense by the divine. In the premodern period, for example, Catholic churchmen typically claimed that Latin was sacred because Divine Providence had chosen the Romans to propagate the Gospel: "The privileged role given to Latin is due in part to the notion that Roman *imperium* is divinely ordained. Roman expansion is willed by God in order to promote the expansion of Christianity, so that under the unity of empire all nations can be brought into the Body of Christ" (Resnick 1990, 64). This belief is echoed as late as 1962 in the papal document *Veterum Sapientia*. What these secondary ("holiness one step removed") languages do is preserve and pass on preexisting revelation. They are connected to great bishops, saints, missionaries, monasteries, patriarchates, and other people and institutions that have played a vital role in salvation history. Consider, for example, this statement about Coptic:

> In the book of Acts [of the Apostles] we read that the handkerchief of St. Paul, a plain ordinary piece of cloth, was able to provide healing to those who touched it in faith. Its mere presence before the Saint was enough to

> impart this blessing; the grace of Saint Paul could not be separated from the garments in which he lived. Coptic is the handkerchief which wiped the brow of the suffering martyrs who endured towards their heavenly reward; it is the relic bearing the everlasting impression of the lives of those who lived and breathed it, and it is the handkerchief infused with the fragrance of the sweet smelling aroma of the sacrifice of the first Christians of the Church. (Younan 2005, 8–9)

Here Coptic is hallowed as the language of the foundational saints and martyrs of Coptic Orthodox Church history, not as a language spoken directly by God. Church Slavonic occupies an intermediate position since, according to Orthodox tradition, it was a divinely inspired instrument for transmitting Christianity to the Slavs and was thus a pure vessel from the start – unlike Latin, which had begun its career as a heathen tongue (Tornow 2009, 71).

Interventionist

Sacred languages do not just reveal the superhuman realm; supporters say that the language is uniquely qualified to communicate with the divine. Sacred languages are celebrated for their role in liturgy, thaumaturgy, and somatology (spiritual disciplines like yoga and meditation). They are called upon to praise God, to envelop believers in a protective aura, to connect with the divine energy slumbering within. This interventionist motif comes in stronger and weaker versions. Sometimes it is claimed that a sacred language has an actual effect on the supramundane realm. Some Zoroastrians contend that prayers in Avestan actually combat evil spirits. According to one tradition, angels do not understand Aramaic, a kind of auxiliary sacred language within Judaism, so prayers said in the language go directly to God. In an ethnographic study of women Sanskrit users, one informant declared, "Sanskrit has a purifying effect on the mind." Another claimed, "I was literally cured of my illness after I began to speak Sanskrit." A third said that she recites Sanskrit mantras while cooking – something that has a noticeable effect on the food and those who consume it (Patton 2007, 28, 30). Such claims show that these are not ordinary linguistic mediums. They have one foot in this world, so to speak, and the other in the spiritual world.

In other cases the claim is weaker. Some Russian Orthodox adherents declare that, because Church Slavonic was intended from the start as a language of worship, it contains no jargon or profanity and is thus a pure and fitting vehicle for communing with God, Mary, and the saints. Sometimes the notion is framed more in stylistic terms. According to one author, "the Christian Latin language has attained such perfection, such plenitude, that the praises of God resonate completely naturally in this mode of expression, elevating souls toward Heaven" (Lécureux 1998, 73). Though such beliefs come in various shadings, the basic idea is that the language relates to – intervenes with – the spiritual dimension in a way that regular vernaculars cannot.

Vehicular

Other beliefs about sacred languages have a more social as opposed to superhuman emphasis. A common claim is that the sanctified language binds together members of the religious community over time and space. It is part of communal history and identity. As we saw in Chapter 1, sacred languages are primarily associated with the so-called world religions. Sacred languages are celebrated as lingua francas (vehicular languages), linking believers who speak different mother tongues. According to *Veterum Sapientia*, Latin has been "a bond of unity for the Christian peoples of Europe" and "a maternal voice acceptable to countless nations." A Conservative Jewish website declares that, "Hebrew unites us with Jews across time and space. It is the eternal language of our people and connects us with Jews in Israel and throughout the world" (quoted in Avni 2012, 176). Its defenders say that Church Slavonic unites all the Orthodox Slavs – Russians, Ukrainians, Bulgarians, Serbians, and so on. The idea here is that the sacred language is uniquely qualified to hold together a dispersed religious community.

Cultural

Related to this more earthly orientation, beliefs about the language are often linked to cultural expressions and artifacts. Here is a good sample from *The Wonder that is Sanskrit*:

> Much like the sacred river Ganga, Sanskrit has flowed across India for thousands of years, embracing and nourishing, but also uplifting and purifying an entire country and its people and creating a unique civilisation and culture. It has been the most perfect instrument for expressing the thoughts, feelings, aspirations, knowledge and experiences of this ancient culture. (Sampad and Vijay 2002, 7–8)

A small lay Catholic association called St. Benedict Patron of Europe Association (*Associatio Sanctus Benedictus Patronus Europae*) aims "to promote and disseminate Christian culture in a spiritually united Europe." This includes Latin, which, according to the group's mission statement, "was once the common language of the whole of Europe and an excellent medium of communication, culture, science and education" (Libreria Editrice Vaticana 2006). Such ideological statements emphasize the far-reaching influence of the sacred language on the community's cultural heritage.

Good Vibrations

With these general comparative observations as a backdrop, let us return to the example of Pali. The name itself shows that it is a bookish or scholastic language. It seems that "Pali" was originally used to refer to a scriptural text as opposed to a commentary on the text. By a kind of slippage, the word came to mean the *language* of the text.

In the Theravada Buddhist world, Pali is mythologized as the language of the Buddha. Now, some scholars doubt that Pali was ever a spoken tongue, since it seems to combine elements of different Indian dialects, as well as a dose of Sanskrit, giving it a kind of synthetic quality. "Most scholars now maintain that Pali is an artificial language, like Esperanto, designed specifically to record the Dharma, and was never the spoken language of anyone" (Morgan 2004, 69). But such judgments are not really relevant to most Theravadins, who associate Pali with the Buddha (with all Buddhas, for there have been multiple Buddhas across the vast eons of time). We are dealing with religious beliefs here, which may or may not tally with scholarly appraisals.

All religions involve some form of alleged disclosure from or about the supersensory order. Pali is also a language of revelation. But, as with most things Buddhist, some qualifications are in order. Keith Ward explains:

> Buddhism is, in one sense, a religion without revelation; there is no active communication from a God in most forms of Buddhism. However, there is certainly an authoritative teaching in Buddhism, derived from the enlightened insight of Gautama. He had a special mode of access to the suprasensory realm, nirvana, and he revealed it to his disciples ... [so] it is not wholly improper to speak of Buddhism as a revealed religion, whose teachings are

> received on authority by virtually all believers, as long as one is careful to note that there is no personal supernatural god who reveals the holy truths that most disciples learn from the Buddha. (1994, 58)

In the Theravada Buddhist world, this revelation is conveyed by Pali. A classic text spells out why Pali is foremost on the Buddhist scale of values. It is worth quoting at length:

> for a mother and father, when their children are small, lay them on a bed or on a chair and, speaking such and such words, do such and such work. The children define such and such speech of theirs thus: "By this that is mentioned, by this that is mentioned." As time goes on, they get to know the whole tongue. The mother is Tamil, the father is Andhaka. The child born of them, if he hears the mother's speech first, will speak the Tamil tongue; if he hears the father's speech first, he will speak the Andhaka tongue. But not hearing either speech, he will speak the Māgadha tongue. And he who is reborn in a great forest without a village and where there is no-one else who speaks, he too, when he creates speech of his own accord, will speak only the Māgadha tongue. And in hell, in the animal kind of generation, in the realm of ghosts, in the human world and in the world of deities, everywhere the Māgadha tongue is foremost.... Also the Fully Enlightened One, in announcing the Buddha word of the Tipiṭaka [the "Three Baskets" of Theravada scripture], did so only in the Māgadha tongue. (Ñāṇamoli 1996, 128)

Three separate but overlapping strands are braided together in this canonical account. First, Pali ("the Māgadha tongue") is the root language, meaning a kind of default linguistic mode of reality. Deprived of all social contact, a child will spontaneously speak Pali. Second, Pali prevails not just among humans but among beings in the unseen order, including ghosts and gods. This gives the language a unique vehicularity, for it is understood not only by people from different countries, but by different life forms! Third, Pali is the word of the Buddha, codified in the scriptures, the Tipitika. According to this line of thought, Pali is that language which denotes things as they really are. Since there is a direct and transparent correspondence between words and things, it represents the surest path to insight and thus to nirvana (Collins 2006, 50).

Contemporary practitioners echo these canonical statements. According to one Theravada teacher: "Pali is extremely necessary, because it permits us to study and teach students. From the very first sentence to the very last sentence, there is meaning in each word of the Buddha. From the lowest level up until the highest level there is [a teaching that will help] surpass suffering." Another says: "Pali is the language of every Buddha. It is the language that is beautiful and gentle. It carries deep meaning" (quoted in Collins and McDaniel 2010, 1395–1396). But the thing is – and here we return to the opening vignette of this chapter – the revelatory truth of this language is the basis for its reputed efficacy. For it is not just the words that bring healing and protection, the *sound* and the *graphic form* of the language are believed to have a kind of magical potency. Here we need to make a detour to understand something important about religion in general and sacred languages in particular.

Religion is a multisensory affair. Religions are not just beliefs, though of course ideas are a necessary part of any religious system. But religions go beyond the mental to the physical – to smells, tastes, colors, and textures (Kermani 2015, vii). They are embodied, material phenomena, involving people, places, practices, and paraphernalia. Christians around the world typically celebrate Christmas not by pondering the doctrine of the hypostatic union, which states that Christ was both fully human and fully divine, but by going to midnight Mass, singing Christmas carols, setting up crèches, and exchanging gifts (or possibly shooting off guns and fireworks, as was the custom in an earlier America). The doctrine is there, of course, but it is submerged in the colors and gestures and smells of the holiday.

Languages, too, are multimodal phenomena. They are not just disembodied information, invisible streams traveling through the air. When spoken, languages are often complemented by gestures, symbols, sounds, and props. When written, they are concretized in particular fonts and increasingly accompanied by images, videos, or music. These different modes work synergistically to convey meaning. Sacred languages are multisensory phenomena par excellence, in two ways.

First, sacred languages like Latin, Coptic, or Sanskrit are typically found in rich tableaux where all the senses are involved. Especially in liturgical settings, sacred languages constitute one ingredient in a ritual choreography that may include stylized gestures (prostrating, shokeling, kneeling, clapping, making the sign of the cross), accoutrements (censers, prayer shawls, altars, foodstuffs), smells (incense, beeswax candles, flowers), and sounds (bells, cymbals, sistrums).

To return to the Buddhist case, Paul Numrich describes Theravada rituals in America, including Ven. Piyananda's temple in Los Angeles:

> Typically, when participating in Pali chanting, receiving a blessing, or listening to a discourse on the Buddha's teaching (*dhamma desanā* or *baṇa*), lay people

> sit at a lower level than the monks, usually on the floor, with feet turned under their haunches and pointed away from the monks; moreover, in such instances laity's hands are held in the *wai* gesture, that is, palms pressed together, at chest level.... Also, at times a sacred string, a *pirit-nūla* or *sincana*, stretches from monks to laity during the chanting; afterwards, the monks may cut the string into small segments to be tied around the right wrist of each participant. (1996, 81)

The respective seating positions of the participants, the string that ties them together, and the unusual mode of delivery (chanting instead of simply speaking) – all these elements work in concert with bits and pieces of Pali, which may be well or poorly understood on a semantic level by different people in the room, to achieve a satisfying performance.

Thus, sacred languages are multimodal affairs because they are typically found in vibrant ceremonial settings that incorporate smell, touch, sound, taste, and feel. But, beyond that, the various sensory properties of sacred languages may be valued in and of themselves. That is to say, it is not only the semantic (informational) level of the sacred language that is important, but the sonic and graphic dimensions as well – how they look and how they sound. This is typically not said about workaday vernaculars. People may praise the elegant sound of French, but that is not the same thing as saying, as Bhante Piyananda does, that the sound waves of Pali can "touch the core beings of sincere listeners who are open to receiving their blessings."

The sonic dimension

It is not just words, but the sound of the words, that may be important for devotees. Sanctified languages are often sung, chanted, or declaimed in a way that marks them off from everyday speech. A religious community may have strict rules governing performance and the sounds of the language. A well-known list of guidelines for those reading in the Orthodox Church includes the following stipulations:

> Reading the prayers for all believers in a holy temple, we fulfill a godly deed, therefore you must read reverently and properly, slowly and clearly.... Secular artistic expressiveness is inappropriate in church reading ... do not impart tenderness, emotion, severity, or any other kind of feeling – a church reader is not an actor. Allow the sacred prayers to act on listeners by their inherent spiritual merit. (Quoted in Vorob'eva 2014, 47–48)

This text is saying that the auditory aspect of church reading – neither negligent nor showy – is integral to a true and proper ritual. But it does not go so far as to ascribe a magical potency to the Church Slavonic language per se.

In Ven. Piyananda's account summarized at the start of this chapter, we learn how chanting restored wellbeing to Todd and his wife. *Paritta* chant is ubiquitous in the Theravada world. The texts typically come from the Pali Canon, so are viewed as *buddhavacana* – the Buddha's revelatory word. Pali, as we have learned, is the language that prevails in all realms (heaven, hell, the animal kingdom, etc.). So chanting in Pali is believed to exert a profound interventionist effect on multiple levels of reality as curative and prophylactic. Chanting sessions are a ubiquitous feature of temple life:

> *Paritta* chant is performed twice daily by monks within monasteries, for whom it is a central practice of asseveration of their core teachings. It is also a vital component of virtually every ritual conducted by monks for laypeople, who believe it brings protection from dangers, blessings on worldly endeavors, and religious merit (*punya*) toward advantageous rebirth. (Greene 2004, 41)

Chanting might mean a single statement or a week-long session. During Buddhist festivals loudspeakers often project the sound – the good vibrations – of Pali to those who are unable to attend. As the opening vignette illustrates, *paritta* chanting in Pali is primarily used in thaumaturgical or magical ways, that is, to accrue boons and blessings in the here-and-now as opposed to the far-off goal of nirvana. Pali chants are thought to ward off evil, protect one from danger, provide relief during times of crisis. They bring blessings to business ventures and weddings alike. The acoustic dimension is critical. The fact that these protective texts are not simply written or read, but chanted, is vital to the whole endeavor. Monks do not sing – they chant. Phonetic accuracy is often viewed as crucial if a ritual is to be considered accomplished and legitimate. Similar to the reading of Church Slavonic, a beautiful sound should be cultivated, but one that is neither theatrical nor showy. Monastic chanters therefore walk a fine line. Their chants should capture the attention of lay listeners, but should avoid becoming a musical performance, which would distract from the meaning and mindfulness of the text (Greene 2004, 54).

If we could construct a sacred language barometer similar to the one discussed in Chapter 2, one criterion would be the extent to which the aural element is considered spiritually effective. There is variation across traditions. The *acoustic nature* of Sanskrit and Pali is of utmost importance. The sound of the Qur'an, being the very words of God, is vital to its place in Muslim cultures, though at the same time there is also a tremendous emphasis on the written word (e.g., calligraphy, inscriptions, amulets). The sonic factor is less important in the case of Church Slavonic and even less so with Latin, where it is largely reduced to a matter of style and propriety. Catholics do not typically say that the sound waves of Latin have an effect on the superhuman realm.

The graphic dimension

Some sacred languages are associated with certain scripts. For instance, Coptic is written in a unique alphabet that consists of Greek letters supplemented with a handful of Egyptian demotic characters. The Avestan script is *sui generis* and only used in Zoroastrian literature. Latin, Cyrillic, and Arabic are connected to missionary religions (Christianity and Islam) and are widely diffused throughout the linguasphere today. As discussed in Chapter 2, the phenomenon of alphabetic charisma is an important one in world history: the aura of scriptures may inspire some communities to switch from one writing system to another, even if there are technical drawbacks to doing so. In other words, the pull of communion may trump the dictates of communication. As Islam spread, people converted to the religion and then converted their language from being written in a local script to the hallowed Arabic alphabet. Pali, by contrast, has no iconic script and is actually written in a number of different graphic systems, depending on the locale – Burmese, Sinhala, Roman, and so on. In Thailand, it has often been written in Khom (ancient Khmer), which looks different than Thai.

The good vibrations of the Buddha's word are believed by Theravada Buddhists to provide a protective aura for devotees, capable of shielding them from harmful spiritual and physical effects. Similar powers are ascribed to the graphic representation of the Buddha's liberating words. The implicit belief is this: if the words of the Buddha eliminate passions and suffering and lead to nirvana, then why not use the letters in which this doctrine is inscribed to ward off evil powers which populate our environment (Becchetti 1991, 31)? One can take the Buddha's words and inscribe them on an amulet or tattoo them on the body: their inherent truth does the rest. Now, it is often the case that the text is illegible to the devotee. In fact, the letters may be taken, rearranged, and recombined with an assortment of shapes and images. But this does not diminish their mystical potency. We might think of it this way: Even though flecks of gold may not add up to an ingot, they are nonetheless real gold; they still glimmer and gleam wherever they are found. So, too, with Pali: no matter how big or small the textual element may be – and it may be just a few letters – Pali, the Buddha's revelatory language, is deemed powerful in and of itself.

This line of thought has analogs in the Islamic and Christian religious traditions. The Arabic-language Qur'an has been appropriated for all kinds of talismans and magical procedures (e.g., Hamès 2007). In premodern Christianity, it was very common for biblical verses to be used as textual amulets which would be kept in the home, sewn into clothing, or worn directly on the body for thaumaturgical purposes, for good fortune and protection from injury in the short term. Various passages from the Old and New Testaments in Latin were selected for their purported effectiveness. From the New Testament, the first fourteen verses of the Gospel of John were widely reproduced on amulets. (This is the same passage that is recited at the end of every Tridentine Latin Mass.) According to one expert, "For whatever reason, early Christians embraced these verses as protective or therapeutic and began to use them, first in Greek and later in Latin, to ward off demons, evil, and misfortune" (Skemer 2006, 87). Two lines in particular were widely used as demonifuges (literally, devil-chasers): "*In principio erat verbum*" [In the beginning was the Word] (John 1:1) and "*Et verbum caro factum est*" [And the Word was made flesh] (John 1:14). Latin prayers such as the Pater Noster (Our Father) and Ave Maria (Hail Mary) were also incorporated into amulets, with the Pater Noster believed to be the more forceful. Sometimes the amulet consisted of a sequence of words snatched from scriptural and liturgical sources, and thrown together seemingly pell-mell, as in this thirteenth-century amulet:

> legion. Messias. sacerdos, propheta.
> sanctus immortalis. Rex. Ihesus. as. sabaoth.
> dues. dominus. pater. filius hominis. spiritus
> sanctus. omnipotens. misericors. redemptor.
> α etc ω. flo[s]. leo. karitas. fides. spes.
> eternus. Creator. primus et nouissi-
> mus. unitas. summum bonum. sother.
>
> (Skemer 2006, 287)

Such amuletic practices seem to have largely vanished from the Catholic world.

By contrast, this kind of religiosity thrives in the Theravada lands of Southeast Asia. Amulets and scriptural texts are closely interlinked. Many amulets are made of metal or clay with snippets of Pali (or Sanskrit) texts inscribed on them. (See Figure 4.1.) Some amulets called *takrut* are actually miniature palm leaf scrolls cached in little glass tubes and worn on the body. These are often *paritta* or protective texts, like the ones mentioned at the start of this chapter. In other cases, clay amulets are actually made from burned texts. The ground-up roof tiles of monasteries may be added to the mix, for it is said that they have absorbed the positive spiritual energy – the good vibrations – from the monastic chanting they have housed. (In this case, the aural power of the Buddha's Pali discourse is transmuted into visual power.) Amulets may bear the image of the Buddha or of a saintly monk, and are usually blessed in monastic ceremonies. They play a major role in contemporary Thai religion, much more than reading the voluminous Pali Canon (McDaniel 2014), which outside observers, conditioned by the Protestant emphasis on scripture, have often focused on. In these popular and widespread thaumaturgical practices, Buddhist temples (*there*) act like spiritual pumps or charging stations, which circulate snippets of Pali throughout the society (*anywhere*).

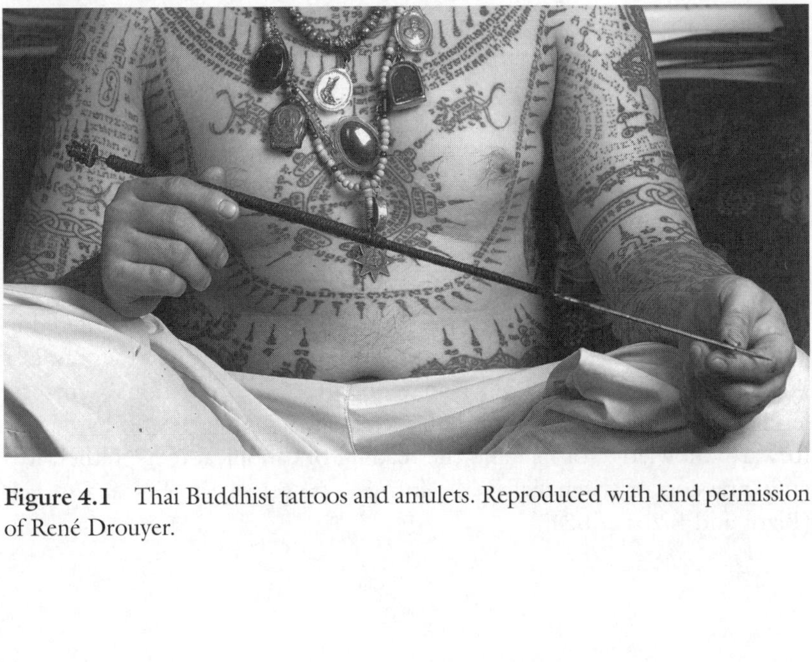

Figure 4.1 Thai Buddhist tattoos and amulets. Reproduced with kind permission of René Drouyer.

Yantra or magical diagrams are another noteworthy medium for the transmission of Pali in society. A *yantra* is a geometric design that provides a visual framework for a mantra, a sacred sequence of syllables. In Thailand, the mantras are in Pali or Sanskrit and are often written using the otherworldly Khom script. They are inscribed on metal tablets and used as amulets, drawn on shirts or headscarves, tattooed on the skin. These Pali-infused sacred diagrams are deployed for thaumaturgical purposes:

> The yant endows the wearer with supernatural protection, love, health and wealth. Sometimes they are also printed on cloths and hung at the entrance of houses in order to protect the inhabitants from evil spirits. Even today in Thailand, soldiers and police officers wear t-shirts printed with the "Yant of the four Buddhas" under their uniforms, to protect them from bullets. In order to bring luck and provide protection, yants are also drawn in the receptions of multinational companies, decorate the entrances of supermarkets, and the interiors of taxis, trucks and airplanes. (Drouyer 2013, 29)

The snippets of Pali are imprinted in ways that defy the tidy categories in which we sometimes try to encase a religious tradition like Theravada Buddhism. In tattoos the Buddha often "rubs shoulders" with Hindu deities like Shiva, Vishnu, Hanuman, and especially the ever-popular Ganesha, remover of obstacles, without apparent trouble or contradiction (Becchetti 1991, 23). There are also snakes, lizards, tigers, and dragons, as well as geometric patterns: squares, triangles, garlands, rosettes. All of these symbolic elements are combined with nuggets of Pali in a design that, for devotees, is both numinous and artistic – "a colorful hotchpotch of religious ideas embedded into skin" (Vater and Thaewchatturat 2011, 5).

These materials also raise the issue of intelligibility, which always seems to be hovering in the background when it comes to sacred languages. On the one hand, these tattoos are felt to be powerful precisely because they are linked to the content of the Buddha's salvational teaching. On the other hand, the letters are often plucked out, scrambled, and reordered in a diagrammatic pattern which can be read in multiple directions, amidst flowers and spirals, all of which may obscure the foundational semantic level (the "meaning"). We cannot understand this in terms of the straightforward knowledge of Pali and the reading of canonical texts; rather, it is an expression of the belief in the intrinsic power of the Buddha-speech (Bizot and Bizot 2002).

***

Peter Pannapadipo (a.k.a. Peter Robinson) was a member of the Buddhist monastic order for ten years. His memoir, *Phra Farang: An English Monk in Thailand*, offers an accessible insider view of contemporary Theravada Buddhism. In several places, he mentions his experience with Pali. "Even now," he writes,

> when I have been present at so many ordinations, I am still moved by the beautiful Pali requests and responses, the chanting of the monks and the traditions involved, by the feeling that this is how it has always been done and it *will* always be done. (2005, 36)

This is one of the things that sacred languages do: they convey a sense of historical memory, of continuity, of communion. But Pannapadipo also says: "All chanting is in the ancient Pali language which, for me at least, is very difficult to learn" (152). By way of example, he introduces the following word:

> *Siridhitimatitejoyasiddhimahiddhimahagunaparimitapunnadhikarassa*

Now, Pali is one of the most syncretic languages on Earth, meaning it packs a great deal of grammatical information into each word (Haarmann 2006, 53–54). This is an extremely long compound term comprising a list of spiritually beneficial phenomena, roughly as follows:

- good fortune
- good intention
- good thought
- energy, fierceness
- power, ability
- supernatural power
- great quality
- perfection, excellence

It concludes with a term meaning "acts of merit." This concatenation would normally be chanted or worn as an amulet for good fortune (Steven Collins, pers. comm.).

Pannapadipo/Robinson makes it clear that he does not go in for that sort of thing. The common people, he says, are drawn to the ritual efficacy of amulets and tattoos. But he personally views such expressions as a disappointing deviation from authentic Buddhism, and argues that monks at least should follow the pure philosophy, the Dharma, discovered and taught by the Buddha. He wants rational communication, not (to him) irrational communion with numinous forces in and through *sacra*: relics, amulets, statues, tattoos, and otherworldly scripts. Interestingly enough, though, he maintains this rather disdainful stance even after he encounters a spectral presence moving past him in a hallway one night – precisely the kind of spooky occurrence that amulets and tattoos are supposed to protect against.

Many of us are probably like Pannapadipo/Robinson. We can accept that an ancient sacred language expresses the sober philosophy of the Buddha, but may look down on more miraculous applications. Yet the two things – the value of language as a repository of doctrine and as an instrument of magic – are not always so easy to separate in the actual lifeworld of believers. Gold is valuable because it can serve as an enduring standard for measurement, but we also know it has been the subject of extravagant mythmaking and mystical speculations.

The belief system of a religion may be encoded in a sacred language. We see this in authoritative texts like the Qur'an or the *Catechismus Catholicae Ecclesiae*. But sacred languages are also the focal point of beliefs. Sacred languages are mythologized as vessels of revelation; as instruments par excellence for liturgy, magic, and meditation; as the glue that helps hold together a diverse religious community; as a font that has nourished literature and culture. Sometimes beliefs about sacred languages are articulated openly and spelled out in official documents. Other times what adherents believe about their sacred language has to be reverse-engineered, as it were, from their behavior.

In the case of Theravada Buddhism, canonical texts explain that the Buddha spoke Pali and that it reverberates among all life forms, from humans to animals, ghosts to gods. That being said, many monasteries do not even possess a complete set of the canon, relying instead on a clutch of handbooks and anthologies. Others may indeed possess the texts, but they remain locked in cabinets or wrapped in their shipping plastic. In some cases the pages are literally gilded together, rendering the book a cultic object of devotion. Elsewhere pages of Pali sacred texts are burned and the ashes inserted into amulets, which are worn for safety and wellbeing (McDaniel 2008; Veidlinger 2006). Protective chants, amulets, and tattoos – these are the ways that the vast majority of Theravadins, including monks, interact with the word of the Buddha. The *sonic* and *graphic* dimensions are as important (or, arguably, more important) than the *semantic* level (McDaniel 2011). The little motor that powers all of these props and practices is a firm belief in the intrinsic truth and therefore power of the Buddha's word in the Pali language. The Buddha spoke Pali. His words divulge the true nature of reality and show a path to nirvana; in the meantime, though, they offer safe passage in a perilous world (cf. Skemer 2006, 1).

References

Avni, Sharon. 2012. "Hebrew-Only Language Policy in Religious Education." *Language Policy* 11: 169–188.

Bachmann, Hans-Gert. 2006. *The Lure of Gold: An Artistic and Cultural History*. New York: Abbeville Press.

Becchetti, Catherine. 1991. *Le mystère dans les lettres. Étude sur les* yantra *bouddhiques du Cambodge et de la Thaïlande*. Bangkok: Édition des Cahiers de France.

Bizot, Catherine, and Bizot, François. 2002. "Buddhist Writings in Southeast Asia." In *A History of Writing: From Hieroglyph to Multimedia*, edited by Anne-Marie Christin, 149–153. Paris: Flammarion.

Collins, Steven. 2006. *Nirvana and Other Buddhist Felicities: Utopias of the Pali Imaginaire*. Cambridge: Cambridge University Press.

Collins, Steven, and Justin McDaniel. 2010. "Buddhist 'Nuns' (*mae chi*) and the Teaching of Pali in Contemporary Thailand." *Modern Asian Studies* 44 (6): 1373–1408.

Crosby, Kate. 2014. *Theravada Buddhism: Continuity, Diversity, and Identity*. Chichester, UK: Wiley Blackwell.

Drouyer, Isabel Azevedo. 2013. *Thai Magic Tattoos: The Art and Influence of Sak Yant*. Photography by René Drouyer. Bangkok: River Books.

Fishman, Joshua A. 2006. *Language Loyalty, Language Planning and Language Revitalization: Recent Writings and Reflections from Joshua A. Fishman*. Edited by Nancy H. Hornberger and Martin Pütz. Clevedon, Buffalo, and Toronto: Multilingual Matters.

Greene, Paul D. 2004. "The Dhamma as Sonic Praxis: *Paritta* Chant in Burmese and Theravāda Buddhism." *Asian Music* 35 (2): 43–78.

Haarmann, Harald. 2006. *Weltgeschichte der Sprachen: Von der Frühzeit des Menschen bis zur Gegenwart*. Munich: C. H. Beck.

Hamès, Constant, ed. 2007. *Coran et talismans. Textes et pratiques magiques en milieu musulman*. Paris: Éditions Karthala.

Kermani, Navid. 2015. *God is Beautiful: The Aesthetic Experience of the Quran*. Translated by Tony Crawford. Cambridge: Polity.

Lange, Uwe Michael. 2012. *The Voice of the Church at Prayer: Reflections on Liturgy and Language*. San Francisco: Ignatius Press.

Lécureux, Bernadette. 1998 (1964). *Le Latin: Langue de l'Église*. New revised edition. Paris: Pierre Téqui.

Libreria Editrice Vaticana 2006. Accessed July 28, 2016. http://www.vatican.va/roman_curia/pontifical_councils/laity/documents/rc_pc_laity_doc_20051114_associazioni_en.html#ST%20BENEDICT%20PATRON%20OF%20EUROPE%20ASSOCIATION

McDaniel, Justin. 2008. *Gathering Leaves and Lifting Words: Histories of Buddhist Monastic Education in Laos and Thailand*. Seattle and London: University of Washington Press.

McDaniel, Justin. 2011. *The Lovelorn Ghost and the Magical Monk: Practicing Buddhism in Modern Thailand*. New York: Columbia University Press.

McDaniel, Justin. 2014. "The Material Turn: An Introduction to Thai Sources for the Study of Buddhist Amulets." In *Material Culture and Asian Religions: Text, Image, Object*, edited by Benjamin J. Fleming and Richard D. Mann, 135–147. New York and London: Routledge.

Morgan, Diane. 2004. *The Buddhist Experience in America*. Westport, CT: Greenwood Press.

Ñāṇamoli, Bhikkhu, trans. 1996. *The Dispeller of Delusion (Sammohavinodanī)*. Revised for publication by L. S. Cousins, Nyanaponika Mahāthera, and C. M. M. Shaw. Oxford: The Pali Text Society.

Numrich, Paul David. 1996. *Old Wisdom in the New World: Americanization in Two Immigrant Theravada Buddhist Temples*. Knoxville: University of Tennessee Press.

Pannapadipo, Phra Peter. 2005 (1997). *Phra Farang: An English Monk in Thailand*. London: Arrow Books.

Patton, Laurie L. 2007. "The Cat in the Courtyard: The Performance of Sanskrit and the Religious Experience of Women." In *Women's Lives, Women's Rituals in the Hindu Tradition*, edited by Tracy Pintchman, 19–34. Oxford and New York: Oxford University Press.

Piyananda, Bhante Walpola. 2001. *Saffron Days in L.A.: Tales of a Buddhist Monk in America*. Boston: Shambhala.

Qutbuddin, Tahera. 2007. "Arabic in India: A Survey and Classification of Its Uses, Compared with Persian." *Journal of the American Oriental Society* 127 (3): 315–338.

Resnick, Irven M. 1990. "Lingua Dei, Lingua Hominis: Sacred Language and Medieval Texts." *Viator* 21: 51–74.

Sampad and Vijay. 2002. *The Wonder that is Sanskrit*. Pondicherry (India): Sri Aurobindo Society, in association with Ahmedabad: Mapin Publishing.

Skemer, Don C. 2006. *Binding Words: Textual Amulets in the Middle Ages*. University Park, PA: Pennsylvania State University Press.

Sneddon, James. 2003. *The Indonesian Language: Its History and Role in Modern Society*. Sydney: University of New South Wales.

Tornow, Siegfried. 2009. *Abendland und Morgenland im Spiegel ihrer Sprachen: Ein kulturhistorischer Vergleich*. Wiesbaden: Harrassowitz.

Vater, Tom, and Aroon Thaewchatturat. 2011. *Sacred Skin: Thailand's Spirit Tattoos*. Hong Kong: Visionary World; Enfield: Publishers Group UK.

Veidlinger, Daniel M. 2006. *Spreading the Dhamma: Writing, Orality, and Textual Transmission in Buddhist Northern Thailand*. Honolulu: University of Hawai'i Press.

Vorob'eva, A. G. 2014. *Uchebnik tserkovnoslavianskogo iazyka*. Third edition. Moscow: Izdatel'stvo PSTGU.

Ward, Keith. 1994. *Religion and Revelation: A Theology of Revelation in the World's Religions*. New York: Oxford University Press.

Younan, Sameh. 2005. *So You Want to Learn Coptic? A Guide to Bohairic Grammar*. Sydney: St. Mary, St. Bakhomious, St. Shenouda Coptic Orthodox Church Kirrawee.

Further Reading

Crosby, Kate. 2014. *Theravada Buddhism: Continuity, Diversity, and Identity*. Chichester, UK: Wiley Blackwell. A masterful overview and introduction; very valuable for placing Pali within the overall context of the Theravada tradition.

Gombrich, Richard F. 1988. *Theravāda Buddhism: A Social History from Ancient Benares to Modern Colombo*. London and New York: Routledge and Kegan Paul. A standard historical work covering Pali and much else.

Terwiel, Barend Jan. 2012 (1975). *Monks and Magic: Revisiting a Classic Study of Religious Ceremonies in Thailand*. New edition. Copenhagen: NIAS Press. An older, accessible anthropological report with many interesting observations about Pali-related beliefs.

Chapter 5

Practices: Religious, Political, Artistic

In 2012 an architectural competition was launched for the design of the National Library of Israel. An important project for the State of Israel and indeed world Jewry, the winning design would be built in a central and symbolic location: a 40,000-square-meter plot of land in Jerusalem's National Precinct, near the Parliament (Knesset), the Supreme Court, the Hebrew University, and the Israel Museum. The goal was a twenty-first-century library that would reflect the history of Israel and the Jewish people while being open to visitors of all faiths and nationalities.

One of the submitted designs that did not win was based on the shape of the first letter of the Hebrew alphabet, aleph (**א**), in its capital form. (See Figure 5.1.) The architects explain their thinking:

> Hebrew scripts, scripture, lettering and calligraphy form the essence of the Israeli National Library.... As Israel is the sole national entity where Hebrew is declared an official language, as well as the only locale where Hebrew is used for all communicational purposes on a daily basis, one may find it desirable to manifest the uniqueness of both the Hebrew lettering and the linkage between language-locale-people, through the design of the building most symbolically and functionally associated with Hebrew worldwide. Through use of shape, material and space, the proposed design strives to demonstrate this idea. (Ronen 2012)

In addition to the overall floor plan, the proposed building also included cutouts in the exterior shell that follow the shapes of the Paleo-Hebrew alphabet, the script that preceded what has become the iconic "square"

Sacred Languages of the World: An Introduction, First Edition. Brian P. Bennett.

Figure 5.1 Conceptual design for the Israeli National Library (2012). Reproduced with kind permission of Ori Ronen, Dany Kazcor, and David Kohan.

Hebrew script currently in use. This particular design choice was meant to symbolize the long history of the Hebrew language.

Now, this proposed blueprint did not invoke Hebrew as a sacred language per se. But the language used in Israel "for all communicational purposes" is actually derived from the "holy tongue," as we will discuss below. For centuries, Hebrew had functioned as a language of liturgy and learning, but was not spoken "on a daily basis." However, starting in the nineteenth century, as part of the Zionist project, the sacred variety was *revernacularized*, that is, converted from a sacred variety into an all-purpose spoken language, namely Modern Hebrew (also known as Israeli or Ivrit). Thus, the sacred language lies behind the vernacular. Moreover, Judaism is very much a textual religion and the letter aleph carries a host of biblical, theological, and mystical significations. A building fashioned according to the shape of the letter 'A' of the Roman alphabet would most likely seem trite or juvenile and unworthy of a national project of this significance. That is not the case here.

The aleph-based proposal did not win the competition and thus will not be built as the National Library of Israel. It remains a conceptual design. Nevertheless, the project reflects an important part of the phenomenon we will discuss in this chapter. To wit: people *do* things with sacred languages – even if those things remain on the drawing board.

Religion is not just a matter of beliefs but of performances in relation to the superhuman realm. Sacralized languages like Classical Arabic, Pali, Latin, and Hebrew are viewed as precious symbolic resources that can be utilized by believers for a range of practices and programs (always, of course, in conjunction with vernaculars such as Italian or Thai). Religious practices are quite varied. *Discursive* practices are those that can basically be done sitting at a desk, like reading, writing, or speaking, the ultimate purpose of which is to explain the nature of the unseen superhuman order and how people should relate to it. *Interventionist* practices involve people engaging with superhuman entities that are said to control our wellbeing and destiny. We can get a handle on the range of practices by grouping them into four categories: the liturgical, somatological, thaumaturgical, and behavioral. They include things like prayer, meditation, yoga, wearing magical amulets, and adhering to certain dietary rules. Practices have to be performed somewhere, and the location matters. We might imagine three spaces: *here* (at home), *there* (in a specially consecrated space such as a mosque or temple), or *anywhere* (on the street, in cyberspace, etc.).

Religions are not hermetically sealed systems, but overlap and interact with other cultural systems, such as politics and art. This can make it hard to determine what exactly counts as Christian or Muslim or Hindu. Where do we draw the line? For our purposes, so-called world religions like Christianity and Islam and Hinduism are best thought of as expansive civilizations that include religious systems in their core but also transcend them insofar as they encompass political and artistic movements and traditions (Riesebrodt 2010, xii). Their boundaries are unclear. *Artistic* projects include music, painting, literature, typography, graphic design, and architecture. The conceptual design for the National Library of Israel obviously belongs to this category. We see *political* projects at work when church and state collude or parties promote a sacred language or implement a policy affecting the language, as when those within the Zionist movement championed Hebrew for the nascent State of Israel.

The purpose of this chapter is to showcase a few of the many diverse ways that sacred languages have been and still are used. Everyone knows that gold is utilized for jewelry and other forms of decoration and adornment. More surprising is the fact that the metal's properties (malleable, reflective, non-corrosive, biocompatible) make it useful for an astonishing array of medical and scientific applications, from facial creams to spaceships.

The equivalent of semiotic gold, sacred languages are used by devotees for a similarly remarkable range of projects and practices. Hebrew is the best example for illustrating this aspect of the phenomenon. It is a vital and highly valued symbolic resource across the multifaceted world of Judaism. According to Sharon Avni,

> From observant (ultra-orthodox to ultra-liberal) to secular (and everything in between), Jewish people appropriate and utilize Hebrew in a variety of ways in the ongoing interactional work of constructing, maintaining, and expressing Jewish selfhood. In some regards then, Hebrew is a language called upon by its users to multitask in that it must simultaneously perform varying roles for its different users. (2011, 56)

The language, now more than three thousand years old, is used in contemporary worship, scholastic learning, art, poetry, meditation, prayer, visualization, yoga, and much else. For example:

> Meditation in a Jewish context sometimes uses the same mantra technique used in transcendental meditation, where the individual repeats a simple word or expression. In Jewish meditation, a Hebrew word or phrase is used, helping the worshiper experience the divine presence. A number of Hebrew prayers are used as mantras, most notably the Shema, the classic prayer that is included in every Jewish prayer service. *Sh'ma Yisrael, Adonai Eloheinu, Adonai Echad!* (Hear, O Israel, Adonai is our God, Adonai is One!) (Kaplan 2013, 289)

Whether all of this counts as Judaism is, of course, a very difficult question to answer. The problem of where to draw the boundary around the religion is perhaps trickier here than in other cases, since Jewish identity may be defined according to religion, ethnicity, civilization, or some combination of these (and other) criteria. Broadly speaking, we might imagine two contrasting viewpoints. For some, Judaism is a belief in God, Torah, and Israel and a concomitant adherence to Halacha (normative observances and rituals). Some suggest that the people who believe in and practice this religion should be called Judaists, which is not the same thing as Jews, not all of whom are actually Judaists (Kaplan 2009, xix). For others, whatever Jews do, by definition, counts as Judaism. This would include attending High Holy Day services, but also practicing forms of tai chi, shamanism, or Zen meditation. Yet some things, such as belief in Christ (e.g., "Jews for Jesus"), are widely deemed as crossing a red line and ending up outside the parameters of Judaism (Kaplan 2013). Jews and scholars (and Jewish scholars) debate these various interlocking issues. Since this book is written from the outside, from the vantage point of an observing comparativist, it operates with the broader definition, while acknowledging that some insiders would stoutly disagree with this decision.

When traditional Judaism from the so-called Old World reached the New World, it fragmented into a colorful mosaic of styles, groupings, and practices. Patterns of observance that worked in a relatively segregated society like the Pale of Settlement in Russia were scrambled in the more open and dynamic climate of the West. The context of American religious pluralism encouraged the development of distinct "denominations" (Sharot 2011, 225). Overall, one third (35 percent) of Jews in the United States are associated with the Reform denomination, 18 percent with Conservative, 10 percent with Orthodox, and 6 percent with Reconstructionist, Renewal, and various other groups. Roughly 30 percent of American Jews do not identify with any particular movement or denomination (Pew Research Center 2013, 10). Each branch or denomination, of course, has its own internal subdivisions and factions. Even Orthodox Judaism – which is all about strict adherence – is a highly fissiparous movement. A tongue-in-cheek listing of different "flavors" of Judaism in the United States includes: Hasidic, Liberal, Liberal Orthodox, Conservadox, Secular Humanist, Orthodox, Non-Denominational, Yekke, Reform, Neolog, Renewal, Progressive Orthodox, Yeshivish, Traditional Egalitarian, Adot HaMizrach/Sephardi, Reconstructionist, Ultra-Orthodox (Haredi) (Kaplan 2009, 113). Some Jews have turned to Buddhism for spiritual inspiration, giving rise to the phenomenon known as Bu-Jews (or Jubus), while others delve into Native American traditions or seek to develop a kind of Hebraic shamanism. The Hebrew language is an ingredient in most of these divergent projects and programs. Serious and playful, traditional and trendy, the "holy tongue" serves as a key symbolic resource in Jewish religious, political, and artistic activities.

In this chapter we will take a broad conspectual view, recognizing a panorama of people, places, practices, and paraphernalia under the umbrella term of Judaism. Our purpose here is to selectively illustrate rather than comprehensively document how some Jewish people do things with sacred Hebrew words. We are not giving proportionate emphasis to the most common Jewish behaviors, like observing Passover. Rather, guided by our conceptual template, our goal is to delineate the diverse *types* of practice that can go with a sacred language. From Torah yoga to the stunning revival of Classical Hebrew as an everyday spoken language in Israel, Hebrew provides the best "e.g." for demonstrating this diversity (cf. Smith 1982, xi).

How to Do Things with Sacred Languages

Thus far, we have made a distinction between discursive and interventionist practices, though this can be hard to maintain when it comes to the study of scriptures. The division is particularly artificial when it comes to Judaism, since there is a long history of study and prayer going hand in hand. A synagogue is traditionally thought of as *beit midrash* (house of study) and *beit tefillah* (house of prayer) (Kaplan 2009, 338), which is not the case with, say, Catholic churches. The purpose of studying the Torah or Talmud may be less about acquiring information per se than being immersed in the sacred text, viewed as a holy endeavor unto itself. Study thus becomes a kind of worship. At the same time, prayerbooks often have scholarly commentaries, providing another connection between liturgy and learning, the discursive and the interventionist (cf. Rabin 1976). Again, that is not the case with Catholic missals.

In terms of *interventionist* practices, Hebrew is used for a host of Jewish liturgical, somatological, and thaumaturgical practices. We will briefly sample each kind. (Obviously, the language has less of a direct connection with behavioral disciplines like adhering to the kosher food system.)

Liturgical practices

Liturgy involves collective, repeated, stylized, multimodal expression directed at the invisible spiritual domain. It is material, embodied behavior, typically performed in designated places *there* (temples, churches, mosques) with special paraphernalia (candles, cymbals, statues, incense). References to the great events of salvation history (the Exodus, Enlightenment, or Resurrection) are typically spliced with expressions of thanksgiving and petition, blessings and litanies. The language policy of a religious community may stipulate that a sacred language is the preeminent, or maybe the only permitted, medium for worship. Over time, the language can come to be seen not only as a hallowed but an essential ingredient in the proceedings.

What is the place of Hebrew in Jewish liturgy? Given the multiplicity of groups and ideologies within Judaism, the answer is by no means straightforward. Far from being monochromatic, Jewish worship varies in colorful ways across sectarian and regional lines. This is not the place for a catalog of Jewish festivals and rites of passage, as there are many handbooks and websites that supply such information. We will restrict ourselves to a few simple observations. First, the quantity of Hebrew used in liturgy is typically an index of broader denominational differences that developed dialectically over the past three centuries. Jews are by no means monolithic when it comes to beliefs about Hebrew. In North America it is common to speak of three or four main denominations: Orthodox, Conservative, Reform, to which some add Reconstructionist. The question of incorporating the vernacular into prayer and liturgy was actively debated among European Jews starting in the nineteenth century. As a general rule, the place of Hebrew in the liturgy correlates with a cluster of other characteristics, including: the relative insularity of the group in relation to broader society; theological views about the nature of God, the authority of the Torah, and the destiny of Israel; the apportionment of gender roles and expectations; and the influence of secular humanism and rationalism. Not surprisingly, the more liberal the denomination, the more likely that the vernacular will be used in synagogue services. According to one study, about half of all Jews in the United States (52 percent) say they know the Hebrew alphabet, can understand all or most of the words (13 percent), or can understand some or a few of the words (35 percent). Only 12 percent overall say they can have a conversation in Hebrew. Proficiency in Hebrew varies by denomination: 66 percent of Orthodox Jews say they can understand all/most Hebrew words (74 percent among the so-called Ultra-Orthodox), compared to 16 percent of Conservative, 4 percent of Reform, and 7 percent of those with no denomination (Pew Research Center 2013, 63–64).

Those who attend a yeshiva or Jewish day school claim the highest proficiency. For those who do not have a good grasp of Hebrew, there are a host of textbooks, seminars, summer camps, afterschool programs, smartphone applications, and websites offering help. Some pedagogical materials are also incorporated more or less directly into the liturgical experience. *Mishkan T'filah* (*A Dwelling Place for Prayer*) is the standard North American Reform Siddur or prayerbook (Frishman 2007). It is a bilingual edition with several special features. The page on the right includes the Hebrew text with an English translation and a transliteration of the

Hebrew words into the Latin alphabet. In general, to pray the traditional liturgy, one proceeds along the right-hand pages. The left-hand page offers poems, prayers, and meditations inspired by the right-hand content, including this interesting metalinguistic prayer for Shabbat (Sabbath):

> I begin with a prayer of gratitude
> for all that is holy in my life.
> God needs no words, no English or Hebrew,
> no semantics or services.
> But I need them. (126)

The very layout of *Mishkan T'filah*, with its bilingual and biscriptal format, represents an attempt to balance the criteria of solemnity and accessibility, communion and communication.

Visual T'filah™ is the name of a program that has been adopted in some Reform congregations in which Hebrew and English can be displayed via large screens placed in the sanctuary. According to the company's website:

> Visual T'filah™ is a way to enhance prayer and help worshipers in finding new or deeper meaning in prayers. It utilizes contemporary technology, such as projectors and screens, to display liturgy for the community intermingled with art and other visual imagery … VT allows the reintroduction of important values of prayer such as integrating art and visual awe as well as liturgical creativity and dynamic prayer experiences. (CCAR Press 2015)

The situation of Hebrew within Judaism is distinctive insofar as a related tongue, Aramaic, plays a vital supporting role in Jewish liturgy and study, representing "a kind of auxiliary holy language" (Rabin 1976, 138). It too has been sacralized. Some chapters from the Bible are in Aramaic (in Daniel and Ezra). The Talmud, a vast compendium of Jewish thought, combines Hebrew and Aramaic. Certain key prayers are also in Aramaic, especially the *Kaddish* and the *Kol Nidre*, which may actually be the most familiar and heartfelt to many Jews. The fact that the *Zohar*, the foundational text of Kabbalah, is composed in Aramaic, further endows this fellow Semitic language with a certain mystique. It is usually considered a mark of learning to know Aramaic in addition to Hebrew.

Another noteworthy aspect of Jewish liturgy is the emphasis on domestic practices. As we have been saying, sacred languages are closely linked to special buildings (churches, temples, mosques, etc.). The situation with Judaism does fit this general pattern. Hebrew is linked to synagogue.

Hebrew is heard there, Hebrew books are held in the hand, Hebraic inscriptions or designs are seen on the walls. Yet unlike other sacred languages, Hebrew is very much at home, so to speak, not just *there*, in consecrated buildings, but *here*, in the family dwelling place. In fact, the elevation of the synagogue to the status of "sacred space" has been influenced in part by Christianity's approach to churches. "Traditional Judaism integrates the holy into every aspect of life. Consequently, prayer and the synagogue represent only one, not particularly privileged, subset of Jewish sacred activities and locations" (Langer 2005, 231).

Now, Hindus may recite snippets of Sanskrit during *puja* (worship) at home, and Zoroastrians may utter their daily prayers in Avestan, but Jewish piety is strongly centered in the home, and therefore so is Hebrew. "On a given day," writes Sarah Benor, "Orthodox men recite several blessings surrounding their dressing, washing, and eating, recite the three daily prayer services, and study biblical or rabbinic texts, mostly in Hebrew (with some Aramaic)" (2012, 82). Sabbath and Passover services have a significant domestic component. Contrariwise, Latin, Pali, and Coptic would seem very much out of place in the kitchen or bedroom.

We turn now to consider some Jewish somatological and thaumaturgical practices. But before doing so, it is helpful to take a detour through the topic of alphabet mysticism.

Alphabet mysticism is a form of religious belief that assigns cosmic, esoteric, or prophetic meaning to the letters of a particular script. This supernatural value may be based on the shape of the letter, the name of the letter, the numerical value of the letter (in some traditions, letters double as numbers), or some combination thereof. Speculating about the numerical symbolism of letters is known as gematria. The mathematical value of the letters in a word or name may be added up and given mystical significance (e.g., a = 1, b = 2). This is not the straightforward semantic meaning of the word, but another kind of meaning thought to be encrypted within the alphabet, regardless of intellectual apprehension. As a general rule, there is a positive correlation between the elevated views of a sacred language as a vehicle of revelation and the practice of alphabet mysticism. The more exalted and mythologized the language, the more likely it will be used by devotees for alphabetical speculation and veneration. This is what we see with Arabic, Hebrew, and Sanskrit, and to a lesser extent with Church Slavonic.

"The Qur'ān," for example, "is regarded by Muslims as the word of Allah (*kalimat Allāh*). It was revealed in the Arabic language and written down in the Arabic script, which is of divine origin" (Dévényi 1996, 279). The script becomes something used in magic, meditation, and mystical speculation:

> The principle of what is known as the science of letters ('ilm al-ḥurūf) is the idea that the nature and secret of letters exist since the letters turned into one another before the creation of the world in order to form words. These words live inside the created things, and before the creation they were identical with the ideas of things. So the secret of every creature resides in the written form of the word which is its name. Hence the letters have a supernatural power from which the universe could be created, in other words, they are the pillars of the universe. (278)

To give one example: There are seven letters in the Arabic alphabet that do not appear in the *Fatiha*, the opening chapter of the Qur'an: th, j, kh, z, sh, ẓ, f (in English transliteration). Interestingly enough, their very absence seems to bestow upon these characters a certain mystique, connecting them to the unseen divine realm, including "the most important names of God, the names of the guardian angels, the seven kings of the jinn, the days of the week and the stars" (278). Not all sacred languages generate such speculation. This kind of thinking is largely absent from Latin. Again, Church Slavonic occupies an intermediate position, because according to legend the script was an inspired creation. It is not surprising to find books dedicated to explaining the divine significance of Church Slavonic letters (e.g., Dmitrieva 2015).

Belief in the potency of the Hebrew alphabet has a long history in Judaism. The shape, sound, numerical value, and alphabetic order of the letters are all said to have cosmogonic power and encode higher spiritual truths. According to Bernard Spolsky, "The rabbis held that the Torah was given in Hebrew, which was also the language of creation" (2014, 51). Such a lofty view naturally leads to all kinds of speculation about the power and holiness of Hebrew letters.

Luxuriant theorizing about the Hebrew alphabet developed in the medieval discourse of Kabbalah, which is often glossed as "Jewish mysticism" (Dan 2006). The last few decades have seen a remarkable growth in interest in Kabbalah among Jews and non-Jews alike. There are attempts to modernize and popularize this ancient and multifarious tradition, blending it with forms of New Age and Christian spiritualities, very much in a postmodern ("Californian") style. A spate of popular books have been published with titles like *Letters of Light: A Mystical Journey through the*

Hebrew Alphabet, *The Wisdom in the Hebrew Alphabet*, *The Hebrew Letters: Channels of Creative Consciousness*, and *Project Otiyot: Healing through Hebrew Letters*. In pluralistic religious settings like North America, individuals can draw on and combine ingredients from different religions (Sharot 2001, 262). This may be referred to as syncretism, hybridity, or bricolage: piecing together things that are readily at hand, including the Hebrew script.

Our detour complete, we can now return to the topic of Jewish somatological and thaumaturgical practices involving the Hebrew alphabet.

Somatological practices

Somatological practices include meditation, visualization, and yoga. The promises offered by such mind–body disciplines range from an enhanced sense of physical wellbeing to actualizing the divine energy within. Though such practices are not usually associated with Judaism, some adherents insist that the religion does indeed have a venerable heritage of meditation, mysticism, and bodily movement. What Jews need to do, they say, is reclaim what is already there lying dormant in the tradition.

Some devotees from the Jewish Renewal Movement – sometimes dubbed New Age Judaism – have cultivated various bodily disciplines that connect the supposed powers of the Hebrew alphabet with practices like yoga or tai chi. These projects draw upon the long tradition of Jewish alphabet mysticism but blend it with elements of Asian traditions. They are capitalizing on the shape or anatomy, so to speak, of the letters – their lines, folds, bends – which they correlate with human anatomy.

A good example of this blended style of spirituality is found in a book called *Aleph-Bet Yoga: Embodying the Hebrew Letters for Physical and Spiritual Well-Being* (Rapp 2002). According to the blurb on the back cover: "Combine the ancient practice of hatha yoga with the shapes and mystical meanings of the Hebrew letters to enhance your physical health and deepen your spiritual life." The author recounts his personal experience with yoga, suggesting that it relieves physical, mental, and emotional stresses and problems, and can help with issues like illness and loneliness. Yoga, he says, is not a religion, but a bodily discipline – a spiritual tool – that anyone can use and benefit from. As for the Hebrew letters:

> Throughout Jewish history, the Hebrew alphabet has always been considered to have many levels of meaning.... In the Jewish mystical tradition, the

> Hebrew letters are considered the divine instruments of God's energy, holy vessels carrying the light of God. For centuries, mystics have read, written, and meditated on the letters in ways that they hoped would bring them closer to the Divine. (12)

In this how-to book, each letter of the Hebrew alphabet is correlated with a specific yoga pose, given in transliterated Sanskrit, for example:

- aleph associated with *utthita trikonasana* (triangle pose)
- beta with *dandasana*, stick pose
- gimmel with *virabhadrasana*, warrior I pose

There is a chapter for each letter, with a verse from Jewish sacred literature and a photograph illustrating the corresponding yoga pose with step-by-step directions ("stand up straight ... inhale ... raise your arms ... slowly reach forward"). According to the author, combining Jewish alphabet mysticism and Hindu yoga in this way enriches one's experience of Judaism and elevates the whole person – body, soul, and mind – and prepares them for the work of *tikkun olam* or repairing the world (14).

Other somatological practices are less demanding in terms of physical movement, emphasizing concentration and visualization instead. Such is the case with a small book called *The Hebrew Alphabet: A Mystical Journey* (Hoffman 1998), where we read: "As Jewish mystics and sages have taught for millennia, the Hebrew alphabet bears a host of hidden significances. In traditional Jewish thought, each letter – its name, pictorial form, numerical equivalent, and respective position in the alphabet – is ordained by God" (18). The book then explains how different letters in the Hebrew alphabet are tailor-made for some of the challenges that people face in contemporary life:

- "To open spiritual doorways that are now hidden or closed in your life, meditate upon the letter *Daled.*" (31)
- "If lately you've been feeling rushed, harried, or impatient, meditate upon the letter *Zayin.*" (40)
- "To experience greater vitality and physical health, meditate upon the letter *Chet.*" (43)
- "To allow yourself more fully to experience spirit guides and angels, focus upon the letter *Mem.*" (58)
- "To experience a sense of peacefulness and harmony in your life, meditate upon the *Shin.*" (82)

Because Hebrew alphabet is positioned as a code or cosmic blueprint, seekers can harness the power of the letters for their own personal betterment and spiritual improvement – "to achieve greater vitality, life purpose, and meaning" (86).

Thaumaturgical practices

Thaumaturgical actions are magical or miraculous in character. They are not intended to bring about a total personal or societal transformation, but seek release from specific ills or bring blessings in the here-and-now. The conditions and constraints of life remain in place. This is the side of religion that involves small benefits, not the big rewards of heaven or nirvana (soteriology). As we saw in the previous chapter, the Pali-language *paritta* chants, being the truthful discourse of the Buddha, are thought to be able to dispel baleful influences and restore mental and physical wellbeing. The use of Pali in amulets and tattoos in Thailand has an apotropaic or protective purpose, meant to protect the person from knives, bullets, sickness, automobile accidents, and other forms of injury or misfortune. They may also be positive and bring romance, health, or luck with the lottery.

Thaumaturgical practices involving Hebrew are relatively common since the "holy tongue" is believed by many adherents to be suffused with divine energy, life, and light. In some social settings, the focus may be less on protection against illnesses and accidents, and more on matters of professional advancement, material success, and improved personal creativity (Sharot 2001, 262).

The Kabbalah Centre, a new religious movement (NRM), has done much to disseminate alphabetic mysticism to the general public, to Jewish and non-Jewish seekers alike. The group has garnered quite a lot of attention in the media, much of it negative, because of the number of celebrities, musicians, and stars of film and television who seem to be involved. Its founder, Philip Berg (also known as Rav Berg), was a popularizer and prolific author. One of his books, *The Energy of Hebrew Letters*, epitomizes his renovated Hebrew alphabet mysticism. He frames a traditional discussion about the Hebrew letters in terms of contemporary science. Science, of course, is a very prestigious discourse, so aligning one's religion with scientific progress can be a strong rhetorical move. Here is a sample of Berg's approach:

> The Hebrew letters – twenty-two distinct and astonishingly powerful energy-intelligences – are animated by a spiritual force more immense than

> the energy contained within the atom. But the *Alef Bet* [alphabet] is of no practical use if we do not understand how to connect ourselves to its inherent energy. Kabbalah is a technology that gives us access to this life-affirming, all-powerful system. (2010, 4)

The role of each letter in the cosmic drama of creation is then detailed. The book combines an elaborate alphabetic mythology with repeated claims to scientific validity.

One of the hallmark practices of the Kabbalah Centre is scanning the *Zohar*, the foundational sacred text of Kabbalah, which is written in the square Hebrew script even though the language is actually Aramaic. The *Zohar Scanning Chart 2013–14* provides this introductory encouragement:

> Kabbalah teaches that each letter is a channel to a unique form of energy – and this is true whether or not we know how the letter sounds, or how it fits into a given word. As you begin your spiritual work with The Zohar, simply scanning the pages allows you to pass over the words and letters – opens a direct connection to the divine spark hidden within each of us. The more you bring The Zohar into your life, the stronger your connection to the Light becomes. (The Kabbalah Centre n.d.)

What follows is an index that relates certain passages of the Zohar (in Aramaic and English) with predominantly thaumaturgical goals:

- Cleansing
- Conflicts in Relationships
- Drawing Your Soulmate
- Finding Real Estate
- Forgiveness
- Healing
- Money/Work Success
- Overcoming Infertility
- Prevent Earthquakes/Natural Disasters
- Protection from Evil Eye
- Removing Dark Forces
- Resolving Legal (Court) Problems

(The Kabbalah Centre n.d.)

Here we note that the index is not just about various indicators of personal success (e.g., Finding Real Estate), but includes some traditional apotropaic goals as well (e.g., Removing Dark Forces).

All of this raises the question, once again, of comprehension. The claim being advanced in this case is that one can gain benefits – spiritual, physical, financial, environmental – by accessing the potent Hebrew alphabet. One does not have to be able to understand what one sees. Comprehension is not an issue, because the letters have a power in and of themselves. Though controversial in the North American context and the media buzz about celebrities and so-called cults, the Kabbalah Centre claims about scanning are ultimately not that different from what we saw in the previous chapter in regard to Pali tattoos and amulets. The sacred language is deemed to be inherently powerful. Just little bits and pieces of it, even if unintelligible to the eye, are spiritually efficacious in helping overcome some human limitations.

Discursive practices

Judaism is a profoundly textual religion. Tanakh (Bible), Talmud, Siddur (prayerbook), Zohar – for centuries much of Jewish life has revolved around these authoritative books (de Lange 2005). It is only natural that constant exposure to a language through ritual and scriptural study would infiltrate the speech and writing of religious adherents, whether consciously or not. Discursive practices involving the sacred language of Hebrew are pervasive in Jewish communities in a way that is simply not the case with Latin in Catholicism or Pali in Theravada Buddhism.

Aureation means to gild or make golden. Not much used any more, it is an old rhetorical term that refers to the practice of introducing elements from a classical language into everyday speech or composition. Since we have been saying that sacred languages are a kind of linguistic gold, it is an apt term to take up and add to our conceptual framework. Just as a touch of gold can enhance the appearance of a person, object, or building, a nugget of sacred language can, in some situations, elevate one's speech into a higher register. Language involves the transmission of content, but also much more. Every word, accent, or grammatical structure sends a signal to others about where the speaker (or writer) is situated vis-à-vis region, gender, religion, culture, and society. Such signaling need not be intentional; in fact, it can hardly be avoided. Introducing bits and pieces of Hebrew (or Aramaic) into one's speech can bring about an almost alchemical reaction, resulting in a sense of affiliation or exclusion for the participants. Thus, Orthodox Jews may use Hebrew and possibly Yiddish terms with coreligionists, with friends and family, while shifting into English for their transactions with non-Jews (Benor 2012, 46). Language always functions as a kind of social positioning system. We can see this clearly with what is sometimes called Orthodox Jewish English, or Yeshivish.

As noted above, Judaism embodies a spectrum that runs from atheist or secular humanist to New Age to Orthodox, which itself is not monolithic but covers a range of subgroups, from Modern Orthodox to Haredi or Ultra-Orthodox. There are 500,000 to 700,000 Orthodox Jews in America, most of whom are Ashkenazi (Eastern European) by background. Their speech and writing are influenced by the traditional languages of Jewish prayer and study, Hebrew and Aramaic, as well as by the historic lingua franca of East European Jewry, Yiddish (Benor 2012, 3–11). Yiddish is a variant of Middle High German with a strong dose of Slavic vocabulary and written in a modified Hebrew script. Long known as a language of the kitchen and the street, not the synagogue and school, Yiddish has been sacralized, at least among Orthodox Jews, by its association with and close proximity to Hebrew and the sages of the shtetl (Fishman 2006). Hebrew is supremely sacred, Yiddish is relatively so.

We know that the use of Hebrew varies across the Jewish spectrum, and usually increases as one moves from liberal to traditional practice. Orthodox congregations use more Hebrew than Conservative ones, which use more than Reform ones, which use more than Reconstructionist ones. However, there is a wrinkle, insofar as many Ultra-Orthodox Jews do not recognize Modern Hebrew (which will be discussed below) as a legitimate form of speech, deeming it a desecration of the "holy tongue." For that reason some Ultra-Orthodox continue to use Yiddish as their daily language, reserving Hebrew for worship and the study of sacred texts. The combination of Ashkenazi Hebrew pronunciation and Yiddish influence results in a jargon known as Yeshivish. This tendency is different from the so-called Modern Orthodox, who favor the Sephardic-Israeli Hebrew pronunciation – for example, *Shabbat* and *tallit* – and use a variety of English that sounds, for want of a better term, more mainstream, while Orthodox Jews are more likely to use the Yiddish-inflected *Shabbos* and *tallis* (Benor 2012, 20, 117).

Quantities of Hebrew permeate the Orthodox Jewish English or Yeshivish variety. There are, for example, some 2500 loanwords, mostly pertaining to rituals, holidays, foods, values, texts, as well as forms of greeting and parting. According to Benor, "Many Orthodox Jews feel it is important to use loanwords, rather than their English equivalents"; to say, for example, *Tanakh* instead of 'Bible'. Expressions like *Kol tuv* ("all goodness") and *Baruch Hashem* ("Blessed [be] God") are common. Moreover, Hebrew words are sometimes integrated into English: they may be given an English plural form: e.g., *tallises* instead of the expected *taléysim*, or the verb form will combine English with Hebrew: 'to *kasher*' meaning to adhere to the kosher food regulations (88–96). There is also the *absence* of certain topics: curse words and sexual innuendos are missing from Yeshivish. All of these linguistic features help create a strong sense of group identity among Orthodox Jews in America.

Aureation in one form or another is common in other religious traditions as well. Buddhist sermons are laced with Pali words. A public oration in a Muslim country will typically draw upon the lexicon and grammar of Classical Arabic. Russian Orthodox adherents often slip in bits of Church Slavonic when speaking or emailing each other (discussed in more detail in Chapter 7). Indian universities and corporations may utilize a smattering of Sanskrit for formal occasions. But the case of the Hebrew revival – or better, revernacularization – in the nineteenth and twentieth centuries is altogether remarkable. The feat would be roughly comparable to turning Ecclesiastical Latin into a bona fide language used in all social situations by millions of people. The project shifted the place of Hebrew from *there* to *anywhere*, and from a discursive practice to an overtly political one. In the words of Eliezer Ben-Yehuda, the pivotal figure in this story, "The Hebrew language will go from the Synagogue to the House of Study and from the House of Study to the school and from the school it will come into the homes and … become a living language" (quoted in Fellman 1973, 49).

Political practices

In some countries, the government lends various forms of support to a sacred language and, in return, it may draw upon the symbolic cachet of the language to help bolster its political authority. But the case of Hebrew and the State of Israel is unique. It is a much-discussed topic in sociolinguistics, especially among scholars and activists concerned with language revitalization. What follows is a highly condensed précis, highlighting the role of Ben-Yehuda.

The revernacularization of Hebrew emerged at a time when many Jews were debating their place in European society. There were questions about whether Jews could (or would ever be allowed to) assimilate in the countries where they lived, or whether they could somehow attain an independent nation of their own. Zionism may be defined as Jewish nationalism, the ideology that looked (and looks) to the creation of a sovereign Jewish homeland. The nineteenth century was a time of nationalistic fervor and movements of independence within the Ottoman and Austro-Hungarian empires. The Greeks liberated themselves from the Ottomans in 1829. Czechs, Poles, Romanians, and Slovenes all strove for autonomy over against the Austro-Hungarian Empire. Ben-Yehuda made the case for Jewish nationalism, arguing that the solution to their struggles lay in their historic homeland of Palestine and their ancient language of Hebrew. Language was a crucial ingredient in European nationalist movements. Most of the newly emerging countries in Europe had a spoken vernacular; the challenge was to create a formal written style. But the converse was true of Hebrew: there was already a "high-status sacred and literary variety," so the problem was developing an informal spoken version (Spolsky 2014, 255). A diglossic (wine/water) division of labor prevailed across the Jewish world, with Hebrew everywhere serving as the H (high) variety, the language of liturgy, learning, and literature, and Yiddish, Ladino, and a host of other vernaculars functioning as the L (low) form of colloquial communication. Yet, remarkably, Ben-Yehuda and others were able to use the ingot of Hebrew as a sacred language to hammer out a language that could be used to talk about politics, agriculture, sex, sports, and just about anything else under the hot Israeli sun. They transformed an H language into an L one.

It is sometimes said that Hebrew was dead and Ben-Yehuda brought it back to life. Indeed, when he started his linguistic project, Hebrew was no one's habitual daily language. It had stopped being spoken as such around 200–300 CE. For the next 1700–1800 years, Hebrew was nobody's mother tongue (Spolsky 2014, 63). But Hebrew was not dead in the sense of museum languages like Etruscan or Sumerian. The language was still used for liturgy and learning, including serious forms of legal, scientific, and philosophical discourse (Berdichevsky 2014, 76–77). In the eighteenth and nineteenth centuries, authors had begun to experiment with adapting Hebrew for more mid-level discourses, such as newspapers and novels. Moreover, Jews in the diaspora occasionally employed a simplified version of the sacred language as a make-do-with-what-you-have lingua franca. In Ben-Yehuda's day, Jerusalem was carved up into three different communities, which spoke Yiddish, Ladino, and Arabic. When people from these different speech communities had to interact, they had recourse to a kind of "Market Hebrew." Ben-Yehuda tried to draw on this variety, which included certain forms of address, questions, and polite phrases. In sum, Ben-Yehuda's project was not starting from scratch; it was more a matter of expanding the domains in which Hebrew was used (Stavans 2008).

Ben-Yehuda realized that speaking the language at home was critical to the success of the project, but doing so was a challenge. Though prayers and blessings were indeed spoken *here*, Hebrew was not used for low-level domestic duties. An early report about Ben Yehuda and his wife gives us a glimpse of the awkwardness involved in modifying Hebrew for such purposes:

> when Ben Yehuda wanted Devora to pour him a cup of coffee with sugar, he was at a loss to communicate words such as 'cup', 'saucer', 'pour', 'spoon', and so on, and would say to his wife, in effect: 'Take such and such, and do like so, and bring me this and this, and I will drink.' (Quoted in Fellman 1973, 38)

In addition to raising Hebrew-language families, Ben-Yehuda's linguistic project involved the creation of Hebrew-speaking societies, the development of Hebrew-only schools, the publication of Hebrew-language newspapers, and the compilation of Hebrew dictionaries.

The creation of neologisms (new words) was a critical component in all of this. As a sacred language, Hebrew had a lopsided vocabulary. According to Meir Madan,

> There was a wealth of words for all matters pertaining to the religion, to emotion and to abstract thought, but none for some of the most elementary accessories of modern living: newspaper, dictionary, street, pavement, railway, train, airplane, screw-driver, corkscrew, and the like.... Needless to say, terms for the machines, appliances and forms of organization of the new age were completely wanting. (Quoted in Fellman 1973, 62–63)

To get around this, the "early adopters" of spoken Hebrew had different strategies. Sometimes they would take a word from Yiddish, German, or Russian, such as *telegraf* or *univerzität.* Other times, they would use a Hebrew word or phrase that approximated the meaning: a *photograph* was "a picture of the image of a pattern"; a *sled* was "a winter wagon which has no wheels." Occasionally, sacred literature could be mined: a line from the prayerbook, "it will go up and come down," was adapted to mean *elevator* (Fellman 1973, 63–64).

Ben-Yehuda created a multitude of new Hebrew terms, which may be categorized by topic, for example:

- clothing: glove, lapel, blouse
- foods: apricot, tomato, beer
- everyday items: brush, bus, chimney, movies, pencil, postcard, sidewalk, shower, soap, clock
- newspapers: editor, print, telegram
- science: barometer, microbe, laboratory, radium
- government: bureaucratic, candidate, commission, communism, declaration, democracy, parliament, organization (67–69)

Comprised of poets, authors, and researchers, the Academy of Hebrew Language still mints roughly 2000 new words a year. Recent neologisms include *biyush* for "shaming" and *netunei atek* for "big data" (*New York Times*, July 29, 2016).

"The revitalization of Hebrew," notes Bernard Spolsky, "took place in the farming settlements set up by Yiddish-speaking Zionist immigrants from eastern Europe" (2014, 255). Ben-Yehuda himself moved to Jerusalem and chose to live among Orthodox families, hoping to convert them to the cause. Instead, they harassed, excommunicated, and even jailed him. The rift continues within Judaism to this day. Ultra-Orthodox Jews

> insist that a vernacular, secular, profane and public Ivrit [i.e., Modern Hebrew] amounts to a sacrilegious and blasphemous transgression and can readily justify this view by pointing out how the modern language is used in advertisements for pornography, the football lottery, detective novels, or sensationalist and bizarre tattoos. On numerous occasions, demonstrations have defaced both the house in which Eliezer Ben-Yehuda lived and monuments to his memory. (Berdichevsky 2014, 83)

Thus, what is called a miracle in some quarters is denigrated as a sacrilege in others – sacredness is in the eye of the believer. From the point of view of comparative religion and sociolinguistics, the transformation of Hebrew in the nineteenth and twentieth centuries is one of the most significant projects involving a sacred language in world history.

Artistic practices

Before delving into this final topic, it is useful to make a preliminary distinction between two kinds of art: liturgical and religious. The creation of liturgical arts and appurtenances (icons, statues, plaques, vestments, tapestries, service books, chalices) may involve the use of a sacred language (see Figures 3.2 and 3.3). Religious art is that which invokes or displays religious themes or images, but is not integrated into religious practice per se. Artists have long been drawn to the aesthetic and stylistic properties of different sacred languages, though they may care more about the graphic and the sonic dimensions – or simply the very idea of the language – than the propositional content. For example, introducing Church Slavonic elements into a piece of literature can "immediately cause the spiritual temperature" of the work to rise in the readers' perception (Gasparov 2004, 139). Even in the postmodern era, Russian poets are drawn to Church Slavonicisms because those words have an elevated, numinous feel to them:

> Whether they are used as direct quotations from religious texts or separately, Church Slavonicisms serve as an instant indication of a different style or a particular epoch (Biblical times, or the Russian past) and point at a contrasting set of values that is either endangered or profaned in the contemporary world. (Khotimsky 2008, 95)

Composers in the Western classical tradition, from Bach to Stravinsky, have long set Latin prayers and rituals to music. More recently this has been done to great effect by Sir Karl Jenkins, one of the most-performed classical music composers in the world. Born in Wales to a family of Presbyterians, Jenkins's career has traversed the worlds of rock and jazz and classical music and advertising jingles. Though he himself is not Catholic, Jenkins starts a number of his most beloved compositions with classic Latin texts, including his *Gloria* and *Requiem*. One of these is *The Armed Man: A Mass for Peace*, composed in 2000. Based largely on the text of the traditional Latin service, spliced with thematically linked prayers and poems from different religious traditions, the piece has proven to be enormously popular. It has been performed over 1800 times around the world; 123,000 copies of the vocal score have been sold, and the CD has been on the bestseller chart for over 700 weeks running. A poll conducted in 2006 ranked it among the top five British pieces, ahead of Handel's *Messiah* and Holst's *The Planets*.

A rather different, but intriguing, use of Latin is found in Jenkins's *Adiemus*. This project, which blends aspects of classical and world music genres, actually began as a commercial for Delta Airlines. The original advertisement jingle was so popular that Jenkins expanded it into a full-fledged album (which eventually became a series of albums), which have sold millions of copies to date. Jenkins drew upon Latin in a number of ways. It is from there that the title *Adiemus* emerged. This looks very much like a bona fide Latin word, but it was actually accidental. Jenkins and his record producers liked the sound of it. Jenkins then added some Latin titles to the parts of the piece. As he explains,

> For some strange reason I gave some of the movements Latin titles, probably to lend an air of gravitas to the proceedings. Also, once we were underway with the first realization (which was the commercial spot), there was always an aura of the spiritual about *Adiemus*, and the Latin language, more so than any other, was apposite and helped promote the feeling and ambience of this quality. (2015, 106)

We see here quite clearly the way that a sacred language like Latin functions as a special symbolic resource that can be used by artists (who may not be believers) in novel ways. The look and feel of the ancient Roman tongue has a degree of cultural clout – "an air of gravitas" – that helps sell records and fill seats in a concert hall. (We will say more about this type of artistic spirituality in Chapter 8.)

Many calligraphers, painters, graphic designers, sculptors, and photographers have been inspired by the visual features of the Hebrew alphabet. Here we will use the example of Marc Chagall (1887–1985) since, among other things, he contributed to both liturgical and religious types of art.

Chagall led an eventful and peripatetic life. Raised in an impoverished Jewish milieu in the city of Vitebsk, then part of the Russian Empire, his life traversed several world capitals, including St. Petersburg, Moscow, Berlin, Paris, and New York. He interacted with major artistic trends and movements such as Cubism, Expressionism, and Surrealism. He crossed paths with major European writers, artists, and composers, including Apollinaire, Stravinsky, and Picasso. Chagall worked briefly as a minister of culture after the Russian Revolution, yet also painted high-profile murals for major cultural establishments like the Metropolitan Opera House. In sum, Chagall was "a witness to the twentieth century" (Harshav 2006, 8). The bits and pieces of languages that he used in his art reflect his life trajectory through these remarkable times and places.

Chagall's mother tongue was Yiddish, which was spoken *here* at home and *anywhere* on the street, but not necessarily *there* in the synagogue, the place of liturgy and learning. According to one of his biographers,

> Yiddish was Chagall's principal language until adolescence, the language of the family home, and its use enshrined a feeling of security and belonging, of participating in an autonomous system of values, religious traditions, and laws, that a Jew in the nineteenth century could find nowhere else. (Wullschlager 2008, 11)

Chagall would continue to speak and write Yiddish throughout his life. Of course, as a Jew, it was only natural that he learned morsels of Hebrew, first with an old teacher in *cheder* (literally "room," an all-male classroom in the teacher's home), where he studied passages from the Bible and prayerbook, and then later with a more erudite rabbi who helped prepare Chagall for his Bar Mitzvah. However, throughout his life Chagall never had a good grasp of Hebrew, with the result that he read the Bible in Yiddish translation.

In 1900 Chagall started attending a Russian imperial lyceum, where he soon found himself in unfamiliar circumstances, surrounded by boys from a higher social class and with different ethnic backgrounds. This alone was discombobulating enough, but the schooling was in a language (Russian) and script (Cyrillic) that he did not actually know. Though he felt in over his head at first, learning Russian "gave him an entrée into a living language of culture that connected him to mainstream European thought, literature, history, and to the society of Vitebsk's Russian-speaking Jewish intelligentsia" (Wullschlager 2008, 39).

Eventually, seeking personal and artistic freedom, Chagall left for France, where he soaked up many of the traditions and new trends in art without committing to any particular artistic movement or manifesto. He learned French and this broadened his horizons even further, making it possible for him to interact with leading artists and writers of the day in the famed City of Light. Once in Paris he switched from Mohska (Yiddish) or Moisei (Russian) to Marc and settled on the spelling of Chagall (as opposed to Шагал or Shagal) for his last name, in part because of its elegant Francophone appearance (Wullschlager 2008, 148). Chased by World War II to America, Chagall enjoyed the shiny progressive dynamism of New York City, but by that point he had no interest in learning English. He continued to use Yiddish, Russian, and French, depending on the context.

Though he gave up the ritual practices of Judaism after his Bar Mitzvah, Chagall never questioned his identity as a Jew. His paintings are replete with ingredients hearkening back to his religious roots: images of rabbis, Torah scrolls, and menorahs, as well as snippets of Hebrew lettering (the content itself being either Hebrew or Yiddish, which is written in a Hebraic script), reflecting the profoundly textual nature of Jewish culture. French or Russian rarely figure in his oeuvre. Although Chagall had only learned fragments of the "holy tongue" as a child, he drew upon Hebrew as a semiotic resource in a number of his paintings. *Jew in Bright Red* (1914–1915), for example, includes an image of a traditional East European Jewish man set against a golden semicircle (a halo? a setting sun?) that contains Hebrew writing running in vertical strips. The verses are taken from Genesis and refer to two key moments of people on the move. On the left are lines describing how the patriarchs Isaac and Jacob left the promised land to return to their homeland, Padan-Aram, in order to find wives; Chagall himself had returned from Paris to wed his old-country sweetheart. On the right is a famous verse in which God commands Abraham to go out of the land. The theme of wandering (often in the form of forced banishment) en route to the Promised Land is a much-repeated theme in Jewish art, literature, and song. It is noteworthy that Chagall has added his own name, in Hebrew letters, to this background text, thus finding a place in the storyline of Jewish salvation history (Rajner 2008).

Though not a major part of his fantastical vision, Hebrew plays a small but significant role in Chagall's artistic projects. Are all of Chagall's paintings, windows, and mosaics *Jewish* art because he was raised in a traditional Jewish milieu and always considered himself a Jew? Or do only those works that contain explicit Jewish themes and symbols (menorahs, rabbis, Hebrew letters, etc.) qualify? Or does the label "Jewish" only apply to that artwork that is found in recognizably Jewish places, like his windows for the Abbell Synagogue in the Hadassah Medical Center in Jerusalem? It is not necessary to adjudicate that here. All we need to say is that artists, like Chagall, look to the sacred language of Hebrew for inspiration. It is precious material used by Jews of all kinds to signify history, identity, and spirituality.

***

Religious adherents draw upon sacred languages (and their associated scripts) for a wide range of projects and practices. An excellent example of this phenomenon is found in Hebrew, perhaps the most versatile sacred language, and Judaism, a tradition which – especially in North America – exhibits an astonishing variety of expressions and formations, from intense Ultra-Orthodox textual studies to lighthearted programs like "Jewdo" martial arts. Hebrew is used for liturgical purposes, for prayer and worship. Of course, there is considerable variety across the spectrum of Jewish denominations. Still, the cultic use of a sacred language is what we would expect. More surprising is the way that Hebrew has been used for somatological practices, such as aleph-bet yoga, and thaumaturgical ones, as in the scanning technique touted by the Kabbalah Centre.

Hebrew also figures in various discursive practices. It is used by Jewish devotees for aureation or linguistic gilding, a way of elevating one's speech by incorporating some of the precious linguistic resource (and it has the side effect of signaling a religious/cultural/social affiliation to one's conversation partners). Again, this is to be expected; we can observe something roughly comparable in a number of other traditions. Altogether remarkable, however, is the way that, starting in the nineteenth century, some Jews were able to revernacularize Hebrew, transforming a cultic and canonical language into a modern-day spoken tongue for the State of Israel. From worship to yoga, nationalism to mysticism – Hebrew has done it all.

References

Avni, Sharon. 2011. "Toward an Understanding of Hebrew Language Education: Ideologies, Emotions, and Identity." *International Journal of the Sociology of Language* 208: 53–70. DOI: 10.1515/ijsl.2011.012

Benor, Sarah Bunin. 2012. *Becoming Frum: How Newcomers Learn the Language and Culture of Orthodox Judaism.* New Brunswick, NJ, and London: Rutgers University Press.

Berdichevsky, Norman. 2014. *Modern Hebrew: The Past and Future of a Revitalized Language.* Jefferson, NC: McFarland.

Berg, Rav. 2010. *The Energy of Hebrew Letters.* Los Angeles: The Kabbalah Centre.

CCAR [Central Conference of American Rabbis] Press. 2015. Visual T'filah. Accessed July 29, 2016. https://www.ccarpress.org/shopping_product_list.asp?catID=3756

Dan, Joseph. 2006. *Kabbalah: A Very Short Introduction.* Oxford and New York: Oxford University Press.

De Lange, Nicholas. 2005. "The Authority of Texts." In *Modern Judaism: An Oxford Guide*, edited by Nicholas de Lange and Miri Freud-Kandel, 243–253. Oxford and New York: Oxford University Press.

Dévényi, Kinga. 1996. "Mysticism in Arabic Writing." In *Tradition and Modernity in Arabic Language and Literature*, edited by J. R. Smart, 273–292. Richmond, Surrey, UK: Curzon.

Dmitrieva, L. O. 2015. *Bozhestvennoe znachenie tserkovnoslavianskikh bukv*. East Longmeadow, MA: Hope and Life Press.

Fellman, Jack. 1973. *The Revival of the Classical Tongue: Eliezer Ben Yehuda and the Modern Hebrew Language*. Paris and The Hague: Mouton.

Fishman, Joshua. 2006. "The Holiness of Yiddish: Who Says Yiddish is Holy and Why?" In *Language Loyalty, Language Planning, and Language Revitalization: Recent Writings and Reflections from Joshua A. Fishman*, edited by Nancy H. Hornberger and Martin Pütz, 233–250. Clevedon and Buffalo: Multilingual Matters.

Frishman, Elyse D., ed. 2007. *Mishkan T'filah: A Reform Siddur: Weekdays, Shabbat, Festivals, and Other Occasions of Public Worship*. New York: Central Conference of American Rabbis.

Gasparov, Boris. 2004. "Identity in Language?" In *National Identity in Russian Culture: An Introduction*, edited by Simon Franklin and Emma Widdis, 132–148. Cambridge and New York: Cambridge University Press.

Harshav, Benjamin. 2006. *Marc Chagall and the Lost Jewish World: The Nature of Chagall's Art and Iconography*. New York: Rizzoli.

Hoffman, Edward. 1998. *The Hebrew Alphabet: A Mystical Journey*. San Francisco: Chronicle Books.

Jenkins, Karl, with Sam Jackson. 2015. *Still with the Music: My Autobiography*. London: Elliott and Thompson.

The Kabbalah Centre. n.d. *Zohar Scanning Chart 2013–14*. Accessed October 15, 2015. http://cdn1.kabbalah.com/files/scanchart13-14.pdf

Kaplan, Dana Evan. 2009. *Contemporary American Judaism: Transformation and Renewal*. New York: Columbia University Press.

Kaplan, Dana Evan. 2013. *The New Reform Judaism: Challenges and Reflections*. Lincoln: University of Nebraska Press; Philadelphia: The Jewish Publication Society.

Khotimsky, Maria. 2008. "Rethinking the High Style: The Uses of Church Slavonicisms in the Works of Contemporary Russian Poets." *Ulbandus Review* 11: 74–98. http://www.jstor.org/stable/25748183

Langer, Ruth. 2005. "Prayer and Worship." In *Modern Judaism: An Oxford Guide*, edited by Nicholas de Lange and Miri Freud-Kandel, 231–242. Oxford and New York: Oxford University Press.

National Library of Israel. 2012. Accessed July 29, 2016. http://web.nli.org.il/sites/NLI/English/library/aboutus/future/architects_comp/Pages/default.aspx

Pew Research Center. 2013. *A Portrait of Jewish Americans: Findings from a Pew Research Center Survey of U.S. Jews*. Accessed July 29, 2016. http://www.pewforum.org/2013/10/01/jewish-american-beliefs-attitudes-culture-survey/

Rabin, Chaim. 1976. "Liturgy and Language in Judaism." In *Language in Religious Practice*, edited by William J. Samarin, 131–155. Rowley, MA: Newbury House.

Rajner, Mirjam. 2008. "Chagall's Jew in Bright Red." *Ars Judaica* 4: 61–80. http://www.academia.edu/854099/_Chagalls_Jew_in_Bright_Red_

Rapp, Steven A. 2002. *Aleph-Bet Yoga: Embodying the Hebrew Letters for Physical and Spiritual Well-Being*. Woodstock, VT: Jewish Lights Publishing.

Riesebrodt, Martin. 2010. *The Promise of Salvation: A Theory of Religion*. Translated by Steven Rendall. Chicago and London: University of Chicago Press.

Ronen, Ori. 2012. "National Library of Israel – Jerusalem." Accessed July 29, 2016. http://orironen.blogspot.com/2012/09/national-library-of-israel-jerusalem.html

Sharot, Stephen. 2001. *A Comparative Sociology of World Religions: Virtuosos, Priests, and Popular Religion*. New York and London: New York University Press.

Sharot, Stephen. 2011. *Comparative Perspectives on Judaisms and Jewish Identities*. Detroit: Wayne State University Press.

Smith, Jonathan Z. 1982. *Imagining Religion: From Babylon to Jonestown*. Chicago and London: University of Chicago Press.

Spolsky, Bernard. 2014. *The Languages of the Jews: A Sociolinguistic History*. Cambridge: Cambridge University Press.

Stavans, Ilan. 2008. *Resurrecting Hebrew*. New York: Nextbook; Schocken.

Wullschlager, Jackie. 2008. *Chagall: A Biography*. New York: Knopf.

Further Reading

Avni, Sharon. 2012. "Hebrew as Heritage: The Work of Language in Religious and Community Continuity." *Linguistics and Education* 23: 323–333. An insightful study of the multiple meanings and applications of Hebrew.

Benor, Sarah Bunin. 2012. *Becoming Frum: How Newcomers Learn the Language and Culture of Orthodox Judaism*. New Brunswick, NJ, and London: Rutgers University Press. A detailed but accessible sociolinguistic investigation.

Drucker, Johanna. 1995. *The Alphabetic Labyrinth: The Letters in History and Imagination*. London: Thames and Hudson. An erudite and richly illustrated historical survey of various forms of alphabet mysticism.

Rabin, Chaim. 1976. "Liturgy and Language in Judaism." In *Language in Religious Practice*, edited by William J. Samarin, 131–155. Rowley, MA: Newbury House. An older but still useful synopsis.

Yardeni, Ada. 2010 (1991). *The Book of Hebrew Script: History, Palaeography, Script Styles, Calligraphy and Design*. Jerusalem: Carta. A richly illustrated volume covering a gamut of topics relating to the Hebrew alphabet.

Chapter 6

Learning a Sacred Language

A short distance from the Niagara River, and thousands of miles from the Nile, the sound of Coptic, the ancient Egyptian language whose millennium-long history stretches back to the time of the pyramids, can be heard amidst the rhythmic clanging of cymbals and the pungent smell of incense. The liturgy unfolds at St. Mary and St. Moses Coptic Orthodox Church, a modest brick building which sits snugly amidst older homes in North Tonawanda (the name means "Swift Running Water" in the indigenous Seneca language), a working-class city in western New York a few miles from Niagara Falls that was once the hub of a thriving lumber industry and home to factories producing carousels and barrel organs.

The elaborate liturgy represents a symbolic reenactment and celebration of Jesus' Last Supper set against the immense backdrop of salvation history, with cascades of prayers, readings, petitions, and hymns to God, Christ, Mary, angels, and saints. Almost entirely sung or chanted by priests, deacons, cantors, and congregants, the ritual is performed here in three different languages written in three distinct scripts: Coptic, Arabic, and English.

Traditional prayerbooks may be found in the pews for congregants to follow the service, but in this case there are also four electronic screens suspended from the ceiling of the nave. The church uses a computer application called Coptic Reader. (See Figure 6.1.) Developed by the Coptic Orthodox Diocese of the Southern United States,

> Coptic Reader has been specifically designed to harness the power of modern mobile computing technologies to deliver a seamless user experience....

Sacred Languages of the World: An Introduction, First Edition. Brian P. Bennett.

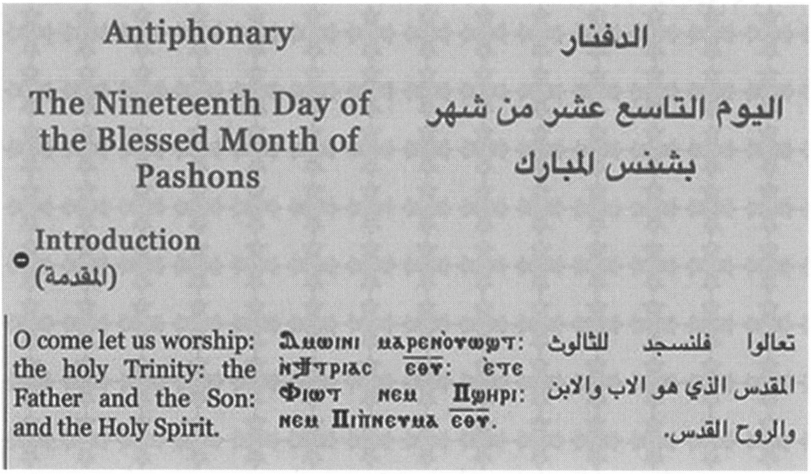

Figure 6.1 Coptic Reader application. Reproduced with kind permission of the Coptic Orthodox Diocese of the Southern United States.

> Thousands of pages from dozens of books have been compressed and included in Coptic Reader allowing effortless access to all the prayers of the Church.... Coptic Reader will dynamically generate the prayers exactly as they should be prayed on that day including all the appropriate hymns and responses of the day. (Coptic Orthodox Diocese of the Southern United States n.d.)

The ancient language of the pharaohs is no longer spoken, but its scion is still in use, many centuries and several major historical transformations later, in the liturgical practice of the Coptic Orthodox Church. New technologies help the parish balance the desire for communion – with the past, with the divine – and communication. The liturgy becomes an occasion not only for prayer and supplication, but a kind of ritual education.

The Coptic Orthodox Church belongs to the Oriental Orthodox branch of Christianity, which also includes the Armenian, Syrian, and Ethiopian churches. It has approximately twelve million members, with some eleven million residing in Egypt, making Copts the largest Christian minority in the Middle East. The current-day Coptic liturgy, in its trilingual and triscriptal form, reflects three large-scale historical processes: Christianization, Islamization, and globalization.

Along with Ge'ez, Arabic, and Hebrew, Coptic is one of the four great sacred languages to emerge from the Afro-Asiatic language family. There are two main dialects, Sahidic and Bohairic, the latter being used in the Coptic liturgy. Much of the vocabulary is actually Greek, reflecting the Hellenization and subsequent Christianization of Egypt. In fact, the alphabet consists largely of Greek letters, with seven characters coming from Demotic, a simplified writing system that ultimately derives from ancient hieroglyphics. Coptic ceased being spoken in the medieval period, though precisely when is subject to debate. There are reports of oases of speakers as late as the nineteenth century, though those are in all likelihood legends (Haarmann 2002, 108–109).

The use of Arabic in Coptic worship reflects the later transformation of Egypt under Islam starting in the seventh century. Arabic eventually overwhelmed Coptic as the dominant vernacular of the region, the autochthonous Egyptian language slowly reduced to being a strictly ecclesiastical phenomenon spoken within church walls. Arabic even entered the liturgy and became sacralized to a certain degree:

> Since the 12th century the liturgy celebrating Holy Communion has been read in both Coptic and Arabic ... and strong emotions are attached to these well-known texts. To many, the beauty of the liturgy is linked to the use of the old Coptic and Arabic hymns and prayers. Many in the older generation are not keen to give up what they see as hallowed tradition. To them, church heritage seems closely or even inseparably linked to both Coptic and Arabic ... the link to Coptic is a link to the distant past and to the golden age of the church. Arabic does not carry these associations, but it is also part of the Egyptian heritage, and, as such, the Arabic liturgy is treasured. (Preston 1998, 97)

It should be noted that most members of the Coptic Orthodox Church, both in Egypt and abroad, speak a variety of Arabic as their mother tongue.

The appearance of English in the liturgy represents a third major historical development, during which the Coptic Orthodox Church has broadened its position from being primarily an Egyptian entity to that of a transnational organization very much involved in the global ecumenical movement. Starting in the 1950s, facing severe social, economic, and political pressures, many Copts left Egypt for England, Canada, the United States, Australia, and other locales. There are currently about 350,000 Copts in the United States, with some 151 parishes, two monasteries, three seminaries, and many educational and benevolent organizations (Saad 2010, 209). Coptic music, architecture, liturgy, and language are now found outside the Egyptian homeland. As the Coptic Church has become globalized, English has assumed greater significance. The church hierarchy seems to have embraced this turn of events and regularly uses English in its liturgies and publications.

As we know, sacred languages are fixed, mythologized, textual languages that serve as precious symbolic resources for a range of religious purposes. In terms of mythologization, Coptic is not considered a primary language of revelation the way that Hebrew, Arabic, or even Church Slavonic is. The Coptic Church does not claim that God delivered scriptures in this ancient Egyptian tongue. Rather, it is a secondary language of revelation, related to the earthly drama of redemption ("holiness one step removed," in Fishman's terms). In particular, it is associated with the golden age of Egyptian Christianity, the idiom of the storied monks and martyrs who are hailed as the founders of the Coptic Orthodox Church. Sometimes, however, the role of Coptic in salvation history is pushed even further back in time. According to one folk tradition, Jesus learned Coptic during his childhood sojourn in Egypt, referenced in the second chapter of the Gospel of Matthew (Preston 1998, 93). Indeed, in some discourses Coptic is pushed all the way to the glorious era of the pharaohs:

> The Coptic language is the bridge that links the Copts with their ancient Egyptian roots. It provides them with a continuous written record of their civilization that spans over 6000 years, the longest in existence. A civilization that has truly been considered, then and now, a marvel of human achievement. Their accomplishments encompassed most areas of human endeavors such as art, architecture, medicine, and of course their remarkable embalming techniques. (Takla 1996)

Of course, it is a point of pride to be able to trace one's heritage back to such a renowned civilization. But this rhetorical move is not unproblematic, since ancient Egypt was a pagan, not a Christian, society. Sacred language ideologies change over time, and the theme of Pharaonism, which the above quotation represents, does not seem to be as common as it once was in Coptic communities.

Religions are collective, organized systems of practices. Discursive practices involve interpersonal communication, while interventionist ones involve communication with postulated superhuman beings. As far as discursive practices go – the kind of thing that could be done at a desk or in an office – new texts are not produced in Coptic to the same degree as Latin or even Pali. And while there have been sporadic attempts on the part of some individuals to revive Coptic as a spoken language – inspired by the Hebrew precedent, enthusiasts of sacred languages often dream of doing this – to date these have not borne fruit. Coptic is above all used for interventionist purposes, especially liturgical as opposed to somatological or thaumaturgical ones. The liturgy, which symbolically reenacts and reaffirms the themes of Incarnation, Crucifixion, and Resurrection, is central to Coptic religious life. Here is how one adherent describes it:

> The church is the house of God, the place where the angels and saints are offering praise to God, the place where heaven and earth meet. The faithful now stand in heaven giving praise to God, accompanying the heavenly realm in praise. The sanctuary is the Holy of Holies, the dwelling place of God Almighty, where the angels, martyrs, and saints are present sharing in the heavenly praise with the faithful. (Farag 2014, 135)

This is the true niche of Coptic, a specially consecrated building *there*, where the language is chanted, sung, and declaimed amidst stylized gestures and sacramental paraphernalia. Coptic is not widely known or studied by average churchgoers, though many certainly know or at least recognize the most prevalent hymns. It is really the intellectual property of – male – clerics. Priests and deacons (boys as young as five may be deacons) learn how to pray in Coptic and must memorize important texts (Preston 1998, 92).

Religions involve not only beliefs and practices but institutions as well. Now, some people are very much against "organized religion." But that is a personal judgment as opposed to a historical or sociological one, for no religion can survive without institutional structures. It is not something that just exists, floating along in the ether, but is embodied in and perpetuated by organizations with street addresses, including places of worship, schools, publishers, retail outlets, cemeteries, benevolent societies, and of course clergies. The so-called world religions are associated with relatively autonomous clerical groups – the Buddhist *sangha*, the Muslim *ulama* – that guide their religious communities in the areas of doctrine and behavior. They are the religious intellectuals, the ones who have the time and opportunity to learn the sacred language and who may even use it as a scholastic lingua franca among themselves.

Institutions are particularly important when it comes to sacred languages. Water is found in nature, in springs and creeks and rainfall. But wine is not a naturally occurring substance. It is the work of human hands, and requires specific tools and procedures to produce. Similarly, Coptic, Pali, Latin, and Classical Arabic are not mother tongues transmitted from one generation to the next by the family, but may be called "father tongues" passed on by artificial means through institutions, often clerical in nature, such as monasteries, seminaries, yeshivas, and Sunday schools. There are many languages that can exist, water-like, without formal academic structures, being passed along organically *en famille*: sacred languages are not among them. This chapter focuses on educational institutions and programs. The basic question we consider is this: How do believers go about learning an ancient language that has been conserved for liturgical, somatological, and other purposes, but is not used in everyday conversation?

When we think of sacred language education, we need to cast a wide net. There are all kinds of different ways that Coptic, Latin, Pali, and the rest are perpetuated, including textbooks, Sunday schools, bilingual prayerbooks, university courses, catechisms, projection devices like the Coptic Reader or Hebrew-language Visual T'filah, summer camps, DVDs, weekend study groups, alphabet primers, and language Olympiads. Increasingly, electronic and multimedia options, including YouTube videos and smartphone applications, help convey the multimodal (sonic and graphic) dimensions that are so integral to sacred languages. Of course, one can also learn nuggets of a sacred language through sheer ritual repetition, which may or may not be complemented by more formal instruction.

It is impossible in the space of one chapter to cover every relevant institution and method of instruction, even in the case of one sacred language, let alone half a dozen. Our goal is to provide a rough-and-ready chart to this sprawling terrain. We will begin with some general comparative observations about the close relationship between sacred languages and religion before delving into the issue of restricted literacy and the question of who studies sacred languages and why and how they do so. Our virtual tour includes several stopovers to peer in on moments of sacred language instruction, separated from the main exposition in boxes.

The ABCs of Faith

For those religious communities that have one, learning a sacred language usually goes hand in hand with learning the rudiments of the tradition. As with all things, there is variation – sacred languages are not the same. As a general rule, though, learning a sacralized language like Hebrew, Arabic, or Pali is considered a prerequisite for advancement in the faith. Indeed, religious literature is full of earnest exhortations for members to learn the sacred language. For example, a Russian primer for children asserts:

> Church Slavonic is the greatest possession of our people, given to us by our ancestors. It is in this very same language that the liturgy is celebrated in the Russian Orthodox Church. It is necessary for an Orthodox Christian to know the Church Slavonic language in order to understand the liturgy. (Arkhipova 2012, 7)

A how-to manual called *The Language of Yoga* states:

> Knowing how to properly pronounce Sanskrit is a crucial skill for serious students and teachers of yoga.... Because Sanskrit is the language of yoga, understanding key Sanskrit terminology and its pronunciation can deepen a practitioner's knowledge of the yogic path. It can also provide a more complete understanding of the meaning and purpose of yoga *āsanas*, or postures – an understanding that is lost when these āsanas are known only by their English names. (Bachman 2005, 1)

In short, knowing the language gives one access to the religion's canonical texts and enables one to participate in its liturgical, somatological, and other activities.

The close connection between learning the ABCs of the language and growing in the faith is manifested in several ways. One example is the alphabet book, sometimes called a primer or abecedary, arguably the quintessential genre of religious pedagogy (cf. Rosowsky 2013). These books typically teach not only the letters of the alphabet but something of the ingredients thought to comprise the religion. The two subjects are intertwined. For example, a Russian Orthodox abecedary will teach the Church Slavonic alphabet, with the name and depiction of each letter providing a kind of verbal peg to hang different words on, accompanied by illustrations (which are absent in Classical Arabic exemplars, due to the aniconic nature of Islam). So, instead of "A is for apple" and "B is for ball," we have:

- *az'* is for angel, Adam, ambon
- *buki* is for *Bog* (God), *Bogoroditsa* ("god-bearer": a term for the Virgin Mary), and *bogosluzhenie* (liturgy)
- *kako* is for *kreshchenie* (baptism), *kadilo* (a liturgical implement), and *kolokol'* (bell)
- *mysliete* is for *monakh* (monk), *molitva* (prayer), and *mitropolit* (metropolitan – a key position in the church hierarchy)

The student thereby learns the Slavonic letters as well as some of the basic terms and concepts pertaining to Russian Orthodox beliefs, practices, and institutions.

Rites of passage are another area where we can see an intimate connection between sacred language and religious tradition. A well-known example is the Jewish Bar (or Bat) Mitzvah, which requires learning enough Hebrew to be able to read the designated weekly scriptural passages before the assembly. In the Theravada Buddhist tradition, when a young boy goes through an ordination ceremony to become a novice monk, he gets his hair shaved while chanting the Pali words *kesā*, *lomā*, *nakhā*, *dantā*, *taco* (head hair, body hair, nail, teeth, skin), which come from a famous meditation on the foulness of the body, in which the various disgusting constituents of the body are enumerated. According to a report from Sri Lanka:

> Prompted by the head monk, the initiates recited a Pāli verse asking permission to go forth. Following this verse – which none of the boys understood, since it was in the ancient language of Pāli and not Sinhaa – the boys were prompted to recite another Pāli verse: "Leaving behind all suffering [and] seeing with my own eyes enlightenment, please, oh reverend sir, having taken this yellow robe, ordain me." (Samuels 2013, 240)

As this suggests, inculcating youngsters in the religion often involves teaching the sacred language – or, more accurately, selected nuggets of the language.

Instruction in a sacred or consecrated language often takes place in a thoroughly religious context:

- Sacred languages are often taught by clerics (priests, monks, imams, etc.).
- Instruction in the sacred language may take place in a structure attached to the consecrated liturgical space (*there*), or even inside it, as is often the case with mosques.
- The classroom where the sacred language is taught may be adorned with religious symbols or icons.
- Lessons may begin and end with traditional prayers, invocations, or ritual gestures like the sign of the cross.
- Learning a sacred language is usually an embedded, multidimensional affair. As young Muslim children study the Arabic alphabet, they also absorb the proper way to behave in a mosque, to sit, and to hold a copy of the Qur'an. Novice monks learn Pali chants at the same time as they acquire the proper way to walk, eat, shave, or sweep the monastery grounds. The sacred language is thus drilled into the body, creating

> certain dispositions and propensities. The language learner becomes "enskilled" (cf. Blommaert 2013, 33).

In these various and sundry ways, learning the religion and the language go hand in hand. There is a corollary: If the language and the faith are interdependent, then their fortunes are intertwined. That means that if the religion is seen to be on the decline, then teaching the sacred language may be viewed as one way of rectifying the situation. The teaching of Hebrew is often viewed as a critical factor in the continuity of the Jewish people. In the past few centuries in Theravada Buddhist countries like Sri Lanka and Thailand, the study of Pali was promoted when monasticism was thought to be in decline or disarray. As we saw in Chapter 3, the decline of Latin studies has led – at least in the eyes of traditionalist Catholics – to empty pews. And as we will see in the next chapter, the revival of Russian Orthodoxy after the collapse of Communism has hinged in part on the revitalization of the Church Slavonic language tradition.

Similarly, the study of Coptic was revived within the Coptic Orthodox Church during a crucial moment in its history. When in the nineteenth century Protestant missionaries from Britain visited different churches in Egypt, they were shocked by what they considered to be the abysmal educational level of Coptic Christians. Blind tutors led their students in rote recital of Coptic verses, much like their Muslim counterparts were doing with the Arabic Qur'an.

> For the CMS [Church Missionary Society] missionaries, the "blind," "ritualistic" recitation that characterized Coptic worship in the nineteenth century was the epitome of "superstition." For them, worship was about grasping a particular message, and how could Christians grasp the message of God if they uttered the Scriptures in a language, Coptic, they could not understand? (Sedra 2011, 107)

The reform-minded Patriarch Cyril IV became head of the Coptic Orthodox Church in 1854. Influenced by British evangelicals, Cyril condemned "blind" incantation of Coptic during church services. He decried the lack of understanding of liturgical Coptic and promoted a grammar-based methodology. Reform of Coptic language instruction was closely tied to the advent of the printing press. When the first one arrived in Alexandria, Cyril ordered "priests and altar boys to greet the press clothed in formal vestments, and to march in a procession with the press, all the time chanting" (Sedra 2011, 112). Coptic texts were henceforth printed, catalogued, and systematically displayed on the shelves of the Patriarchal headquarters. Ever since the nineteenth century, Coptic has been studied and cultivated within the Coptic Church, including at the Institute of Coptic Studies in Cairo.

Before we continue on this path, we should pause to confirm what we have seen thus far: namely, in some traditions, sanctified languages are believed to be tied to the religion as a whole, such that the two entities rise or fall together. We see this interconnection in alphabet primers, rites of passage, and the physical location and trappings of sacred language instruction. Not teaching the language is viewed as a recipe for disaster, while revitalizing it – instilling the ABCs of the faith – is often trumpeted as a way to boost religious participation and ensure the ongoing vitality of the community.

The traditional greeting of *Shabbat shalom* (Sabbath peace) is repeated as members of the congregation gather for Torah study on a Saturday morning in an urban Reform Temple (synagogue). The session takes place in a room lined by museum-style cases housing historical mementos and manuscripts, many bearing Hebrew lettering, conveying a palpable sense of Jewish cultural history. Participants, who range in age from college students to senior citizens, grab a copy of the Torah and gather round a long conference table. Some use iPads or other electronic readers. A few sip coffee. After a song and blessing for Torah study, the erudite and convivial rabbi launches into an exegesis of the first verses of the biblical book of Leviticus, chapter 6. He parses the text, explaining the Hebrew involved and comparing different translations, pausing at one point to make sense of a rare word, *mokdah*, meaning something like "hearth," with an unusual piece of orthography: it is scribal tradition that the starting *mem* (m) is written smaller than the other letters. The rabbi makes semantic connections between words in the Torah and other terms the group would be familiar with, and traces interpretations of the passage through a string of influential premodern rabbis, walking the group through their arguments and counter-arguments. Then, in Socratic fashion, the discussion spirals out to ponder the institutions of sacrifice and priesthood in Judaism, as well as broader questions about history, psychology, and the inherent value for the Jewish people of rabbinic argumentation.

Restricted Literacy

Sacred languages are not used for everyday communication. Although there are a few instances of popular learning methods being applied to these venerable tongues – there is a Latin edition of the computer-based Rosetta Stone program, and both Latin and Sanskrit versions of the French Assimil system – in general, the acquisition of a sacred language does not follow the pattern of a spoken vernacular. Sacred languages are secondary, bookish varieties that are usually studied in special schools, often attached to a sacred space (*there*), with a strict curriculum heavy on scripture and ritual. The focus is cultic as opposed to conversational (although there are exceptions to the rule, as we will see later in this chapter). The goal is usually quite targeted: to perform the daily prayer in Classical Arabic, to read a portion of the Hebrew-language Torah, to celebrate the Slavonic version of the Liturgy of St. John Chrysostom. Learning a language – any language – is never an all-or-nothing proposition. People pick up (and may later lose) a truncated version of the language, involving competence with certain words, accents, and styles, but not touching many other zones. No one knows it all. This general principle is *a fortiori* the case with sacred languages, where we are dealing with a highly restricted form of literacy, where the focus is on performance, not grammar, on practice, not theory.

In a way, acquiring bits and pieces of a sacred language is similar to the way that people learn a few snippets of other languages for their hobby, work, or travel. Fluency is not the objective. A manual called *Prayerbook Hebrew for Adults* (Cardin, Kaye, and Lyons 2006) aims to simply help people get over their fear of the Hebrew alphabet and make them feel more comfortable participating in Jewish worship. The Easy Sanskrit Online Course "has been designed in a manner that any individual regardless of their mother tongue or age will get acquainted with the salient aspects of Sanskrit language without being unduly burdened with details and nuances that could overwhelm a beginner" (Chinmaya Publications 2016). The purpose of a DVD on Coptic is to enable churchgoers to pronounce the words in Bohairic Coptic texts, learn some phrases used in the liturgy (e.g., pray, kneel, peace, have mercy on us), and become familiar with some rudimentary grammatical principles (Makar n.d.). Modest goals in every case.

Moreover – and this can be baffling to people outside the tradition – intellectual understanding of the material may not be emphasized, even for clerics. The "Rolls Royce" version of reading, with full comprehension and explication, is not always considered necessary or attainable for the faithful (Rosowsky

2013, 76). In some cases, the form of literacy involved is better understood as a kind of decoding: the devotee is able to decipher the script (which may be foreign to them), and correctly pronounce the words, but without necessarily understanding the meaning, let alone being able to explain the grammar involved. A decoding approach to sacred languages is actually widespread around the world and is by no means restricted to lay people. Theravada monks often memorize voluminous *paritta* chants (see Chapter 4) but not be able to explain their meaning. This runs counter to our Protestantized form of educational common sense. But we must recognize that we are dealing with a different mode of religiosity, one that finds beauty, mystery, and efficacy in canonical texts, even where straightforward intelligibility is lacking.

Nestled in a subdivision of pleasant middle-class homes, the mosque boasts basketball courts, a volleyball net, a barbecue, a swing set, and other staples of American suburbia. Parents in minivans drop off their children for Classical Arabic class. About ten boys, ages five to seven, sit around low benches converted into tables within the prayer space of the mosque. Unlike the imam, the boys are dressed in typical "American" style: t-shirts, jeans, sweat pants, and the like. After a long day at their regular school, they are fidgety, often requesting diversionary breaks to go to the toilet or get a drink of water. The students are all working at their own pace, using a variety of primers and simplified scriptural readers. Some delve into their lesson for the day, others procrastinate, a couple stare into space. The imam must be a deft multitasker, keeping up with students who are all at different levels, with some just learning the Arabic letters, others able to read sentences, and the most advanced reciting directly from the Qur'an. When the students recite simultaneously, it is a polyphonic verbal experience. The boys come from different backgrounds, but all know English, even if their parents speak another language (such as Kashmiri) at home. The imam uses colloquial English to instruct, praise, and at times admonish his charges:

"Good job"
"Read it again"
"Sit over there"
"Get to work"
"No – that's *ta*"
"Why aren't you reading?"

(*Continued*)

The lesson is interrupted by the late afternoon prayer, one of five stipulated for Muslim daily practice. The boys shuffle over and form a line behind the men who have come to the mosque after work. The sound of the Arabic *adhan* (call to prayer) resonates in the space, the walls of which are richly decorated with pious Arabic inscriptions.

His gruff demeanor softened, the imam doles out candy to the boys when the lesson is concluded.

What, Who, Why, and How

Let us now consider some of the basics of sacred language education. *What* someone learns depends on *who* they are (for example, cleric or lay person) and *why* they are learning it (for example, to perform a liturgy or say one's daily prayers). These factors are cross-tabulated with *how* the language is learned (more on that below). Sawyer provides a helpful distinction:

> The retention of such sacred languages has some far-reaching sociolinguistic and religious consequences. In many cases it means that there arises a class of priests or other experts who are the only people who can translate and interpret, and this gives them a unique status and power over the rest of the community…. Alternatively, where the people are permitted or encouraged to learn the sacred language and participate more fully in the religion, education is inevitably dominated from an early age by language-learning. Mnemonics are devised to make the learning and memorizing of language easier. (Sawyer 1999, 24)

Painting in broad-brush strokes, we can say that Hinduism, Zoroastrianism, and some branches of Buddhism and Christianity fall under the first type, which we may call the sacerdotal type, while Islam and Judaism belong to the second.

In Theravada Buddhism, the clergy subsists in a symbiotic relationship with the laity. Monks need to know Pali, while "householders" (lay people) do not. The reliance on this sacralized variety has had the effect of making monks rather like priests, that is, ritual experts (Gombrich 1988, 155). In Russian Orthodox Christianity, priests are distinct from parishioners. Church Slavonic is recommended for churchgoers, but required for priests and other ecclesiastics (readers, deacons, etc.). Russian priests will learn the sacred language, to a greater or lesser extent, within the context of a seminary curriculum, along with courses on theology, church history, homiletics, pastoral care, and so on. Russian churchgoers, on the other hand, may learn snippets of Church Slavonic through Sunday school or possibly a program of self-study. To be sure, church leaders are constantly encouraging or hectoring parishioners to crack the books and learn some of the sacred language, but this does not necessarily translate into the desired result.

There may be further distinctions within the clergy. For example, in Theravada lands, there is often a division between the majority of monks who follow the traditional route of reciting Pali verses without much knowledge of the meaning of the texts, and a minority who are involved in scholastic endeavors. In Thailand there are approximately 20,000 *mae chi* (female renunciants or "nuns"), 25,000 monks, and 70,000 novices (Crosby 2014, 233). All learn and memorize some Pali. Yet few monks (only 1 or 2 percent) actually pass the highest level of the royally sponsored Pali exams (McDaniel 2008). In the case of Russian Orthodoxy, more advanced academic students will attend one of the elite "spiritual academies" instead of a seminary.

The model in Islam is different. According to tradition, "there is no priesthood in Islam." There are certainly imams and religious scholars who know Arabic much better than average believers. Yet, that being said, since Arabic is understood as the language of revelation and the medium par excellence for communion with God, all Muslims should try to learn something of the language, even though most are not native Arabic speakers. This has profound social and religious consequences, since a whole educational network needs to be constructed, not just a handful of seminaries for the clergy, as in the sacerdotal model.

Of course, gender differences are also significant. Sacred languages have historically been the purview of male clerics and have been passed on through a kind of artificial dissemination. Obviously, there are variations across and even within religious traditions. All the officiants in the Coptic liturgy described at the start of this chapter, including the priest, deacons, choir, and altar servers, are male. In Orthodox Jewish enclaves, men are expected to be engrossed in learning (Talmud study) and *davening* (praying), while women are often discouraged from such pursuits (Benor 2012, 10–11), though, of course, there are women rabbis and cantors in other denominations of Judaism. Women are not allowed to be priests in the Russian Orthodox tradition, but they will study Church Slavonic if they plan to become a choir director, Sunday school teacher, or icon painter.

Thus, there are important distinctions between who studies sacred languages (priest or lay person, male or female) and why. As for methodology, studying sacred languages is primarily about gaining access to a fixed corpus of holy literature. The point is to read, memorize, recite, chant, or perform texts that have been consecrated and passed down within the religious tradition. Fishman provides a handy typology of three ways that sacred languages can be learned:

> In some cases, these languages are "target" (i.e. textual) languages to which ample school time is devoted over the course of many years. In other cases, they are "merely" learned by virtue of repeated use in religious services and in home rituals with no explicit school time being assigned to them. In some cases, the power of the secular state authority is added to that of religious authority, in order to require and to subsidise school attention to these languages. (Fishman 1991, 360)

We will organize our discussion around these three points.

Ritual repetition

Liturgical practices like prayer and worship are often learned "merely" by means of ritual repetition. Liturgy is sometimes said to be a school of prayer. The fact that rituals have a calendrical (daily, weekly, yearly) regularity makes them conducive to learning relevant bits (prayers, hymns, chants) of the sacred language involved. This manner of language learning has not actually been studied much by sociolinguists, so we do not really know how it works. But we do have reports from believers that, the more they attend worship services, the more they understand what is going on. This should not be surprising.

Sometimes textual aids like bilingual prayerbooks or projection screens like the Coptic Reader can help. Consider, for example, a slim volume of the Divine Liturgy of St. John Chrysostom, with parallel Church Slavonic and Russian texts. This little book was produced by Metropolitan Hilarion, a well-known church figure who is concerned about relating the faith to Russians in the post-communist world. He writes in the foreword to this volume:

> One of the difficulties, which a person runs into upon first entering into an Orthodox temple is the lack of intelligibility of the liturgy. For a person in contemporary culture it is necessary to spend time and energy in order to understand the theological depths of the poetic images contained in the liturgical

> texts of the Orthodox Church. Making it even more difficult is the fact that in the Russian Church the divine service is celebrated in the Church Slavonic language, which has been reverentially preserved almost without change for many centuries. All officiants without exception are required to know Church Slavonic to a certain degree – although in the scope of a seminary course. Many lay people also possess a zeal for the study of the Church Slavonic language, though for some it turns out to be beyond them. (Alfeyev 2013)

Hilarion explains that this little tome is for those who wish to better understand the Orthodox liturgy. It is intentionally designed in a compact format so that it may be consulted during a church service, though of course it is not for official use.

Things like bilingual prayerbooks to projection screens attempt to preserve the overall shape of the ritual, but to insert into it an element of pedagogy, teaching how the words are pronounced or what they say and mean. The ritual context stays the same – candles are lit, hymns sung, incense fills the air – but a kind of real-time instruction occurs simultaneously. Such apparatuses represent a stepping-stone between ritual repetition and more deliberate textual study.

Like all activities at the seminary, the class on Church Slavonic begins with a prayer chanted in unison by faculty and students, facing an icon of a sacred personage. The class consists of one student who has already been a priest for a number of years, and two priests-in-training. All speak different mother tongues – Russian, English, and Georgian. The gerund (past tense: e.g., "having arrived") is the subject of the day. After a discussion of the general forms delineated in the textbook, students try their hand at identifying examples in practice sentences, then in a selection from scripture. They are used to reading, hearing, and singing Church Slavonic in the sacred space, but not necessarily analyzing it from a grammatical perspective. The professor moves easily back and forth between English and Russian (which the Georgian also speaks) as she provides explanations, makes corrections, and generally encourages the students.

With the grammar lesson behind them, the class turns to the Great Canon of St. Andrew of Crete, a classic text recited during the Lenten season leading up to Easter. The focus now is on performance, not

(*Continued*)

grammar. The pressing need is for these clerics to be able to read this notoriously difficult text in its proper liturgical context. The instructor provides guidance with regard to pronunciation as the students try to make their way through the Great Canon. The bell rings; time is up. The class rises, faces the icon, and concludes with another chant-like prayer – in Church Slavonic, of course.

Targeted study

Sometimes sacred languages are the object of intentional study in the classroom, not just a result of attending church or synagogue on a regular basis. There is a wide range of educational settings: Bar Mitzvah preparation programs, maktabs and madrasas, seminaries and Sunday shools. Sometimes the targeted study of a sacred language takes place across a sequence of age-appropriate scholastic settings. We can see this illustrated clearly, as well as a number of other topics discussed thus far, in the educational program of the Ethiopian Orthodox Tewahedo Church. Long affiliated with the Coptic Orthodox Church, it received its autocephaly (ecclesiastical independence) only in the twentieth century. Its sacred language is Ge'ez (Classical Ethiopic).

Education proceeds along two tracks in contemporary Ethiopia: state schools teach Amharic and English, whereas church schools teach Ge'ez. Training in Ge'ez language and literature is part of a four-stage curriculum. The *Nebab Bet* ("House of Reading") is roughly comparable to primary school. The goal is to teach reading – which means reading Ge'ez religious texts. There are thousands of such schools throughout the country, many attached to churches or monasteries. The school typically consists of one instructor with up to twenty pupils. The main instructional text is called *fidel hawariya*, the First Epistle of St. John from the New Testament. Step by step, month after month, students learn the complex Ge'ez syllabary, which consists of 231 characters. Students progress from characters to words and then phrases complete with proper intonation for church reading. Once the student has mastered this foundational exercise in Ge'ez literacy, he (or possibly she) moves on to other religious texts like the epistles of St. Paul or St. James, the Gospel of John, or Acts of the Apostles. Literal comprehension is not vital; more important at this stage is proper reading. When this stage of reading has been mastered, then the student moves on to reading "David," the book of Psalms, a key devotional text in

Ethiopian Christianity. When the student completes his course of study in the "House of Reading," this is a major occasion for the student and the whole community. The graduate – even though just a child – enjoys a certain prestige in the community.

The next stage, for those (males only) who pursue it, is called *Qidasse* (or *Qedasse*) Bet. Here the training involved is ritualistic, not literary. A student who has gone through this practical hands-on training is qualified to be an altar priest. But this does not necessarily involve understanding the sacred texts. The next level is *Zema Bet* (Music School), perhaps akin to college. This involves the seminarian leaving home and becoming a wandering scholastic. The content to be mastered consists of the voluminous liturgical hymns and the different ways of singing. There is also a more advanced topic called *akwakwam*, a kind of slow-motion choreographic expression of the liturgy with drums, rattles, and staffs. Finally, in *Qene Bet* (Poetry School) students learn the *qene* genre, which is an improvised form of allegorical poetry performed in liturgical and para-liturgical contexts. Students at this level must really know all the nuances of Ge'ez well and must be able to speak and compose (and perhaps concoct new words) in the ancient language. There are approximately 200 different types of *qene* (Binns 2013).

As the Ethiopian system suggests, the targeted study of a sacred language – as opposed to learning it simply through ritual repetition – may involve some combination of decoding, memorization, and recitation. Let us expand a little on each of these factors.

Decoding Learning to read ancient texts in a sacred language can be a formidable undertaking. To begin with – and this is no small thing – there may be a new script to learn. Many Jews do not live in Israel, so do not use the Hebrew alphabet in their everyday lives. Most Muslims are not Arabic speakers. The Church Slavonic script overlaps with the modern Russian Cyrillic alphabet, but it can still be daunting for churchgoers, especially newcomers, given the extra letters and accent marks that are involved.

Once the script has been deciphered, the student can then try to read the text, but this is not reading in the sense most of us are accustomed to. Decoding means being able to correctly decipher and pronounce the words. Now, the student may not understand the words at all, let alone be able to translate them, yet that may not matter much. What counts is being able to puzzle out and pronounce the letters, syllables, words, and phrases. The implicit belief is that the language has a spiritual meaning and power all on its own. Just being able to see the words and recite them aloud is considered beneficial, curative, salutary. However, this makes little sense according to our prevailing Protestant assumptions regarding reading and scripture. Like the British missionaries recoiling from Coptic instructional techniques in the nineteenth century, we are tempted to think that simply decoding or memorizing texts without really understanding them seems useless.

Memorization Even though missals, projector screens, and bilingual prayerbooks may be readily available, memorization of traditional prayers and chants is still considered a productive exercise in a number of religions. Knowing the words "by heart" means just that: it is believed that memorization can lead to a more heartfelt and sincere expression of traditional religious formulae. Moreover, memorization may be deemed preliminary to scriptural understanding and interpretation. We tend to think that learning a subject comes before memorization; but other pedagogical traditions say that one must memorize before moving on to interpretation. In this alternative educational vision, memorization is logically and practically prior to textual comprehension (Boyle 2004).

For example, consider the task of a Brahmin boy training at a traditional Sanskrit school in India, where prodigious amounts of lexical and grammatical information must be committed to memory before he can approach the study of actual texts. The Mysore Sanskrit College has students ranging from eight-year-old beginners to advanced graduate students. The goal is to produce a pandit, a scholastic expert in Sanskritic wisdom.

The elementary level in this program requires memorization of copious linguistic information. This is done orally, without the aid of texts. The first thing to be learned is a kind of thesaurus in the form of 3000 verses referencing some 13,000 terms. This step alone takes about four years. But despite the effort, the student does not yet learn the meaning of the terms (though he might know some through his vernacular, just as an Italian speaker can guess the meaning of many Latin words). This is quite unlike teaching methods used in the West: "Learning Sanskrit in this way is thus more akin to learning a musical score than it is to learning a language. To a pundit, our method of emphasizing always 'meaning' seems a bit like beginning your musical study with a Mozart sonata" (Gerow 2002, 666).

Next comes grammar. Sanskrit is a highly inflected language, which means that different nouns change their shape depending on their number, gender, and grammatical function. Here is an example of the most common form of nouns, namely, masculine stems ending in short –*a*.

Rāmaḥ	*Rāmau*	*Rāmāḥ*
he Rāma	*he Rāmau*	*he Rāmāḥ*
Rāmam	*Rāmau*	*Rāmān*
Rāmeṇa	*Rāmābhyām*	*Rāmaiḥ*
Rāmāya	*Rāmābhyām*	*Rāmebhyaḥ*
Rāmāt	*Rāmābhyām*	*Rāmebhyaḥ*
Rāmasya	*Rāmayoḥ*	*Rāmāṇām*
Rāme	*Rāmayoḥ*	*Rāmeṣu*

The verb *bhū* "to be" boasts a total of ninety forms, which have to be repeated daily. After the lexicon and the grammar comes syntax, followed by literary and philological studies. All of this is preliminary to discussing classical texts in terms of their poetic and theological content – a daunting curriculum indeed! But the study and memorization of Sanskrit is considered a dharmic activity for Brahmins. That is to say, it is in keeping with the socio-cosmic order of things as traditionally defined by and for Brahmins. In short, learning the sacred language in this way is a good deed and a religious and social obligation.

Recitation The goal of sacred language learning in some traditions is the proper and aesthetically pleasing recitation of scriptural texts, regardless of whether or not the contents are well understood on an informational level. We see this especially with languages that are viewed as primary instruments of revelation, such as Arabic, Sanskrit, and Pali. From Brahmin priests to Theravada monks to ordinary Muslims, the point of schooling is to learn to buff and polish the linguistic gold, so to speak, that contains eternal truth. We do not see the same attention to recitational detail with secondary languages of revelation like Latin, which is understood to have been an imperial language "repurposed" for a divine goal (to spread the Gospel).

Islam provides a clear example of the tendency to focus on the propriety and beauty of scriptural recitation. According to one study of madrasas in Singapore, the best students are those who can attain an Arabic-style pronunciation with proper intonational contours. "Accuracy," notes the researcher, "is prized over meaning and understanding" (Chew 2014, 55). Similarly, an anthropological study of Islamic schooling in Cameroon notes: "The primary goal in the first years of schooling was the faithful – verbatim, fluent, and reverent – rendering of Qur'anic texts by the child" (Moore 2008, 643). This happens through constant and extensive imitation of the teacher, repetition, and performance.

Yet the vehicularity of sacred languages – the fact that they have been carried across social and political borders and serve as linking languages between people who speak different mother tongues – can pose problems. To take one example: Indonesia is home to the largest number of Muslims in the world. Since the 1990s, there has been a great revival of interest in Qur'anic recitation, evidenced in various projects including books, audio tapes, and recitation competitions. Yet many Indonesians struggle with certain aspects of Arabic phonology.

> A first, and ongoing, goal in learning to read the Qur'ān in Indonesia was to be able to vocalize Arabic phonemes without any trace of the characteristics of local languages in pronunciation. Native speakers of Indonesian languages concentrate on certain sounds in particular: for instance, pronouncing correctly the Arabic '*fā*' (not '*pā*') and '*thā*' (not '*sā*'). (Gade 2004, 115)

Some common mistakes in pronunciation can result in quite radical differences in meaning. The word *al-ḥamd* meaning "all praise" is often mispronounced as *al-hamd* meaning "to put out a fire." The Arabic word *ḍāllīn*, meaning "those who go astray," may come out as *dālīn*, "those who follow the right path" (Gade 2004, 127). This is but one tiny example of the difficulty of transmitting a sacred language across the world.

Issues of translation and transliteration There are cases where the sacred language is taught in the sacred language itself. In an earlier period of Catholic history, Latin composition and conversation were everyday affairs. Jesuit seminarians studying for the priesthood were expected to know Latin fluently. They were required to converse in Latin, debate theological topics in Latin, and compose public recitations in Latin. This is no longer the case, though there are attempts to return to that golden age (see below). The ability to translate Thai texts *into* Pali is still part of the nine-tiered examination system for monks in Thailand (Sammapanno 2007). As noted above, the composition of new poems in Ge'ez is the culmination of the decades-long Ethiopian Orthodox method of schooling. But those are high-level achievements. For most adherents, the purpose of learning a sacred language is reading and recitation, not composition and conversation.

Questions of translation and transliteration (transposing the sacred language into a local vernacular script for ease of pronunciation and comprehension) come up frequently in connection with sacred languages, especially in the educational and liturgical domains. Within a given religious tradition, one typically observes recurring debates among clerics and lay people about the theological, pastoral, and educational value of resorting to these expediencies for learning a sacred language.

Transliteration and translation are common enough in certain denominations of Judaism. *Mishkan T'filah*, the prayerbook of Reform Judaism, uses both throughout: Hebrew is transliterated into the Roman alphabet, along with translations (stricter and more poetic) of the Hebrew liturgical text, though some rabbis worry that such measures reduce the incentive to learn the Hebrew alphabet. The ornate Church Slavonic characters can be difficult even for native Russian speakers to decipher; accordingly, devotional materials are increasingly being published in the streamlined "civil" script (i.e., the Cyrillic alphabet, which is used for Russian), even though traditionalists and teachers often object to this concession on ideological and pedagogical grounds (some grammatical details are lost or obscured in the simpler Cyrillic system). Coptic is often accessed through Arabic and/or English translations and transliterations. Transliterating Classical Arabic into the Latin alphabet as a teaching aid is making inroads in some Qur'anic schools (Rosowsky 2016), a surprising turn of events, given the holy aura that surrounds the Arabic script.

Not surprisingly, translation poses more of a threat to sacred languages than transliteration. The relationship between sacred languages and translation might be described as that of frenemies. A frenemy is "one who pretends to be a friend but is actually an enemy" (Merriam-Webster). Many religionists feel that translation may be beneficial in the short term but threatening in the long term. Vernacular translation, whether in a bilingual prayerbook or projection screen like the Coptic Reader, can help people get by in the sacred language. These aids may contribute to the maintenance of the sacred language in the tradition. But if they become too helpful, then questions may arise. Why not just go over to the vernacular altogether? Why not transliterate the mystical script all of the time? As we will see in the next chapter, questions about the educational merit of translation usually play a role in the sacred language debates that from time to time convulse religious communities.

Inspired by the papal document known as *Veterum Sapientia* (discussed in Chapter 3), this Ecclesiastical Latin camp is a full-immersion (*Latine tantum*) week-long course for members of the Catholic clergy, including priests, monks, and nuns. The aim of the program is not only to better understand some of the canonical texts of the Roman Church, but to help revive Latin as the grand lingua franca of the Catholic world. To that end, Latin is both the object and the medium of instruction. The ancient tongue is spoken at all meals and during recreational activities and excursions. Students play Scrabble and other games in Latin, and compose and act out skits in the ancient language based on famous biblical stories (e.g., Moses and the Red Sea). All of this is made possible because the instructors speak Latin with remarkable fluency. The academic tasks are framed by liturgical practice: the schedule includes Mass (in both its "ordinary" and "extraordinary" forms) in the morning, grace before meals, and vespers in the late afternoon – all in Latin, of course. A kind of traditional Catholic piety prevails, yet with moments of levity and laughter, including plentiful Latinate jokes and puns bandied about, perhaps aided by the availability of *vinum rubrum Burdigalense* (merlot). Hearing the participants carry on conversations in Latin, one would be hard pressed to consider Latin a dead language.

State involvement

In some cases, governments get involved in the teaching of sanctified languages. This happens when there is a state religion or at least an alliance of secular and sacred authorities. History records many instances when the Thai monarchy intervened in Buddhist monastic education, including regulating the Pali exam system for monks (Dhammasami 2004). In Egypt, the state supports the teaching of Classical Arabic. In fact, the 1980 Constitution enshrines Classical Arabic as the official language – with no mention of the Egyptian Arabic variety. The Ministry of Education promotes materials that teach pupils how to pray in the sacred language (Haeri 2003). Church Slavonic was taught in state schools before the Russian Revolution. The Bolsheviks did away with that. Now, the sacred language is finding its way back into some public school systems under the heading of "culturology" or "cultural history." In India, the government supports Sanskrit through an array of publications, cultural events, radio broadcasts, and educational institutions (Ramaswamy 1999). Rashtriya Sanskrit Sansthan is an official government agency set up in 1970 to help promote the cause of Sanskrit in India. It overseas the teaching of the sacred language in special "deemed" universities and thousands of pathshalas (traditional Sanskrit schools). Its activities include research, publications, correspondence courses, and curricular development.

It is interesting to see in these cases how sacred languages become the subject of governmental management, with various bureaucratic directives issued about standards, textbooks, and examinations. What is ostensibly a matter of divine revelation becomes subject to state regulation. Yet this underscores, once again, one of the key facts about sacred languages compared to ordinary vernaculars: Coptic, Pali, Church Slavonic, Sanskrit, Classical Arabic, and the rest are secondary, bookish languages, preserved and promoted from one generation to the next not by families, but by institutions.

References

Alfeyev, Hilarion, ed. 2013. *Bozhestvennaia liturgiia sviatitelia Ioanna Zlatousta, s parallel'nym perevodom na russkii iazyk*. Moscow: Izdatel'stvo Moskovskoi Patriarkhii Russkoi Pravoslavnoi Tserkvi.

Arkhipova, I. G. 2012. *Tserkovnoslavianskii iazyk dlia detei. Uchebnoe posobie*. Dolgotrudnyi: Izdatel'skii dom "INTELLECTiK."

Bachman, Nicolai. 2005. *The Language of Yoga: Complete A to Y Guide to Asana Names, Sanskrit Terms, and Chants*. Boulder, CO: Sounds True.

Benor, Sarah Bunin. 2012. *Becoming Frum: How Newcomers Learn the Language and Culture of Orthodox Judaism*. New Brunswick, NJ, and London: Rutgers University Press.

Binns, John. 2013. "Out of Ethiopia – A Different Way of Doing Theology." *International Journal for the Study of the Christian Church* 13 (1): 33–47. DOI: 10.1080/1474225X.2012.754137

Blommaert, Jan. 2013. *Ethnography, Superdiversity and Linguistic Landscapes: Chronicles of Complexity*. Bristol and Buffalo: Multilingual Matters.

Boyle, Helen N. 2004. *Quranic Schools: Agents of Preservation and Change*. New York and London: RoutledgeFalmer.

Cardin, Nina Beth, Terry Kaye, and Lori Lyons. 2006. *Hineni: Prayerbook Hebrew for Adults*. Springfield, NJ: Behrman House.

Chew, Phyllis Ghim-Lian. 2014. "Language Choice and Religious Identities in Three Singaporean Madrasahs." *International Journal for the Sociology of Language* 229: 49–65. DOI: 10.1515/ijsl-2014-0017

Chinmaya Publications. 2016. Easy Sanskrit Online Course. Accessed July 29, 2016. http://www.chinmayapublications.com/easy-sanskrit-online-course

Coptic Orthodox Diocese of the Southern United States. n.d. Coptic Reader. Accessed July 12, 2016. https://suscopts.org/coptic-reader/

Crosby, Kate. 2014. *Theravada Buddhism: Continuity, Diversity, and Identity*. Chichester: Wiley Blackwell.

Dhammasami, Khammai. 2004. *Between Idealism and Pragmatism: A Study of Monastic Education in Burma and Thailand from the Seventeenth Century to the Present*. PhD thesis, University of Oxford, St. Anne's College.

Farag, Lois M. 2014. "Spirituality: In God's Presence." In *The Coptic Christian Heritage: History, Faith, and Culture*, edited by Lois M. Farag, 132–142. London and New York: Routledge.

Fishman, Joshua A. 1991. *Reversing Language Shift: Theoretical and Empirical Foundations of Assistance to Threatened Languages*. Clevedon and Philadelphia: Multilingual Matters.

Gade, Anna M. 2004. *Perfection Makes Practice: Learning, Emotion, and the Recited Qur'an in Indonesia*. Honolulu: University of Hawai'i Press.

Gerow, Edwin. 2002. "Education in Sanskrit: Methods and Goals." *Journal of the American Oriental Society* 122 (4): 661–690. DOI: 10.2307/3217609

Gombrich, Richard F. 1988. *Theravāda Buddhism: A Social History from Ancient Benares to Modern Colombo*. London and New York: Routledge and Kegan Paul.

Haarmann, Harald. 2002. *Lexikon der untergegangenen Sprachen*. Munich: C. H. Beck.

Haeri, Niloofar. 2003. *Sacred Language, Ordinary People: Dilemmas of Culture and Politics in Egypt*. New York: Palgrave Macmillan.

Makar, Kyrillos Fr. n.d. *The Coptic Language*, Part 1: *Introductory Lessons*. Des Moines, IA: St. Mary Coptic Orthodox Church. DVD.

McDaniel, Justin. 2008. *Gathering Leaves and Lifting Words: Histories of Buddhist Monastic Education in Laos and Thailand*. Seattle and London: University of Washington Press.

Moore, Leslie C. 2008. "Body, Text, and Talk in Maroua Fulbe Qur'anic Schooling." *Text & Talk* 28 (5): 643–665. DOI: 10.1515/TEXT.2008.033

Preston, Nora Stene. 1998. "Multiple Choice? Language-Usage and the Transmission of Religious Tradition in the Coptic Orthodox Community in London." *British Journal of Religious Education* 20 (2): 90–101. DOI: 10.1080/0141620980200204

Ramaswamy, Sumathi. 1999. "Sanskrit for the Nation." *Modern Asian Studies* 33 (2): 339–381. DOI: 10.1017/S0026749X99003273

Rosowsky, Andrey. 2013. "Faith, Phonics and Identity: Reading in Faith Complementary Schools." *Literacy* 47 (2): 67–78. DOI: 10.1111/j.1741-4369.2012.00669.x

Rosowsky, Andrey. 2016. "Heavenly Entextualisations: The Acquisition and Performance of Classical Religious Texts." In *Navigating Languages,*

Literacies and Identities: Religion in Young Lives, edited by Vally Lytra, Dinah Volk, and Eve Gregory, 110–125. New York and London: Routledge.
Saad, Michael. 2010. "The Contemporary Life of the Coptic Orthodox Church in the United States." *Studies in World Christianity* 16 (3): 207–225. DOI: http://dx.doi.org/ 10.3366/swc.2010.0101
Sammapanno, Phramaha Somjin. 2007. "Introduction of Pali Studies into Thailand." Accessed July 29, 2016. http://atbu.org/node/23
Samuels, Jeffrey. 2013. "Ordination (*Pabbajjā*) as Going Forth? Social Bonds and the Making of a Buddhist Monastic." In *Little Buddhas: Children and Childhoods in Buddhist Texts and Traditions*, edited by Vanessa R. Sasson, 229–246. Oxford: Oxford University Press.
Sawyer, John F. A. 1999. *Sacred Languages and Sacred Texts.* London and New York: Routledge.
Sedra, Paul. 2011. *From Mission to Modernity: Evangelicals, Reformers and Education in Nineteenth Century Egypt.* London and New York: I. B. Tauris.
Takla, Hany N. 1996. "The Value of Coptic." Accessed March 2, 2015. http://www.coptic.org/language/stshenouda2.htm

Further Reading

The Claremont Coptic Encyclopedia. http://ccdl.libraries.claremont.edu/cdm/landingpage/collection/cce. A treasure trove of information about Coptic Christianity and civilization, with a number of articles concerning linguistic matters.
Preston, Nora Stene. 1998. "Multiple Choice? Language-Usage and the Transmission of Religious Tradition in the Coptic Orthodox Community in London." *British Journal of Religious Education* 20 (2): 90–101. DOI: 10.1080/0141620980200204. A vital contribution to our understanding of the place of the sacred language in Coptic Orthodox Christianity.
Rosowsky, Andrey. 2008. *Heavenly Readings: Liturgical Literacy in a Multilingual Context.* Bristol and Buffalo: Multilingual Matters. A sensitive in-depth account of how non-Arabic-speaking Muslims learn Classical Arabic.
Zakrzewska, Ewa D. 2014. "The Coptic Language." In *Coptic Civilization: Two Thousand Years of Christianity in Egypt*, edited by Gawdat Gabra, 79–89. Cairo and New York: The American University in Cairo Press. A clear and accessible historical overview of the topic.

Chapter 7

Communities and Controversies

In August 2012, Russian Orthodox Christians celebrated the 200th anniversary of the founding of Fort Ross, a small settlement with a chapel perched on the rocky coast of Sonoma County, north of San Francisco. Priests and pilgrims came from across the country and abroad to mark the occasion with a Divine Liturgy and festival. The three different Russian-related ecclesiastical jurisdictions in the United States were represented: the Russian Orthodox Church-Moscow Patriarchate (ROC MP), the Russian Orthodox Church Outside of Russia (ROCOR), and the Orthodox Church in America (OCA). Two local choirs sang: one from Saint Seraphim Church (OCA) in English and the other from Holy Virgin Mary Cathedral (ROCOR) in the consecrated language of Church Slavonic. After the Divine Liturgy, there was a procession of the cross around the fort to the cemetery, where a prayer service was sung for the Russians and native Kushaya buried there. A banquet with performances of traditional Russian music and dance followed.

This event illustrates an important aspect of sacred languages: they can unite as well as divide. On the one hand, a sacred language can serve as a banner of collective identity, helping to forge a sense of solidarity among members who live in different parts of the world and speak different mother tongues. It can do this by shared liturgical as well as visual means, with the sacred script functioning as a kind of logo for the religious "brand." On the other hand, a sacred language can become a source of linguistic estrangement among adherents, leading to controversy and division. During unsettled times (cf. Swidler 2001), sanctified languages can

Sacred Languages of the World: An Introduction, First Edition. Brian P. Bennett.

become proxies or substitutes for broader disagreements about religion, culture, and politics. In sum, though they can contribute to social chemistry, sacred languages can also be combustible, sparking conflicts among the faithful. Church Slavonic is a good "e.g." to illustrate these conflicting dynamics.

Church Slavonic (or Church Slavic) is the sacred language of the Russian Orthodox Church, as well as a number of other Orthodox and Eastern Catholic communities. It is sometimes referred to as Old Church Slavonic (OCS), though this designation is best reserved for the earliest stratum of the linguistic tradition. Codified in the ninth century by the missionary brothers Saints Cyril and Methodius and their disciples, Old Church Slavonic was from the start a textual, not a colloquial, language. One Russian churchman has compared it, rather provocatively, to Tolkien's invented languages of orc and elvish, as well as to Esperanto:

> The Church Slavonic language always was a language of the temple [*khram*]; that is, it was never a language of the street. From the start it was an artificial language, which people did not converse in with each other. It's an Esperanto. (Kuraev 2005, 189)

Church Slavonic, which evolved out of OCS, functioned for centuries as a bookish lingua franca across swaths of Eastern Europe and the Balkans, a cultural zone known as *Slavia orthodoxa* or Orthodox Slavdom. Cozy interaction with local vernaculars resulted in several different "recensions" (sub-varieties), for example Croatian Church Slavonic and Russian Church Slavonic.

In the sixteenth and seventeenth centuries, with the Balkan countries under Ottoman rule, the Russian variety prevailed and became the standard used throughout *Slavia orthodoxa*. In the eighteenth century, the language was basically fixed with the publication of the so-called Elizabethan Bible. (Elizabeth was the daughter of Peter the Great.) This variety is sometimes called New, Modern, or Synodal Church Slavonic, a reference to the Holy Synod, which was the governing council of the Russian Church in that era. From that point on, the sacred language became something of a closed system (MacRobert 2005).

Russian and Church Slavonic are related, but Church Slavonic is not simply an older form of Russian – more like a relative from out of town who speaks with a sophisticated accent. Up until the modern era, Slavonic and Russian coexisted in a roughly diglossic (high/low, wine/water) relationship.

> The closer a certain text came to the perceived ideal of Church Slavonic purity, the stronger would be the aura of piety, spirituality, and didacticism that it exuded. By the same token, the prevalence of indigenous [Russian] linguistic material would draw the text towards the sphere of the worldly, the practical, and the material. (Gasparov 2004, 139)

With the painstaking development of the Russian literary language in the eighteenth and nineteenth centuries, Church Slavonic slowly lost its elevated position in much the same way Latin had in Western Europe, eventually being reduced to the cultic domain. However, Slavonic's pre-modern "bulge" was never as prominent as Latin's. "The use of Church Slavonic … rarely expanded outside a limited range of genres relating to liturgical services and pious reading, from the Gospels and the Psalter to sermons, prayers, and hagiography" (Gasparov 2004, 134). The language was never really used for mathematics, diplomacy, or drama, the way Latin was. Church Slavonic was further sidelined under the atheistic ideology of Soviet Communism. Since the implosion of the USSR, however, there has been a revitalization of the sacred language in Russia and elsewhere. In this chapter we will concentrate on the Russian situation, setting aside the question of Slavonic in Bulgaria, Serbia, Belarus, and other Orthodox lands.

The first Russian Orthodox adherents arrived in the New World from the West. In this they were unlike all other Christian groups, including the Latin-wielding Spanish friars who set up the Catholic mission system in California (e.g., at Santa Clara). In the eighteenth and nineteenth centuries, Russian fur trappers and Christian missionaries trekked across Siberia, hop-scotched across the Kurile, Aleutian, and Alaskan islands, and made their way down the west coast of North America, ending in the colony known as Fort Ross (from the word *Rossiia*, meaning Russia). Along the way, they altered the linguasphere by disseminating two lingua francas: secular Russian and sacred Church Slavonic. A kind of triglossic situation emerged in the indigenous communities impacted by this imperial and missionary venture, with three different languages slotted to perform different functions. Church Slavonic was the golden resource reserved for prayer and worship. Russian was the instrument of official business, for example, correspondence with St. Petersburg, the capital of church and state in imperial Russia. Meanwhile, day-to-day interactions took place at least partly in native tongues such as Alutiiq, Fox, Tlingit, and Yupik (Ivanov 1997).

A number of Russian missionaries paid considerable attention to learning these indigenous languages. They devised alphabets, composed grammatical treatises and dictionaries, and then translated Church Slavonic literature (liturgical, scriptural, catechetical) into them. However, this "indigenizing" approach was not without its critics. Those in favor of it argued that Orthodox Christianity has always translated its message into vernacular languages. They emphasized the importance of evangelical communication. But others worried that this method could lead to dangerous forms of syncretism, with indigenous languages serving as a pathway for shamanistic beliefs and practices to infect the pure Orthodox faith. They insisted on the sanctity of Church Slavonic and the value of imposing Russian civilization on native peoples (Znamenski 1999).

It would be misleading to suggest that Church Slavonic continued to be used in California without interruption for two hundred years. In fact, a number of dramatic developments occurred between 1812 and 2012. The Russian American Company abandoned its overseas venture, which had become unprofitable, and shuttered Fort Ross in 1841. Russia sold Alaska to the United States in 1867. The profile of Orthodoxy in America would change radically from its modest Alaskan beginnings when, starting in 1890 and lasting for several decades, millions of Orthodox believers came to America from Europe and the Middle East – Albanians, Arabs, Bulgarians, Georgians, Macedonians, Romanians, Russians, Serbians, Ukrainians, and above all Greeks. In 1905, the Russian Orthodox Church transferred its administrative headquarters in the United States from San Francisco to New York, to better serve this influx of new immigrants. A bit later the Russian Revolution of 1917 triggered a massive new wave of Russian Orthodox immigration to America. Thus, for much of the twentieth century, the experience of Russian Orthodoxy in the United States was shaped by a number of factors, including the trauma of the unprecedented Communist attack on the Russian Church, the medley of Orthodox ethnicities present in the United States and the confusion over ecclesiastical jurisdictions, and nostalgia for the vanished world of Tsarist Russia and recriminations against those who allegedly capitulated to Soviet atheism (Stokoe and Kishkovsky 1995). Disputes about Church Slavonic certainly did not cause these divisions, but tended to dovetail with them.

The debate over the status of Church Slavonic within Russian Orthodoxy had started even before the Bolshevik Revolution of 1917. Some clerics and churchgoers argued that Slavonic was no longer intelligible and should be replaced by Russian or at least Russified to a certain extent. Others insisted that Slavonic is a sacred tongue inextricably linked to the beliefs, practices, and institutions of the Orthodox faith. The debate was basically shelved within Russia itself as a result of the Revolution, when there appeared to be far more pressing concerns. What happened, though, was the debate was exported to the United States, where immigrants were dealing with a tricky new kind of triglossia (Church Slavonic, Russian, English). The issue became, not only whether Church Slavonic should be replaced by Russian – the mother tongue of the émigrés – but also by English, the dominant vernacular of the surrounding culture. This *linguistic* dispute also become entangled in a longstanding and complicated debate over (among other things) *institutional* jurisdiction – basically, who has the ecclesiastical authority to represent Orthodoxy in the United States. Three different groups claim that privilege, each with a different linguistic profile. The Orthodox Church in America (OCA) has emphasized accessibility and adaptability: it has been the most "American" in its approach; 95 percent of parishes currently use English in the liturgy. Meanwhile, the Russian Orthodox Church Outside of Russia (ROCOR) long maintained a more insular stance, wary of interactions with the wider culture and emphasizing the sanctity of Church Slavonic in the liturgy; only 49 percent of churches use English (though that number has been growing due to converts). In between these two poles are those parishes that are part of the ecclesiastical infrastructure of the Moscow Patriarchate (the headquarters of Russian Orthodoxy): 77 percent use English as the main liturgical language (Krindatch 2011).

The two decades since the demise of the USSR have witnessed the restoration of numerous Orthodox places and practices neglected or suppressed under Communism, a trend that extends to Russia's cultural and religious legacy abroad. This includes the reconciliation in 2007 between the Moscow Patriarchate and ROCOR, brokered in part by President Vladimir Putin. Russians have also found it important to symbolically reclaim Fort Ross as part of the story of Orthodox Christianity in America. Hence the ceremony in 2012. What transpired on the coast of Northern California that day reflects some of the broader dynamics involving sacred languages and communities. Orthodox Christians from different parts of the world who speak different mother tongues were able to come together and participate in a celebration using a common liturgical language. Indeed, one can hear Church Slavonic not only in Russia and California but also in many countries all around the world, from Finland to Mongolia, Paraguay to North Korea, Cuba to Canada. But the presence of different churches with their respective choirs singing in both English and Church Slavonic suggests that fault lines are still there beneath the surface. In what follows we will look at these two propensities of sacred languages – to unite and to divide – relying on Church Slavonic as the prime example, while taking a comparative foray into Avestan, the sacred language of Zoroastrianism.

United We Stand

A lingua franca is a linguistic go-between, a mediating language used by people who cannot communicate directly because they speak different mother tongues. The term lingua franca is preferred in English-language discourse, while vehicular language (*langue véhiculaire*) is more common in French. The term "vehicular" is helpful because it can be turned from an adjective into a noun: vehicularity. We can then talk about the degree of vehicularity for this or that language (as Calvet does in his barometer of world languages: see Chapter 2).

Vehicular languages have played a major role in human history and continue to be crucial arteries in the linguasphere. The world, after all, is a Babel of tongues. How can traders plying the seas communicate with their customers? How can diplomats from different countries conduct negotiations? How can missionaries preach to potential converts? The answer: through lingua francas or vehicular languages, which are used to bridge the gap, to expand communication across frontiers, to overcome Babelization (Chew 2009). The rise and fall of the great vehicular languages across the linguasphere, including Arabic, Aramaic, English, French, Greek, Latin, Persian, and Spanish, is a major theme in world history (Ostler 2010).

In theory, any language can become a lingua franca. Vehicularity is not based on the inner workings of the language, by its nouns and adjectives, but is brought about by social, political, religious, commercial, and other factors. The oldest existing lingua francas are closely linked to the axial age. Sanskrit, Arabic, and Latin are vehicular languages that go with the so-called world religions. (In retrospect, perhaps a better name would be "vehicular religions." For one thing, it would avoid the triumphalist connotations of the term "world religions," which sounds like a *fait accompli*. Religious vehicularity is relative; it waxes and wanes and can be measured empirically.) As discussed in Chapter 2, this period in history witnessed a gradual shift in religious topography, from a focus on ritual sacrifice performed in civic temple complexes (as in ancient Roman religion) to more spatially dispersed multiethnic communities linked by a network of symbols and texts and the promise of salvation (as in Roman Catholic Christianity). In the premodern period, sacred languages and scripts helped tie together these geographically spread out communities, facilitating the flow of information between speakers of different mother tongues. Benedict Anderson's classic description of this era is worth quoting:

> Few things are more impressive than the vast territorial stretch of the Ummah Islam from Morocco to the Sulu Archipelago, of Christendom from Paraguay to Japan, and of the Buddhist world from Sri Lanka to the Korean peninsula. The great sacral cultures (and for our purposes here it may be permissible to include "Confucianism") incorporated conceptions of immense communities. But Christendom, the Islamic Ummah, and even the Middle Kingdom … were imaginable largely through the medium of a sacred language and written script … All the great classical communities conceived of themselves as cosmically central, through the medium of a sacred language linked to a superterrestrial order of power. Accordingly, the stretch of written Latin, Pali, Arabic, or Chinese was, in theory, unlimited. (1991, 12–13)

Vehicularity is an important aspect of sacred languages, though to varying degrees. Latin used to have a very high quotient. After Vatican II, however, its vehicularity dropped precipitously, though prayers and liturgies are still performed in Latin in Rome and in some parishes around the world, and the international character of Latin remains an ideal, especially among Catholic traditionalists. By comparison, the vehicularity quotient of Coptic is much more modest, since the language is largely confined to Egypt. However, we should note that in the diaspora Coptic helps bring together people of different backgrounds. For example, the parishioners of St. Mary and Moses Church in North Tonawanda (discussed in the previous chapter) are not all Egyptian and do not necessarily know Arabic. Coptic helps unite a congregation reflecting "at least 11 nationalities, including Serbian, Egyptian, Lebanese, Iraqi and African, as well as Irish and Italian members" (*The Buffalo News*, August 15, 2016).

Vehicularity – the use of the language by people who speak different mother tongues – can lead to controversy over intelligibility, the issue that seems to shadow sacred languages. This is a problem faced especially by the world/vehicular religions with universalist aspirations (see Ostler 2016). How do you transmit one message (the Gospel, the Dharma) to peoples of different cultures and languages? What parts of the religion are essential and, as it were, linguistically non-negotiable? When is translation considered legitimate, expedient, impossible? In sum, how close is the link between the faith religion and one particular linguistic vessel? We have already touched on how Russian Orthodox believers have struggled with this issue in the New World, first vis-à-vis indigenous peoples during the missionary ventures of the eighteenth and nineteenth centuries and then in relation to twentieth-century American society. But even Muslims have grappled with it. Why "even"? Because the assumption is that Islam is intransigent when it comes to maintaining Classical Arabic as the language of scripture and liturgy. But that has not always been the case. During the interface of Islam and Persian civilization in the tenth and eleventh centuries,

> Muslim theologians and jurists sought to balance the catholicity of the Qur'an with its particular Arabic form. The universality of the call to Islam is a motif running throughout the Qur'an. Thus, the question of how the Arabic message was to be delivered to the diverse linguistic populations of the world served as a repeated site of concern in the early constitution of Islamic societies. (Zadeh 2012, 11)

Tensions may arise with regard to the nobility of local vernaculars: are they worth nothing compared to the sacred language? Who determines this scale of values?

Before we discuss those tensions in connection with Church Slavonic, we need to first look at the ways that sacred languages foster solidarity in international faith communities. It is helpful to distinguish at least three different modes of vehicularity: the liturgical, the visual, and the conversational.

Liturgical

Interventionist practices, which aim to connect the human and the superhuman for the purpose of either sanctification or salvation, form the core of any religious system. For the sake of analytic convenience, we have divided these practices into the liturgical, somatological, thaumaturgical, and the behavioral (having to do with food, dress, and hygiene, as well as ethics). Sanskrit is the language par excellence of yoga and is thus a somatological lingua franca. Snippets of Sanskrit are read, spoken, chanted, or displayed in ashrams and yoga studios around the world. For its part,

Classical Arabic is a kind of liturgical Ethernet connecting the Muslim *ummah* or worldwide faith network. Whether in Hong Kong, Pakistan, Indonesia, France, or Saudi Arabia, with or without some kind of bilingual textual aid, Muslims endeavor to recite the Qur'an and say their daily prayers in the sacred language.

Church Slavonic may not be as strong numerically as those languages, but it is still an impressive liturgical vehicle among the Slavic Orthodox nations, including Serbia, Bulgaria, and Russia. The Russian Orthodox Church (Moscow Patriarchate) alone boasts some 165 million members worldwide (World Council of Churches 2016). It currently has 426 parish churches in the following countries (the number is listed after the name), the vast majority of which list Church Slavonic as their liturgical language, sometimes in combination with English, French, German, or another local language:

Andorra (1)
Antarctica (1)
Argentina (23)
Australia (39)
Austria (6)
Belgium (16)
Brazil (5)
Bulgaria (1)
Cambodia (2)
Canada (53)
Chile (4)
China (5)
Costa Rica (1)
Cuba (1)
Cyprus (1)
Czech Republic (2)
Denmark (5)
Dominican Rep. (2)
Ecuador (1)
Egypt (1)
Finland (6)
France (38)
Germany (127)
Great Britain (42)
Haiti (7)
Hungary (9)
Iceland (1)
India (1)
Indonesia (26)
Iran (1)
Ireland (8)
Israel (17)
Italy (45)
Japan (2)
Jordan (1)
Lebanon (1)
Luxembourg (1)
Malaysia (1)
Malta (1)
Mexico (2)
Mongolia (1)
Morocco (2)
Nepal (1)
Netherlands (11)
New Zealand (4)
North Korea (1)
Norway (7)
Pakistan (1)
Panama (1)
Paraguay (1)
Portugal (13)
Serbia (1)
Singapore (1)
South Africa (1)
South Korea (3)
Spain (20)
Sweden (8)
Switzerland (14)
Syria (1)
Thailand (5)
Tonga (1)
Tunisia (2)
Turkey (1)
Uganda (1)
United Arab Emirates (1)
USA (231)
Venezuela (6)

(Moscow Patriarchate 2016)

Extended across the linguasphere, Church Slavonic provides a transnational medium for prayer and worship. Church members traveling abroad would be able to attend the liturgy and understand, or at least feel comfortable with, the same liturgy in the same language (though, as always, regional accents can complicate the task of understanding). The global range of Church Slavonic is well symbolized by its most extreme outpost, the Holy Trinity Church, perched on King George Island near the Russian Bellingshausen Station in Antarctica, some 9600 miles from Moscow.

Visual

Liturgies are usually performed in specially consecrated buildings (*there*) decorated to some extent with the sacred script. Such is the case with Russian Orthodoxy and Church Slavonic. Russian churches (often called temples: *khramy*) may be marked inside and outside by the ornate script. Doors and gateways may bear Slavonic lettering, while inside the sanctuary, tiny bits of the sacred language may be found on icons (often just abbreviations for Christ, Mother of God, and the like) as well as larger inscriptions on the walls (Deschler 2008). Sometimes these inscriptions are executed in a style called *vyaz*, in which the letters are intertwined and sometimes set inside each other, often in an exaggeratedly condensed way, with characters stretched, stacked, pressed together, and interlocked. The end result can be visually powerful, almost like hieroglyphics, though challenging to decipher even for cognoscenti. Mystery trumps intelligibility. The ornate Church Slavonic lettering seems of a piece with the rich cultic setting – the array of flowers, beeswax candles, silver-covered icons, and golden liturgical vessels – inside the temple. Thus, aside from its content, the very *appearance* of Church Slavonic, which also occurs on books, prayer cards, and other accoutrements of devotional life, provides a connecting thread for Russian Orthodox believers around the world.

The way that certain sacred scripts reinforce religious identity is hard to measure and quantify, but is not something we should take for granted. In Chapter 2, we mentioned how many communities around the world have converted their language into the charismatic Arabic script. The writing system creates a civilizational scriptworld. This involves a kind of branding, "a process whereby a specific visual/graphical element of written language such as an alphabetic character becomes emblematic of a group of people who use that element in their writing practices." Such branding can be done by insiders or outsiders (Sebba 2015, 6), and may play on stereotypes in a humorous or prejudicial way. Branding works by lifting and separating, using a linguistic marker to distinguish *this* group from *those* groups. A certain script (or a piece thereof) becomes the icon or "logo" of the religion as a corporate entity. Consider the ubiquity of OM (or AUM), according to some interpretations the primordial generative syllable of the universe and a key element in mantras. This little bit of Sanskritic writing, symbolizing India and/or Hinduism, is found all around the globe, on tattoos, jewelry, signs for yoga studios, temple websites, and much else. (See Figure 7.1.)

Religious communities can capitalize on their own "brand" identity by using sacred scripts. For example, the unique Coptic writing system sometimes appears on Coptic Orthodox publications. "In these instances, the intent may not be to present a text that should be read, but to give a reference to the common heritage and glorious church traditions that the Coptic language represents" (Preston 1998, 93). Nowadays, this technique has gravitated online to the websites of churches, temples, and mosques. Again, intelligibility is not necessarily the main criterion – it is the very *idea* of the language that is crucial.

If the script is a kind of logo or emblem of communal religious identity, then it stands to reason that those within the religion who are intensely concerned with enforcing communal borders will resort to an equally intense use of the script. We see this at work among religious extremists. For example, the flags, banners, and logos of dozens of Muslim jihadist

Figure 7.1 Faux Sanskrit writing. Reproduced with kind permission of the Saratoga Hindu Temple and Community Center, California.

groups almost invariably incorporate elements of Classical Arabic alongside images of mosques, books (the Qur'an), globes, swords, guns, and clenched fists, usually against a backdrop of black or green, two colors identified with Muhammad and early Islamic victories. As far as the language goes, particularly common are the *shahada* ("There is no god but God [Allah], and Muhammad is His messenger") and the *takbir* ("God is [the] Greatest") (Beifuss and Bellini 2013). Less well known, but in a similar vein, Russian nationalists often drawn upon extravagantly ornate Slavonic lettering in their periodicals and websites in order to symbolize Orthodoxy and/or Russianness (Bennett 2011).

A related issue is the phenomenon of typographic mimicry, sometimes called faux fonts (Sutherland 2015). This is when one language is "dressed up" to look like another. Different typefaces may be used to look like Cyrillic or Devanagari or Mandarin. The words are still English, and can be read by Anglophone speakers, but the appearance is meant to convey something foreign or exotic. Again, this typographic technique can be done by insiders or outsiders, often playing on clichés for marketing purposes. During the Cold War, for instance, books and movies about espionage often used fake Cyrillic to convey something vaguely Soviet. Indian restaurants, yoga studios, and Hindu temples sometimes resort to faux Devanagari in their signage and advertising. (See Figure 7.1.) These typefaces are often derided as at best stereotypical, and at worst racist. But it may be a bit more than just a marketing gimmick. In fact, we might think of it as a rather subtle way of negotiating the push-and-pull between unity and diversity. The words are readable in, say, English, but the script has a translocal symbolic significance, connecting the local group to the wider religious community. Faux fonts can thus be identity markers and makers.

The Hebrew script is one of the things that links Jews around the world. Historically, the charismatic script was used to write a number of regional Jewish vernaculars, including Yiddish and Ladino. More recently, elements of Hebrew writing are applied in more playful, punning, and provocative ways to signal Jewishness. For example, the Hebrew word for life, *Chai*, is now a common symbol, comparable in a way to the Sanskrit OM as a popular religious logo. The fact that American pronunciation of Hebrew makes it a homophone with "hi" or "high" can be exploited in witty ways, as in a "Getting [Chai]" t-shirt or "[Chai] Tech" business card. Indeed, bits and pieces of Hebrew show up on lapel pins, sports jerseys, beer labels, bumper stickers, coffee mugs, and various other tchotchkes – in sum, just about *anywhere*. Sometimes their usage is clever; other times subversive or even salacious, as in fake Hebrew lettering that actually says "Go F@$% Your Self" backward. The laugh or frisson that is achieved is the result of subverting or playing with the sacredness of the Hebrew script. The actual content or informational level is beside the point. All of these bits and pieces of real or faux Hebrew may be viewed as kind of insider code signaled by Jews to other Jews, who can appreciate and understand the gist of these mischievous linguistic manipulations. Faux Hebrew might actually be a community-building device. That is to say, those who have struggled through Hebrew school in preparation for their Bar or Bat Mitzvah get the joke and together experience a fleeting sense of *communitas* (Avni 2015).

Conversational

Sacred languages are used for interventionist practices – prayer, worship, chanting – which entail communicating with supposed superhuman powers. They may also be called upon for discursive practices, such as papal encyclicals and Dharma talks, the purpose of which is to explain the nature of superhuman forces as they relate to human welfare. Over time, this dimension has gradually dwindled for most sacred languages. For example, Sanskrit and Latin were once widely used for a whole range of genres, including lectures and theatrical dramas. They are still used for such things – Sanskrit far more than Latin – but the scope has been drastically reduced since the premodern era.

Pali is the vehicular language of Theravada Buddhism. Monks who speak different mother tongues (Sinhala, Thai, Khmer, Burmese, etc.) have used it as a lingua franca for conversations and letter-writing since at least the fifth century (Crosby 2014, 86–87). In the early part of the twenty-first century, a number of conferences were conducted in Pali in Thailand and Myanmar (Burma), with both monks and "householders" (i.e., lay people) participating. At the 2009 conference, held in honor of the Thai Sangharaja (Supreme Patriarch of the Monastic Order), scholars from six different nations delivered some thirty-four papers in Pali. At the 2014 conference in Myanmar, over one hundred scholars participated as speakers and observers. Twenty-three scholars from nine different countries presented their papers in Pali. Everything, including the opening and closing ceremonial speeches, as well as the keynote address, was delivered in Pali. Thus, the adviser to the conference, the Ven. Prof. Dr. Khammai Dhammasami, claimed it was the first international conference in the contemporary era conducted completely in Pali (Ven. Nyanasamilankara, pers. comm.).

One potential problem is the way that vehicular languages like Arabic or Sanskrit are domesticated by speakers of different mother tongues. For example, Burmese and Thai monks pronounce certain Pali words differently. Such local inflections may slow down, but usually do not completely obstruct, communication. Another tricky aspect of this is that new words are necessary for discussing many aspects of the contemporary world. (We saw this in Chapter 3 with Latin.) How Pali speakers form those neologisms varies and there is no fixed way for devising new words; sometimes a vernacular word simply has to be imported into the conversation (Kate Crosby, pers. comm.). The use of Pali in conferences is a relatively new (and thus far, small-scale) phenomenon. Nevertheless, it is remarkable to think of a language that is thousands of years old and reputedly spoken by Gautama Buddha himself being employed for academic conferences in the age of information.

Unlike Pali, Latin, or Sanskrit, Church Slavonic has never really worked as a spoken clerical language. It is used for liturgies, not lectures. And yet, there are ways that the sacred language does enter into everyday conversation, contributing to a sense of camaraderie among Russian Orthodox devotees. At Easter time, for instance, it is common for believers to exchange the traditional Paschal greeting in Church Slavonic:

Khristos voskrese! (Christ hath risen!)
Voistinu voskrese! (Verily, he hath risen!)

These words (sometimes just the abbreviation *Kh V*) will also be seen on Easter eggs, greeting cards, children's books, and other items sold at church kiosks.

More substantively, some scholars contend that there is a distinctive Ortho-Russian "religiolect" – a kind of Russian dialect that is informed by Orthodox liturgical practices and theological ideas about God, salvation, church, death, holiness, and so on. We saw something similar to this in the case of Yeshivish (Chapter 5). It is a kind of insider code, a Slavonic-influenced jargon or patois. In terms of who use this Slavonicized variety, we might imagine concentric circles. In the innermost circle are Russian Orthodox monks. Because they are the most removed from the world and the most immersed in the liturgy and ecclesiastical teachings, their speech is the most influenced by Church Slavonic. Next come Orthodox priests. They are obviously connected to the church's ceremonial and doctrinal traditions, but they also move about in the broader society. Their language can switch, becoming more or less Slavonicized, depending on the situation and audience. Next would be the circle of the "churched," those who regularly attend liturgical services, read devotional literature, watch ecclesiastical programs on TV. Outside them would be people of varying degrees of "churchness" (Bugaeva 2008, 206).

This Slavonic-infused variety is detectable on different levels:

Lexicon: Speakers may use words according to their Church Slavonic, as opposed to their Russian, meaning; for instance, in Russian *podvig* means a sacrifice or heroic feat, while in Slavonic it has to do more with a personal effort exerted for the sake of salvation.

Word formation: Speakers tend to favor words that have a Slavonic ending, like *zashchítitel'* instead of the standard Russian *zashchitnik*, meaning defender.

Pronunciation: The same word in Church Slavonic and Russian may have a different stress; speakers may intentionally or inadvertently choose the *izbávitel'* instead of the Russian *izbavítel'* (deliverer) (Bustanov and Kemper 2013, 262–263).

When it is written, this Slavonic code also involves many abbreviations. Those "in the know" recognize and understand them: for example, V.P. for *Velikii Post* (the "great fast" before Easter), r.B. for *rab Bozhii* ("servant of God," used as a term of humility: e.g. *r.B. Natasha*), i/m for *ieromonakh* (hieromonk, a level in the clerical hierarchy) (Bugaeva 2008, 140–141). When Orthodox devotees use these abbreviations in emails or other form of writing, it creates a kind of social bond between them.

To recap: sacred languages are also vehicular languages. They have a remarkable ability to foster communal ties through liturgical, visual, and occasionally even conversational means. At the same time, they can become a source of bitter polemics within a faith community.

Divided We Fall

A language ideology is the more or less consistent, consensual set of beliefs, assumptions, and attitudes that places one language (and, by extension, its users) on a scale of values in relation to other languages (and, by extension, their users). To fans, French is elegant; to critics, Indonesian is simplistic. Perpetuated within a speech community by teachers, novelists, policy makers, and other influential voices, language ideologies come to appear natural and self-evident. However, because they are in fact human constructs and not natural occurrences, these beliefs may be challenged. Resistance comes in all shapes and sizes. Practitioners may grumble about meaningless prayers and liturgies, while students may complain about the time and energy (or lack of practicality) involved in learning a sacred language. In *Geek Sublime: The Beauty of Code, the Code of Beauty*, Vikram Chandra reflects:

> Sanskrit – as it was taught in the classroom – smelled to me of hypocrisy, of religious obscurantism, of the khakhi-knickered obsessions of the Hindu far-Right.... As soon as I was offered a choice – a chance to learn another contemporary language to fulfil requirements – I fled from Sanskrit and never looked back. (2014, 186–187)

Except: later in life, he came to appreciate the poetic beauty and algorithmic logicality of the language.

Long-simmering grievances may flare up into what sociolinguists call language ideological debates (Blommaert 1999). These disputes are not just about the language. It is not really syntax or phonology that is being contested. Rather, the language typically becomes a kind of screen onto which broader theological, cultural, and political concerns are projected. The social critic Antonio Gramsci put it this way: "Every time the question of language surfaces, in one way or another, it means that a series of other problems is coming to the fore" (quoted in Suleiman 2013, 5).

As linguistic estrangement grows, the community becomes divided. Sometimes this becomes a contest between one sacred language and another particular language (e.g., Sanskrit vs. Tamil); other times it may be a question of the sacred language vs. vernaculars in general. Debates over sacred language can become particularly fraught affairs, with charges even of heresy, schism, or apostasy made against opponents. These debates have some common denominators in their overall shape, but the specifics must be examined on a case-by-case basis. The questions put to Sanskrit are not the same ones put to Slavonic. (Incidentally, we should not assume that clerics are always supporters of sacred languages and lay people of vernaculars. In fact, some of the staunchest advocates of reform may come from within the clergy, while dedicated enthusiasts of the sacred tongue are often found among the laity.)

Beliefs about languages are also, by extension, beliefs about the people who use (or do not use) them. The language "iconizes" or symbolizes the group, so that statements about the language are applied or extended to its users. This process is called *iconization* (Irvine and Gal 2000). "Those who customarily speak refined or sacred words may themselves be credited with essential qualities of refinement or sacredness" (Keane 1997, 54). A vivid example of iconization appears in Veronica Chater's memoir, *Waiting for the Apocalypse*, the story of a family in suburban San Jose, California, ruled by a conspiracy-addled traditionalist Catholic who becomes increasingly unhinged by the changes wrought by Vatican II. The shift from Latin to the vernacular, in this case English, is of course the most visible aftereffect of the Council. Chater writes:

> A controversy is raging in the form of two languages. It's like a war, but it's not a war. It's a battle of ideas. And those ideas represent the heart and soul of the believer. And even though we treat each other with courtesy outside the church, inside we are engaged in linguistic self-defense: two sides convinced they are right. (2009, 24)

Note the slippage here. There is a subtle shift in focus from the war-like controversy over "languages," to a battle of "ideas," to the representatives of those ideas: us vs. them. The contest is personalized. Early on in the memoir, we get thumbnail sketch of the kind of churchgoers who seem to embody the drastic changes involved:

> Modern people. "Progressives," Dad calls them. Women who don't wear scarves, some of them in slacks or miniskirts, men in everyday clothes, jewelry peeking out from their chest hair. People armed with the new missal, the Novus Ordo missal, circa 1970, boldly printed in English, with no scapular or rosary in their possession. Vatican II people. (Chater 2009, 13)

The brash, informal, inappropriate style of the "Vatican II people" seems to match their reckless use of English in the Mass. This is not just the idiosyncratic perspective of a memoirist. Language ideological debates often involve *ad hominem* rhetoric. In the remainder of this chapter, we will look at the long-running ideological debate about Church Slavonic, and for comparative purposes take a quick lateral glance at the case of Avestan.

Church Slavonic

In a remarkable twist of history, Orthodox Christianity, which for decades was vilified by Communist propaganda, has, since the collapse of the Soviet Union, emerged as a kind of Russian civil religion. "Orthodox narratives, holidays, and moral values have quietly but inexorably replaced the discredited social ideology of Russian Communism" (Burgess 2009, 7). As mentioned earlier, during this religious renewal, Church Slavonic has also been revitalized. The language had never stopped being used and studied during the Soviet era. But now it is being widely taught again in seminaries and Sunday schools. New dictionaries and textbooks have been published, while websites and smartphone applications present fresh ways of approaching the ancient language. One notices a newfound appreciation for the traditions of Slavonic chant and calligraphy. There is even a national holiday – the Day of Slavonic Writing and Culture, held every May 24 – dedicated to Saints Cyril and Methodius, the creators of Church Slavonic, and the profound influence their alphabet (now known as Cyrillic) has had on Russian history and civilization (Bennett 2011).

But this revitalization has also reignited a longstanding language ideological debate about the intelligibility of Church Slavonic for regular churchgoers. Already at the end of the nineteenth century, there were complaints about the opacity of the Slavonic liturgy. The early twentieth century saw considerable discussion of the topic, both in ecclesiastical journals and in the popular press. The church hierarchy initiated a project to make the liturgical service books more intelligible, but it ended up being shelved due to the Revolution of 1917 – and exported with émigrés to America. In the early Soviet era, a Bolshevik-supported movement known as Renovationism advocated replacing Church Slavonic in the liturgy with vernacular Russian, but that venture failed. The debate was rekindled in the 1990s in connection with the efforts of a maverick priest, Fr. Kochetkov, to introduce Russian into the liturgy. His translation project proved to be exceptionally controversial at a time of tremendous social and cultural turbulence and was ultimately quashed by the church hierarchy. Defenders of Church Slavonic sometimes label those favoring reform as "Neo-Renovationists" or "Kochetkovites." Both of these terms are toxic among many Russian Orthodox believers.

Members of the Russian Orthodox Church appear to be divided on the question of Church Slavonic as a liturgical language. According to one survey, 37 percent of adherents favored replacing Slavonic with Russian,

36 percent thought Slavonic should be retained, and 27 percent found it hard to decide (Interfax-Religion 2011). Those who believe that the Church Slavonic liturgy should be "Russified," in whole or in part, emphasize the importance of communication. They tend to make the following arguments:

- Comprehension of the liturgy is essential.
- Slavonic began as a vernacular – that was the very *raison d'être* of the mission of Saints Cyril and Methodius.
- Slavonic is no longer intelligible to ordinary churchgoers, even to many clerics; it is a real impediment to newcomers and converts.
- All languages, including Russian, are legitimate vehicles for worship.
- There are parishes within the global Russian Orthodox Church that use vernaculars (English, French, Japanese, etc.), so Russian *a fortiori* should be permitted.

Emphasizing the value of divine communion, those who believe that the Church Slavonic liturgy should be maintained contend:

- Church Slavonic is a special, sacral language created by Saints Cyril and Methodius under divine inspiration, and further hallowed by a millennium of prayer by both Russian saints and common pious folk.
- Church Slavonic unites Russians with their ancestors and with other Orthodox Slavs; changing it could well result in church schisms.
- The language *is* intelligible to those who regularly attend the liturgy.
- If it is not, then it is up to people to study the sacred language – there are many books and courses for doing so.
- What is needed is more "churching" and catechesis.

Another flare-up in this long-simmering debate occurred in 2011, when the Moscow Patriarchate published a kind of white paper entitled "The Church Slavonic Language in the Life of the Russian Orthodox Church of the 21st Century" (Moscow Patriarchate 2011). The document acknowledges that comprehension of the sacred language is a problem and outlines a program of stylistic simplification, supplemented by educational measures, as a solution.

The document begins by affirming the centrality of the sacred language for the faith, calling it an "inseparable part" of the liturgical tradition of the Russian Orthodox Church. But, since languages constantly evolve, comprehension is now a problem for people. The document summarizes the history of Church Slavonic and previous, unsuccessful, attempts to modify the language to make it more intelligible. It calls for a body of experts to revise those parts of the liturgy that are the most opaque. At the same time, the document says, much can also be done in the realm of education. Noting that most churchgoers learn Church Slavonic in an unsystematic way, through ritual repetition, it calls for more targeted study, including:

- the creation of educational aides in modern media formats – audio and video courses, television programs, etc.
- research efforts leading to the publication of dictionaries and grammar books
- roundtable discussions of the role of Church Slavonic in the life of the Slavic peoples, to be held in conjunction with the May 24 celebrations

In many ways, the document simply rehashes ideas that have been discussed in Russian Church circles for over a century. What was interesting in this case was the fact that the debate was carried out online. Despite its reputation for extreme conservatism, the Russian Orthodox Church in the post-Soviet period has become quite savvy in its use of modern media technologies. Television and radio programs explore the relationship between Orthodox Christianity and Russian history, culture, and society. There are hundreds of Orthodox periodicals and thousands of Orthodox websites (*New York Times*, December 24, 2008).

The text of "The Church Slavonic Language in the Life of the Russian Orthodox Church of the 21st Century" was disseminated not only to parishes throughout Russia but posted on Orthodox websites in order to solicit feedback from ordinary parishioners. It appeared on www.Bogoslov.ru, LiveJournal, a blogging platform that is immensely popular in Russia, and the Russian Patriarchate's own website. It was then reposted on more conservative sites like www.Pravoslavie.ru, where there is staunch support for maintaining Church Slavonic in the liturgy (*Pravoslavie* means Orthodoxy). Many adherents, both lay people and clerics, weighed in on these various websites with an array of opinions, quips, fulminations, counter-proposals, conspiracy theories, and disquisitions on theology, linguistics, or church history. On www.Bogoslov.ru, there were roughly 1800 posts averaging 418 words in length. The debate became personal, with traditionalist defenders identifying Slavonic (and themselves) with the values of faithfulness, reverence, and unity, while stigmatizing their opponents as outsiders and agents of unwanted change, profanation, and division. That is what we mean by iconization.

Critics on conservative websites posted comments like the following:

- For God's sake, there's no need to change anything!
- Tyrants! Leave us our CS [Church Slavonic] language! Hands off the soul of the Orthodox people!
- All Orthodox folk are against changes in CS
- ONLY CHURCH SLAVONIC. DON'T EVEN BRING UP THIS TOPIC!
- IT IS FORBIDDEN TO CHANGE OUR LANGUAGE!!!
- CATEGORICALLY in favor of CS – yea now and henceforth

(Pravoslavie.ru 2011)

Defenders of Church Slavonic supported each other by using elements of the "religiolect" described above. This reinforced their in-group solidarity against the purported outsiders who advocated liturgical modification.

In the end, church authorities backpedaled from the plans sketched in the white paper. It is interesting that, although the ecclesiastical document in no way suggested abandoning Church Slavonic, but rather, recommended stylistic simplification and expanded education, many participants in the debate interpreted it in the direst possible way. In their minds, it became an all-or-nothing, zero-sum proposal. It is noteworthy how often military terminology ("war," "battle") figures into these sacred language debates. That is because, in part, languages are not just languages. They become stand-ins for a whole constellation of historical, aesthetic, theological, and political concerns and anxieties.

Avestan

In the nineteenth century, a number of Parsis (or Parsees) in India began to rethink the nature of their ancient religion, Zoroastrianism. The impetus came from two interlinked sources: British colonialism and Protestant missionary work.

The origins of Zoroastrianism go back to the figure of Zoroaster (Zarathustra). The religion that developed in his name involved (and involves), among other things, a sprawling corpus of sacred texts written in various languages, including Avestan, an ancient tongue akin to Sanskrit; a hereditary priesthood; and a complex system of liturgies and temples. Inspired by Western-style schools and Protestant Christian critiques, Parsis (especially those in the merchant, as opposed to priestly, class) began to promote reform. The goal was to show how "true" Zoroastrianism was compatible with "progress and civilization," just like (or even more so than) Christianity. A kind of rescue effort was launched. Parsi apologists were anxious to show that Zoroastrianism represented an ancient and pure form of monotheism – in fact, the purest and most ancient of them all. In this reformed version of the faith, the Supreme Being was to be accessed primarily through individual reading of scriptures made accessible in vernacular tongues and through an ethical lifestyle that was conducive to productive and loyal citizens of the British Empire. Such a wholesome faith would be compatible with science, proper hygiene, and the other trappings of modern life.

The model of Protestant Christianity is evident in this discourse. Just as Protestant leaders castigated the Catholic version of Christianity, Parsi reformers challenged the preeminence of ritualism and priesthood in the then-dominant form of Indian Zoroastrianism. Rituals were viewed as irrational and inauthentic, and the priestly monopoly contested. The role of Avestan was also implicated in this critique, since "The Zoroastrian priesthood was traditionally hereditary and required the memorization of large quantities of Avestan language liturgies that were often poorly understood" (Ringer 2011, 36).

Parsi critics absorbed the lessons of Protestantism and offered their own appraisal of the ritual-priest-sacred language system. According to Monica Ringer,

> Reformers broke with their orthodox brethren especially over the issue of the Avestan language and its use in prayer. Citing lack of familiarity with Avestan, both by the priesthood and by the laity, reformers refused to recite prayers in Avestan and demanded a translation of canon prayer into the local language of Gujarati as well as English. (2011, 73–74)

According to the Parsi reformers, translation of sacred texts into living languages would enable the true monotheism and ethical message of Zoroaster to shine through, and would cancel out the power of the priesthood and their ritualistic obfuscations.

However, this reformist challenge did not go unopposed. Traditionalists rallied to the defense of the sacerdotal system and the sacred language of Avestan:

> For orthodox Zoroastrians unwilling to dismiss long-standing traditions, reformers' abandonment of Avestan in prayer was tantamount to a renunciation of the religion itself. They believed that Avestan was a holy language and that prayers in Avestan had an effect on the Divine. They defended the priests' mediating role as the guardians of the Avestan language and the performers of rituals that alone could affect the Divine. (Ringer 2011, 74)

Avestan is still part of the linguasphere and continues to be used to this day, although controversy also lingers on. A website dedicated to "Traditional Zoroastrianism" (2016) lists seven tenets of the faith, the first of which is as follows:

> All our Scriptures are sacred, including the Gathas, Yashts, and the Vendidad. We pray all of them in our Fire temples, before the Sacred Fire, and they have immense spiritual power, their very utterance in the sacred Avestan language serving to further righteousness and fight evil.

Many Zoroastrians say their daily prayers almost wholly in Avestan. But some clearly still struggle with the place of the sacred language in the Zoroastrian scale of values. As one Parsi says,

> While I do believe, very much, in the power of prayer, the Almighty Ahura Mazda, still what I personally have always felt [to be a pity] is that the prayers have never been made known to us in layman's language. If you read the Bible it is in a language you can understand. I realize that this may be due to the language in which our prayers were first spoken, the very fact that ours is the oldest revealed religion and all that. (Quoted in Kreyenbroek 2001, 185)

The reference here to the Bible and the valuation of "layman's language" shows the pervasiveness of a Protestant language ideology, one that keeps challenging the status of sacred languages, even in non-Protestant contexts.

***

The San Andreas earthquake fault line, where the Pacific and North American tectonic plates meet, runs right through Fort Ross. When the fault shifted in 1906, San Francisco was leveled. Fort Ross itself was not untouched. The Orthodox chapel collapsed, though the roof and towers remained largely intact. The chapel was rebuilt by 1918 but burned to the ground in 1970. The chapel bell even melted in the fire. The chapel was rebuilt, incorporating pieces of wood salvaged from the original chapel, and the bell was recast with bits of metal from the original bell. It has an inscription in Church Slavonic that reads, "Heavenly King, receive all, who glorify Him" (Fort Ross Conservancy 2016).

Church Slavonic has had a long and eventful history, having been carried across the vast expanse of Siberia and the Pacific Ocean to the New World. It has been adapted to different locales and mixed with different languages, from Russian to Tlingit to English, but has also suffered the equivalent of several social earthquakes. For centuries it has been the holy lingua franca of Russian Orthodox believers dispersed across the planet. Yet fault lines run through it, based on competing interpretations of salvation history and the respective values of communion vs. communication. Occasional tremblers are reminders of this instability.

The axial age saw a general shift in the topography of religion:

> In contrast to older groups focused on a specific temple, city, cult place, or sacred locale, which they served and from which they took their identity, the increasingly international, multiethnic, and geographically disparate population of post-ancient religious communities was held together – often rather loosely – not only by shared symbols, beliefs, and practices, but also by itinerant leaders and mobile texts… (Lincoln 2012, 80)

Sacred languages are vehicular languages for vehicular religions. Spread by missionaries, refugees, diplomats, traders, and colonizers, they link people into transcontinental religious communities. They do this in several different ways: as a liturgical medium shared by people who enter the sanctuary speaking different mother tongues; as a distinctive visual marker and symbol for the religious "brand"; more rarely these days as a spoken lingua franca. Even when poorly understood in terms of content, sanctified languages can contribute to the social rapport that is vital to the functioning of a religious system.

But sacred languages can also be divisive. They have an imperialist track record (Williams 2008). The ideology that exalts a sacred language does so at the expense of other tongues: Church Slavonic over Russian, Sanskrit over Tamil, Avestan over Gujarati. The values associated with this or that language are linked to these or those people. Language debates usually get personalized; opponents may be condemned as heretics or even demonized. If, according to one Orthodox tradition, the Devil loathes Church Slavonic, what does this say about those who wish to remove it from the liturgy (Naumov 2012)?

We have said throughout this book that sacred languages involve beliefs, practices, institutions, and communities. Reviewing these points can help us appreciate why polemics over sacred languages can become so bitter:

- Sacred languages are esteemed for their perceived beauty, purity, solemnity, antiquity; but more than that, they are mythologized as vessels of revelation and instruments of salvation history.
- Sacred languages are employed in liturgical and other practices, the repetition of which reinforces their status; for devotees, they become part of the rhythm of life, an accepted feature in the visual and sonic landscape.
- Sacred languages are supported by institutions like priesthoods, schools, publishing firms, and, in some cases, even the state – they have friends in high places.
- Finally, as we saw in the first part of this chapter, sacred languages can contribute in numerous ways to group solidarity.

To question a sacred language is, in a way, to question this whole fourfold system. When this is done during unsettled times – the turmoil of the 1960s, the traumas of post-Soviet Russia, the intrusion of foreign missionaries in nineteenth-century India – all kinds of extra-linguistic issues can enter the fray. A religion can survive a language ideological earthquake, but visible signs of rupture and offset will remain.

References

Anderson, Benedict. 1991. *Imagined Communities: Reflections on the Origin and Spread of Nationalism.* London and New York: Verso.

Avni, Sharon. 2015. "Hebrew in the North American Linguistic Landscape: Materializing the Sacred." In *Challenges for Language Education and Policy: Making Space for People*, edited by Bernard Spolsky, Ofra Inbar-Lourie, and Michal Tannenbaum. New York and London: Routledge.

Beifuss, Artur, and Francesco Trivini Bellini. 2013. *Branding Terror: The Logotypes and Iconography of Insurgent Groups and Terrorist Organizations.* Foreword by Steven Heller. London and New York: Merrell.

Bennett, Brian P. 2016 (2011). *Religion and Language in Post-Soviet Russia.* Abingdon and New York: Routledge.

Blommaert, Jan, ed. 1999. *Language Ideological Debates.* Berlin and New York: Mouton de Gruyter.

Bugaeva, I. V. 2008. *Iazyk pravoslavnykh veruiushchikh: V kontse XX – nachale XXI veka.* Moscow: RGAU – MSKhA imeni K. A. Timiriazeva.

Burgess, J. P. 2009. "Orthodox Resurgence: Civil Religion in Russia." *Religion in Eastern Europe* 29 (2): 1–14. http://digitalcommons.georgefox.edu/ree/vol29/iss2/1

Bustanov, Alfrid K., and Michael Kemper. 2013. "The Russian Orthodox and Islamic Languages in the Russian Federation." *Slavica TERgestina* 15: 259–277. Accessed July 29, 2016. http://hdl.handle.net/11245/1.436789

Calvet, Louis-Jean. 1981. *Les langues véhiculaires.* Paris: Presses universitaires de France.

Chandra, Vikram. 2014. *Geek Sublime: The Beauty of Code, the Code of Beauty.* Minneapolis, MN: Graywolf Press.

Chater, Veronica. 2009. *Waiting for the Apocalypse: A Memoir of Faith and Family.* New York: W. W. Norton.

Chew, Phyllis Ghim-Lian. 2009. *Emergent Lingua Francas and World Orders: The Politics and Place of English as a World Language.* New York: Routledge.

Crosby, Kate. 2014. *Theravada Buddhism: Continuity, Diversity, and Identity.* Chichester: Wiley Blackwell.

Deschler, Jean-Paul. 2008. *Abkürzungen in kirchenslavischen Texten auf Ikonen, in Handschriften und in liturgischen Büchern mit deutscher Übersetzung.* Basel: Verlag Fluhegg.

Fort Ross Conservancy. 2016. "Fort Ross Chapel." Accessed July 20, 2016. http://www.fortross.org/chapel.htm

Gasparov, Boris. 2004. "Identity in Language?" In *National Identity in Russian Culture: An Introduction*, edited by Simon Franklin and Emma Widdis, 132–148. Cambridge and New York: Cambridge University Press.

Interfax-Religion. 2011. "Bolee treti rossiian – za izmenenie iazyka pravoslavnogo bogosluzheniia." Accessed February 11, 2014. http://www.interfax-religion.ru/?act=news&div=42341

Irvine, Judith T., and Susan Gal. 2000. "Language Ideology and Linguistic Differentiation." In *Regimes of Language: Ideologies, Polities, and Identities*, edited by Paul V. Kroskrity, 35–84. Santa Fe: School of American Research Press.

Ivanov, Vyacheslav. 1997. *The Russian Orthodox Church of Alaska and the Aleutian Islands and its Relation to Native American Traditions: An Attempt at a Multicultural Society, 1794–1912.* Washington, DC: Library of Congress.

Keane, Webb. 1997. "Religious Language." *Annual Review of Anthropology* 26: 47–71. DOI: 10.1146/annurev.anthro.26.1.47

Kreyenbroek, Philip G., ed., in collaboration with Shehnaz Neville Munshi 2001. *Living Zoroastrianism: Urban Parsis Speak About Their Religion*. Richmond: Curzon.

Krindatch, Alexei. 2011. "Usage of English Language, Ethnic Identity and Ethnic Culture in American Orthodox Christian Churches." Accessed July 30, 2016. http://hirr.hartsem.edu/research/UsageOfEnglishLanguageEthnicIdentity.pdf

Kuraev, Andrei. 2005. *Otvety molodym*. Saratov: Izdatel'stvo Saratovskoi eparkhii.

Lincoln, Bruce. 2012. *Gods and Demons, Priests and Scholars: Critical Explorations in the History of Religions*. Chicago and London: University of Chicago Press.

MacRobert, C. M. 2005. "Church Slavonic." In *The Encyclopedia of Language and Linguistics*, edited by E. K. Brown et al. Second edition. Amsterdam and Oxford: Elsevier.

Moscow Patriarchate. 2011. "Proekt dokumenta Tserkovnoslavianskii iazyk v zhizni Russkoi Pravoslavnoi Tserkvi XXI veka." Accessed January 16, 2013. http://www.patriarchia.ru/db/text/1542499.html

Moscow Patriarchate. 2016. "Zarubezhnye uchrezhdeniia Moskovskogo Patriarkhata." Accessed August 7, 2016. http://karta.patriarchia.ru/

Naumov, S. A. 2012. "Tserkovnoslavianskii iazyk. Lektsiia pervaia." YouTube video. Accessed July 30, 2016. https://www.youtube.com/watch?v=3qPgbTn-1dc

Ostler, Nicholas. 2010. *The Last Lingua Franca: English Until the Return of Babel*. New York: Walker.

Ostler, Nicholas. 2016. *Passwords to Paradise: How Languages Have Re-Invented World Religions*. New York: Bloomsbury Press.

Pravoslavie.ru. 2011. "Tserkovnoslavianskii iazyk v zhizni Russkoi Pravoslavnoi Tserkvi. Diskussiia." Accessed January 8, 2013. http://www.pravoslavie.ru/polemika/48636.htm

Preston, Nora Stene. 1998. "Multiple Choice? Language-Usage and the Transmission of Religious Tradition in the Coptic Orthodox Community in London." *British Journal of Religious Education* 20 (2): 90–101. DOI: 10.1080/0141620980200204

Ringer, Monica M. 2011. *Pious Citizens: Reforming Zoroastrianism in India and Iran*. Syracuse, NY: Syracuse University Press.

Sebba, Mark. 2015. "Iconicity, Attribution and Branding in Orthography." *Written Language and Literacy* 18 (2): 208–227. DOI: 10.1075/wll.18.2.02seb

Stokoe, Mark, and Very Rev. Leonid Kishkovsky. 1995. *Orthodox Christians in North America 1794–1994*. [Syosset, NY]: Orthodox Christian Publications Center. https://oca.org/history-archives/orthodox-christians-na

Suleiman, Yasir. 2013. *Arabic in the Fray: Language Ideology and Cultural Politics*. Edinburgh: Edinburgh University Press.

Sutherland, Paul. 2015. "Writing System Mimicry in the Linguistic Landscape." SOAS Working Papers in Linguistics 17: 147–167. Accessed February 2, 2016. https://www.soas.ac.uk/linguistics/research/workingpapers/volume-17/file105419.pdf

Swidler, Ann. 2001. *Talk of Love: How Culture Matters*. Chicago and London: University of Chicago Press.

Traditional Zoroastrianism. 2016. "Tenets of the Religion." Accessed December 22, 2015. http://tenets.zoroastrianism.com/index.html

Williams, Alan. 2008. "The Continuum of 'Sacred Language' From High to Low Speech in the Middle Iranian (Pahlavi) Zoroastrian Tradition." In *Religion, Language, and Power*, edited by Nile Green and Mary Searle-Chatterjee, 123–142. New York and London: Routledge.

World Council of Churches. 2016. "Russian Orthodox Church (Moscow Patriarchate)." Accessed July 30, 2016. https://www.oikoumene.org/en/member-churches/russian-orthodox-church

Zadeh, Travis. 2012. *The Vernacular Qur'an: Translation and the Rise of Persian Exegesis*. Oxford: Oxford University Press; London: The Institute of Ismaili Studies.

Znamenski, Andrei A. 1999. *Shamanism and Christianity: Native Encounters with Russian Orthodox Missions in Siberia and Alaska, 1820–1917*. Westport, CT: Greenwood Press.

Further Reading

Bennett, Brian P. 2016 (2011). *Religion and Language in Post-Soviet Russia*. Abingdon and New York: Routledge. Describes the significance of Church Slavonic after Communism and explains (among other things) how the sacred language both defines and divides Russian Orthodoxy.

Blommaert, Jan, ed. 1999. *Language Ideological Debates*. Berlin and New York: Mouton de Gruyter. An important theoretical and comparative work on the topic.

Gasparov, Boris. 2004. "Identity in Language?" In *National Identity in Russian Culture: An Introduction*, edited by Simon Franklin and Emma Widdis, 132–148. Cambridge and New York: Cambridge University Press. A nuanced explanation of the relationship between Church Slavonic and Russian.

Ostler, Nicholas. 2010. *The Last Lingua Franca: English Until the Return of Babel*. New York: Walker. Informed by a remarkable mastery of linguistic and historical data, provides a panoramic view of the trajectories of different lingua francas around the world.

Chapter 8

Borderlines: Sacred Languages, Fundamentalism, and Globalization

The chanting of Sanskrit is not what one would normally expect to hear emanating from a Christian place of worship in a well-heeled section of London. The Temple Church in London is a medieval structure built by the legendary Knights Templar and situated within an enclave of stately buildings in the heart of London, not far from the Thames, St. Paul's, and Big Ben. But on the morning of June 28, 2003, attendees emerged from the sanctuary into the morning light after an eight-hour musical vigil that culminated in a colossal finale complete with resounding brass and timpani and a mantra-like chant in Sanskrit.

The event was a performance of *The Veil of the Temple*, composed by Sir John Tavener (1944–2013), a dashing figure who first came to public attention in Britain in the 1960s and was actually signed to the Beatles' Apple record company for a short while. In 1977 he converted to Orthodox Christianity and shifted to pieces based on religious texts and themes. The performance of his *Song for Athene* during the funeral of Princess Diana in 1997 catapulted Tavener to worldwide fame. His religiosity later veered in a universalist direction, embracing the essential unity of the major world religions. The 800-page score for *The Veil of the Temple* is supposed to represent a mystical journey of individual enlightenment and collective redemption. Blending elements of Christianity, the legend of the Knights Templar, and religious universalism, the piece is intended "for those of any faith or of none" (*The Veil of the Temple* 2004).

Sacred Languages of the World: An Introduction, First Edition. Brian P. Bennett.

The Veil of the Temple is comprised of eight cycles of prayers, hymns, acclamations, and canonical texts sung in English, Greek, Aramaic, Church Slavonic, and Sanskrit. There are long recitations from the Gospel of John, the letter of Paul to the Romans, and the Beatitudes of St. Isaac the Syrian. The Jesus Prayer ("Lord Jesus Christ, Son of God, have mercy on me, a sinner"), a classic of Orthodox spirituality, provides a choral refrain. (See Figure 1.1.) The cycles rise in pitch and intensity. "The *Veil*'s listeners are taken from darkness to light, from death to rebirth. Cycle VIII represents the eighth day of the week, and so the first day of the new creation. In the rising light of dawn, the tomb of Christ becomes the Easter Garden" (*The Veil of the Temple* 2004). The climax centers on the veil of the Temple, which, according to the Gospel, was torn asunder at Christ's death. That moment of salvation is recounted, but also layered with a metaphysical interpretation: all illusions have been destroyed and we now see the divine oneness behind the world's multiplicity. In the preface to the score, Tavener wrote:

> Although The Veil of the Temple is mainly Christian, it attempts to remove the veils that hide the same basic truth of all authentic religions. It begins for instance in the words of the Sufis, and ends in the Hindu world, with the Upanishad Hymn. The 'Logos', that mysterious substance inside the Godhead, reveals itself in many forms, whether it be Christ, Krishna, or 'the word made book' in the form of the Koran. (2002)

It is at this point, at the long-awaited denouement, that the libretto switches from Greek, Aramaic, and Church Slavonic, some of the traditional languages of Christianity, to Sanskrit, the sacred language of Hinduism. The basses repeat a famous phrase from the Chandogya Upanishad: *Tat tvam asi*, "that you are," which is usually interpreted to mean that the individual soul (*atman*) is divine and of a piece with the ultimate godhead (*Brahman*).

Then the chorus chants in Sanskrit:

> Púrnam adah, púrnam idam, púrnat púrnam udacyate, purnasya púrnam ádáya púrnam evavashishiate. Aum.
> Shántih, shántih, shántih.
>
> [That is full, this is full (or "abundant" or "infinite"). The full proceeds from the full. Taking the full from the full, the full remains. Aum.
> Peace, peace, peace]

Meanwhile, the sopranos, altos, and tenors sing a line in English from the prophet Isaiah: "Shine, shine, O new Jerusalem, for the glory of the Lord hath arisen upon thee." Thus ends the monumental musical and metaphysical opus (*The Veil of the Temple* 2004).

The Veil of the Temple is hard to classify. It is liturgical in complexion but is not a liturgy in the strict sense of the word. It was intended for a sacred space, the Temple Church, but has also been performed at the Hamburger Bahnhof in Berlin, a former train station and now museum of modern art. It seems to hover between the classical and the ecclesiastical, ritual and theater, East and West. Canonical texts in Church Slavonic and Sanskrit are combined, something that does not happen in "real" liturgies, whether Christian or Hindu. *The Veil of the Temple* is, in short, a borderline phenomenon – something in-between and ambiguous. Sanskrit, a language associated for many in the West with yoga, chanting, being "spiritual but not religious," is a key symbolic ingredient in Tavener's musical metaphysics. It is noteworthy that in this piece he retains the actual Sanskrit, and does not use an English translation, the way that Gustav Holst, another famous British composer, did in his *Vedic Hymns* written a century earlier (Ghuman 2014). In fact, Tavener had the Temple Church singers coached by a Hindu priest.

***

The linguasphere, the mantle of languages that encircles the earth, is being compressed and corkscrewed by the forces of globalization. Travel, trade, and technology have increased connections across the globe. Missionaries, NGO workers, athletes, bankers, refugees – all are on the move. Images, text messages, corporate logos, musical genres, clothing styles, not to mention pathogens, drugs, and weapons, circulate with unprecedented speed. Of course, the world has gone through various phases of globalization before, for example, with the emergence of the so-called world religions and then during the modern era of European colonialism, both of which profoundly reshaped the linguasphere. Yet the current phase of globalization seems to involve an extraordinary intensification of planetary connections, aided by the transformative impact of the Internet (Dalby refers to this as the neolinguasphere). Moreover, there is a growing consciousness regarding the phenomenon of globalization, an awareness of the wider world and its different cultures, political systems, and religious traditions. What we may call "globality" has its own symbol: "the big blue marble" that is "the inevitable backdrop to television news as the logo for international conferences, sports events, and commercial enterprises" (Chew 2009, 61).

As for the religious landscape, some suggest we are seeing not only the transformation of global religions (plural) but the emergence of a global religious consciousness (singular). However, the picture is complicated and by no means uniform around the world. In addition to globalization, which engenders different results and reactions, we can also observe, in some places, trends in secularization (for example, the decline in church attendance in mainstream denominations like the Church of England), commercialization (the marketing of yoga, Kabbalah, and New Age spiritualities), and democratization (the growth of do-it-yourself online religion) (Turner 2011). This is the era of postmodernity, what Gellner dubbed the "Californian" stage of world history where "anything goes."

Sacred languages are being pushed and pulled in opposite directions during the postmodern moment in history. For one thing, they can slip out of their traditional religious environments and become free-floating symbolic resources appropriated by people, who are not necessarily believers, for various projects – projects that elude straightforward classification, being amalgams of religion and commerce, art and spirituality. Unlike the way they are presented in the table in Chapter 1, sacred languages have never been completely locked into one-to-one correlations. Many Christians revere Hebrew, while Ethiopian Jews have long used Ge'ez. Sanskrit enjoys prestige in Buddhist and even some Muslim nations like Indonesia. But in an era of quickening globalization, the more or less stable lines of correlation seem to become zigzags.

It is especially during this postmodern era that sacred languages can hop from *there* (mosques, temples, churches) to just about *anywhere* (tattoo studios, museums, concert halls, type foundries). Removed from their primary context, they may end up cohabitating in ways that are contrary to orthodox tradition. We see this, for example, in the novel combination of Aramaic, Greek, Church Slavonic, and Sanskrit in *The Veil of the Temple.* A less rarefied example can be found in (or on) Tavener's fellow Englishman, David Beckham. This footballer and global celebrity is famous, among other things, for his numerous tattoos, all of which engender considerable speculation and interpretation in print and online. What is noteworthy for our purposes is the blithe mixture of distinct sacred scripts. On Beckham's left arm is the name of his wife, Victoria, written in Devanagari – though it mistakenly came out as "Vihctoria." He also has several tattoos in Latin: *Ut Amem Et Foveam* ("So That I Love and Cherish") and *Perfectio in Spiritu*, or "Spiritual Perfection." Two Hebrew quotations come from the Bible: "I am my beloved's and my beloved is mine" (Song of Songs) and "My son, do not forget my teaching but keep my commands in your heart" (Proverbs). These combine with Christian symbols (cross, angel, Jesus) and sayings ("Pray for me"), a Chinese maxim ("Death and life have pre-determined appointments; riches and honor are from heaven"), as well as the names of his wife and children (*The Daily Mail*, August 4, 2015).

A trivial example, perhaps – and yet one senses that Beckham's much-photographed body is perhaps emblematic of the Californian stage of history, with its global awareness, the weakening of traditional religious boundaries, the commercialization of spirituality, and the dominance of imagery and celebrities around the world.

This mixture of different sacred scripts may also find more sophisticated institutional expression. The Contemporary Museum of Calligraphy in Moscow is located in the expansive Sokolniki Park, amidst bike paths, zip lines, and cafés – an oasis of recreation in the midst of a busy megalopolis. The museum houses samples of Russian and Church Slavonic calligraphy, as well as Arabic, Tibetan, Hebrew, Japanese, Chinese, Armenian, and Georgian exemplars. These languages and scripts would normally never be found under the same roof of sacred space (*there*). The very existence of such a museum reflects the processes of secularization (removing items from their natural – sacred – habitat and placing them under glass for observation), globalization (bringing together artifacts from across the planet), and commercialization (charging for admission, among other things). Yet, a kind of alternative sacred space is created. According to its website, "In the museum you find yourself in a wondrous world consisting of beautiful symbols, perfect lines and absolute harmony. Every variety of calligraphy creates its own specific mood." In addition to its permanent holdings and rotating exhibitions, the museum offers calligraphy classes for different ages and skill levels, which is endorsed as a kind of spiritual therapy:

> Mastering the art of calligraphy will not only help you develop the skill of writing beautiful letters and words; you will discover a new way of relaxing, submerging into your private world and managing the stresses of the everyday world. (Contemporary Museum of Calligraphy 2016)

The museum combines art and spirituality in a tolerant, multicultural milieu. But this raises a key question: If a sacred language or script is taken out of its "natural habitat," is it still sacred?

The well-known scholar of comparative religion, Jonathan Z. Smith, has argued that sacrality (or sacredness) is not an inherent quality, but a situational one. Things are made sacred (sacralized, sacrated) by their location – their "emplacement," as he terms it. Songs and texts are sacred when performed in a temple or other similar venue; outside that, they are not (Smith 1987, 104). A good example is the pipe organ, which seems to epitomize piety when played in a church service, but means something quite different in a baseball stadium. Yet it is not quite that simple, for sacrality does not simply toggle on or off like that. Carried out of sanctuaries into museums and concert halls, sacred things (including languages) do not simply lose their perceived holiness. The sacredness lingers on, in a vestigial fashion, at least for a while. Thus, even when a sacred language or script is used in a blatantly meretricious way (as in some of the jokey Hebrew objects described in the previous chapter), the jolt is predicated on the sacred "charge" or "charisma" of the alphabet. Just because it is placed in a lavatory does not mean that one cavalierly would use a golden toilet without giving it a second thought. A residual prestige seems to cling to the object or language wherever it goes. It will be interesting to track the long-term effects on sacred languages of their displacement from sacred locations.

During this postmodern period in history, consecrated languages like Latin and Hebrew may now be found in strange new combinations in unexpected places. At the same time, people use sacred languages for putting limits to change and innovation. We see this especially with various forms of religious fundamentalism. This term, which is almost impossible to avoid, has been stretched to fit many disparate situations and as a consequence has lost some of its analytical usefulness. The sociologist Stephen Sharot prefers the term *neotraditionalism*. As he sees it, neotraditionalist movements

> self-consciously attempt to represent or reassert what they regard as their authentic religious tradition against what they perceive as threats in modern developments. A past society is believed to have embodied the authentic tradition, and this provides a model to be reconstituted or emulated. (2011, 203)

Sacred languages are traditional languages insofar as they have been used for centuries and passed on from one generation to the next. Neotraditionalism is different because it involves a dose of extra intentionality – of purposely striving, in the wake of some disruption or challenge, to recapture a glorious past, even though this often entails the use of modern technologies. It is noteworthy how often a sacred language comes to symbolize this vanished golden age. We see different kinds of neotraditionalism at work in those Catholic organizations that celebrate the Tridentine Latin Mass and long for the world of pre-Vatican II Catholicism. We likewise see it in Muslim groups that favor an elaborate Arabic style in their sermons and websites as an emblem of the golden age of Muhammad. A similar dynamic, though with more of a nationalist tincture, is observable in those organizations which contend that Sanskrit is, was, and shall be the essence of Indian civilization. This is not to say, of course, that every individual or group that favors a sacred language shuns modern developments and wants to turn back the clock. We should envision an ideological gradation from conservatives to neotraditionalists to extremists. Here we are simply registering the fact that sacred languages often figure prominently in neotraditionalist rhetoric, as opposed to millenarian or messianic discourses, which look forward, not backward, for a resolution of contemporary troubles.

Sanskrit is a good case study because it is a language that knows a thing or two about both erecting and erasing borders. In what follows, we will look at two different phenomena. One consists of nationalistic discourses and practices which promote Sanskrit as the most spiritual – yet also, the most scientific – language on Earth. This plays into the narrative of India's superiority over against the materialistic, superficial West. The other trend involves artistic efforts that deploy Sanskrit to symbolize a tolerant interfaith religiosity. Both nationalistic revivalism and artistic experimentation are predicated, not so much on any specific linguistic content, but on the *idea* of Sanskrit.

The World of Sanskrit

Sanskrit is an Indo-European language closely related to Pali and more distantly to Latin and Church Slavonic. Like other sacred languages, Sanskrit (a label encompassing Vedic, Classical, and other sub-varieties) has been both a medium for the expression of Hindu beliefs and an object of Hindu theorizing and veneration. For centuries Hindu philosophy, mythology, poetry, theater, grammar, logic, mathematics, medicine, aesthetics, and architecture have been expressed by means of Sanskrit, either in the form of full-fledged works or as key terms embedded in vernacular texts. The name "Sanskrit" means something like cultured, refined, sophisticated, or perfected, in contradistinction to supposedly uncouth vernaculars. Some enthusiasts declare Sanskrit the most nuanced and sophisticated language in the world, its exquisitely logical structures being the ideal code for today's technological needs. Of course, what distinguishes sacred languages from ordinary ones is not the fact that they are beautiful or logical, euphonious in sound or capacious in vocabulary, but rather that they are elevated to the superhuman level and connected to divine disclosure and salvation history, however those are understood within the particular religious tradition. Indeed, Sanskrit has been lacquered by a thick coat of myth and mysticism (Poggi 2012). In Hindu discourse it has often been called the language of the gods. It is said to exist, in monocoque fashion, with the substance of divine revelation, the Vedas. The two are one. From this perspective, Sanskrit words are hierophanic, manifesting the divine sounds of the cosmos and, as such, are untranslatable. As a consequence, Sanskrit mantras and formulae must be recited absolutely correctly if they are going to do their job. This is not to say, for example, that priests always understand what they are reciting. In fact, "A priest may be able to recite a text flawlessly without comprehending the meaning of that text" (Deshpande 1996, 404). Similar in this respect to the Pali *paritta* chants discussed in Chapter 4, intelligibility is less of an issue because the sounds of Sanskrit are said to possess intrinsic holiness and potency. The meticulous transmission of the language from one generation to the next is considered vital to preserving this sacred power intact.

Sanskrit is still widely used in Hindu interventionist practices from yoga to *puja* (worship). In general, the sacred language is mythologized more for its sonic than its graphic power. In fact, it has been said that Hinduism is not really a book religion in the mold of Islam or even Christianity. From ancient Vedic mantras to the latest Bollywood ditties, oral performance is paramount. Beloved texts like the *Ramayana* and Bhagavad Gita are critical to the lifeworld of many Hindus, to be sure, but they come into their own when sounded out, chanted, staged, performed, filmed. Sacred sound pervades the Indian tradition, and is a common thread running through Hindu hymns, rituals, mythologies, and artistic forms. Hinduism is characterized by an "acoustic piety" (Wilke and Moebus 2011, 12).

Sanskrit continues to be used for reading, writing, speaking, and other discursive practices. Imagine if the tradition of Classical Latin (the language of Vergil and Sir Isaac Newton) had been maintained alongside of, sometimes crisscrossing with, Ecclesiastical Latin (the language of Aquinas and papal encyclicals) – that is roughly the situation with Sanskrit. Poetry, short stories, plays, and works of philosophy are still composed in the language. A classical tongue, it has adapted to new themes, for example, the life of Russian revolutionary Vladimir Lenin (*Lenināmṛtam*) (Tripathi 1995, 183–184). In fact, there are still daily radio broadcasts in Sanskrit, requiring new words to describe new realities (Poggi 2012, 42). Interestingly, quite a few terms have actually entered Sanskrit from English, though usually mediated by a modern Indian tongue like Hindi. For example, "camera" becomes *kaimaram*, though Sanskrit purists might prefer *chāyā-citra-yantram* (literally, "shadow-picture-machine") (Hock 1992, 166). More broadly, Sanskrit is used as a font for the creation of new words in modern Asian languages:

> Just as terms for technological innovations are created from Latin and Greek for Western languages (*television* = Greek *tele-* far, Latin – *vision* 'seeing'), Sanskrit is the source of designative cultural and technical innovations in SA [South Asia] and beyond. Consider, for example, the terms for prime minister (*pradhaan mantrii* = *pradhaan* 'head, principal' + *mantrii* 'minister') [and] president (*raashTrapati* = *raashTra* 'country' + *pati* 'husband')... (Bhatia and Ritchie 2013, 851–852)

Sanskrit also comes into play in the rhetorical technique of aureation, providing linguistic gilding for ceremonies or solemn situations:

> Because of its prominent religious and spiritual character, Sanskrit is always held with esteem and its use is regarded as adding dignity and solemnity to an occasion by those who respect the cultural heritage of the country … It is being used as a mark of high taste in different communications from marriage invitations to obituary notes. Use of Sanskrit verses as mottos, as headings on different magazines to reflect their ideologies, at the entrance of public institutes and offices such as theatres and even banks, shows a growing popularity of Sanskrit. (Bhate 1996, 398, 397)

From about a thousand years, from roughly 300 to 1300 CE, there emerged what the scholar Sheldon Pollock has called the "Sanskrit cosmopolis" (2006). This is when Sanskrit moved from being a sacred language used by clerics in sacred precincts for interventionist purposes (liturgical, thaumaturgical, somatological) to become, additionally, a political and artistic idiom diffused throughout South and Southeast Asia.

Sanskrit was then a language not only of priests but of poets (like the great epic *Ramayana*) and politicians (there are plentiful Sanskrit inscriptions hailing royal achievements throughout this civilizational zone). As a vehicular language, Sanskrit was a precious linguistic resource that was adopted by different cultures, mixing with – but not eliminating – local vernaculars. From India to Cambodia to Java, Sanskrit helped knit together various languages, cultures, and peoples into a broad hemispheric community. But this diffusion was not like that of other well-known vehicular sacred languages, such as Latin or Arabic. As Pollock explains:

> No organized political power such as the Roman imperium, or coherent, scripture-based religious idea-system such as Islam, was at work here. Sanskrit's spread was effected by traditional intellectuals and religious professionals, often following in the train of scattered groups of traders and adventurers, and carrying with them disparate and decidedly uncanonized texts of a wide variety of competing religious orders. (Pollock 2006, 198)

There is another key difference. Both Christendom and the Islamic *ummah* (the worldwide community of Muslims) were united by a single script. The Latin alphabet, of course, predated Christianity, but it soon became part and parcel of the missionary faith. (It has since lost most of its religious resonance, now being associated in the minds of many people with modernity and the West.) In Chapter 2 we saw how the spread of Islam entailed the expansion of the Arabic scriptworld. However, for most of its history, Sanskrit was not identified with any one script, but was encoded in different regional writing systems, including Sinhala, Thai, Khmer, and Javanese. This flexibility contributed to the accommodation between the one and the many, the center and the periphery, the H and L language varieties in the Sanskrit cosmopolis. Devanagari has since become the sacred "logo" of Hinduism and India, but this is a comparatively recent development (Pollock 2006, 273–274).

Sanskrit still has a golden reputation in some of the areas of its former expansion. Even though Indonesia boasts the largest Muslim populace in the world, and Arabic has left a decisive imprint on the Indonesian language, Sanskrit continues to have considerable symbolic cachet there. It "has a magical quality for many people, who see it as reinforcing the power and legitimacy of the state, being controlled as it is by powerful people with esoteric knowledge." Thus, *perwira* means officer (from Sanskrit *pravīra* 'hero') and *purnawirawan* means veteran (from Sanskrit *purna* 'complete' and *vīryavān* 'warrior'). Awards for public service tend to have grandiloquent Sanskritic titles, like *Mahaputra Adipradana* (from *mahaputra* 'great son', *adi* 'superior', and *pradana* 'first'). The name of a proposed aircraft was *Gatotkaca*, taken from the Hindu epic *Mahabharata*. Beyond the military and political domains, Sanskritic words have a commercial appeal, for example, *Hotel Kartika Candra* (meaning 'Star Moon Hotel') or *Surya Jaya* ('Victorious Sun') for a bicycle shop (Sneddon 2003, 167–172).

Even further afield, Sanskrit continues to be promoted by various Hindu-based outreach movements, including Transcendental Meditation and the Chinmaya Mission. The remarkable popularity of yoga in the West has further disseminated the "language of the gods."

Back "home" in India, many associate Sanskrit with priestly borderlines. As one author puts it:

> Sanskrit has principally been associated with Brahmins through most of the known periods of Indian history. Brahmins have always been a minority in society – and not a minority espousing a philosophy of equality, or seeking unity, with others at that. (Aklujkar 1996, 60)

A preliminary ethnographic study indicates that Sanskrit is being used in fresh ways by Hindu women in the domestic sphere (Patton 2007). That would be a remarkable and unpredicted transformation of the sacred language's position in Indian society. Our focus, however, will be on the phenomenon of neotraditionalism, which identifies Sanskrit with Hinduism and India in the strongest possible way. According to one critic: "Hindu nationalism has attempted a sweeping appropriation of both the Sanskrit language and Sanskrit literature in seeking to create an Indian nation gathered around the idea of *Hindutva* or Hindu-ness" (Sawhney 2009, 14). It is interesting, and perhaps ironic, that an elite sacerdotal language has been used by some nationalist groups to rally the masses.

The ideology of the Hindu right suggests that Sanskrit is part of India's ancient and dazzling civilization, one however that has been undermined by external invaders: first Muslims, then Europeans (Nussbaum 2007, 213). Hindu neotraditionalists often speak as if they are engaged in a new kind of war, an intellectual battle to wrest control of Sanskrit from American academics who denigrate the language as political, oppressive, and dead, when in fact it is sacred, liberating, and alive (Malhotra 2016). India's return to glory is dependent on a recognition of the manifold glories of Sanskrit: "It will not be an exaggeration to say that if India has to rise, Sanskrit will have to rise once again" (Sampad and Vijay 2002, 134). Yet this is not the first time that such claims have been made about the "language of the gods."

The first decades of the twentieth century saw renewed interest in Sanskrit, coinciding with the rising tide of Indian nationalism over against British rule. The period saw a profusion of publications and conferences dedicated to the sacred language, as well as the creation of Sanskrit-based schools and research institutes (Bhate 1996, 389–390). After that, however, there was a period of stagnation, as more pragmatic and utilitarian interests intensified in the period of Independence (1947).

After 1947 politicians debated the place of language in the new independent nation. One argument put forth in favor of Sanskrit was that it was equally fair – or unfair – for all. Some Sanskrit supporters held up Hebrew as a model to emulate, observing how the ancient scriptural language of Judaism had recently been converted into the secular language of the State of Israel.

In 1956 a commission was formed to explore the question of language, nation, and education. Members were well-respected scholars who toured the country, conducting interviews, visiting schools, attending performances. Concerned with the dangerous fissiparous tendencies in Indian society at that time, they urged recourse to the sacred language for its connective qualities. Emphasizing Sanskrit's vehicularity, they contended it was the "Supreme Unifier" and the "Great Unifying Force" – the ideal lingua franca and the only viable "all-India" language. Moreover, the Commission said, it was Sanskrit that linked India to the wider world, to Tibet, Thailand, Burma, China, Cambodia, and beyond. This was the "empire" of Sanskrit, but – unlike the recently exited British Empire – this was an empire of peace, love, and the quest for truth and salvation.

The Commission claimed that, unlike Latin in Europe, Sanskrit had once been spoken throughout India. It was thus conceivable to make a return to that state of affairs. For that to happen, though, Sanskrit had to lose some of its ideological trappings. Hierarchy had to give way to democracy, elitism to popularism. Instead of being the liturgical language of the Brahmin priesthood, "Sanskrit should be on the lips of every Indian, regardless of caste, class, religion, gender, occupation or age" (Ramaswamy 1999, 350).

Such proposals received mixed feedback. Some countered that Sanskrit was not capable of serving the needs of a modern nation, being ill equipped to handle matters of science and technology. The Commission maintained that Sanskrit was not inimical to progress – as a matter of fact, it is the most scientific language in the world and very much connected to Indian contributions to mathematics and physics. (We hear echoes of this today with the claims that Sanskrit, though of inestimable antiquity, is actually the language most perfectly suited to computer programming and artificial intelligence.) Meanwhile, conservatives at the time of the Sanskrit Commission worried that moving in a populist direction would actually reduce the sacredness of the language. In the end, Sanskrit was not chosen as the official language of India, though this does not mean that it has not received governmental support.

Hindu nationalists tend to be strong and vocal supporters of Sanskrit (Deshpande 2011, 226). At times their rhetoric sounds like the findings of the Sanskrit Commission. According to one proponent, Sanskrit is "the source of our identity, a language that unites us, a language that links us with our past, a language that is the repository of our sacred texts, a language in which so much knowledge and learning from the past is stored" (Paranjape 2009, 93). As such, it should be given explicit recognition as the national tongue of India. Sanskrit can contribute to India's self-enhancement and its "soft power." It is a vital part of Indian history and culture, "the indispensable bedrock that constitutes the national heritage of India." It reflects "the deeper self of India" (Paranjape 2009, 109).

Samskrita Bharati ("Sanskrit Cultivation") is a group that works to revive Sanskrit as an everyday spoken language. According to their mission statement:

> Samskrita Bharati is an organisation committed to the exposition of the richness and beauty of the Samskrit language and its relevance to the modern world. Spearheaded by a team of spirited volunteers, Samskrita Bharati conducts various programmes aimed at enabling people from all sections of society to discover the joy of speaking Samskrit, providing a glimpse into the scientific heritage and spiritual wisdom embodied in Samskrit literature and highlighting the need to preserve its knowledge for posterity. (Samskrita Bharati 2016)

The group, whose US headquarters are located in Silicon Valley, sponsors various publications and programs, including immersive conversation camps and correspondence courses. Their online store sells a range of audiovisual materials and books, including a Sanskrit work on the history of Eliezer Ben-Yehuda and the revival of Hebrew (*Bhuvamānītā Bhagavadbhāṣā*). A camp may consist of a dozen people meeting in someone's house for a three-day program. The group claims that Sanskrit united all Indians in the past, regardless of their religious, linguistic, caste or ethnic identities. It was a golden age when Sanskrit prevailed and India flourished. The group would like to see Sanskrit return to glory. This entails reorienting Sanskrit away from being some kind of esoteric ritual language, and leveling it out, so to speak. One of the ways they hope to do this is through something called "simple Sanskrit." Rather like BASIC (British-American-Scientific-International-Commercial English), an instrumental form of English based on a grand total of just 850 lexical units which was promoted in the early twentieth century, the "simplified Sanskrit" project strives to pare down the number of forms to be learned for any given word (Hastings 2003, 511), "so that a speaker of this modern Sanskrit can talk about trains, plains, universities, politics, and computers" (Deshpande 2011, 226). Words are chosen that are very close to regional languages like Hindi, thus reinforcing the sense that Sanskrit is the true "mother tongue" of all Indians.

A related project is the encouragement of Sanskrit households, the idea being that the movement will progress from house to house, and spread from village to village, town to town, with the end result being "a nation of Sanskrit speakers." According to the 2001 Indian census (the most recent published), some 14,000 people self-identified as Sanskrit speakers. It is hard to know what to make of this datum. Imagine if a survey of Europe turned up thousands of people claiming to be native Latin speakers. It seems that such declarations are probably best understood as being devotional or aspirational in nature. According to one observer:

> The users of such modern Sanskrit are on the one hand ideologically committed to Sanskrit, and prone to declaring Sanskrit as their first language for the census-takers, but are in all cases fluent bilinguals, and in a large number of cases are engaged in modern professions like engineering and information technology. For such users/speakers of modern Sanskrit, Sanskrit becomes an important tie to the inherited Indian tradition, without yanking them from their essential modernity. (Deshpande 2011, 226)

The household program encourages putting labels on all the objects in one's household: toothbrush is *dantakūrcaḥ*, glasses are *upanetram* (literally 'toward' + 'eye'). In a kind of ritual fashion, members of the household should practice moving these objects, and naming them, in a deliberate fashion: "I now put the pot down on the table," and so on (Hastings 2008, 30). (One recalls Ben-Yehuda's stilted attempts to first speak Hebrew with his wife: see Chapter 5.) Samskrita Bharati has also published a booklet that contains various phrases that might be used in a day in the life of a (somewhat beleaguered) middle-class Indian family. The preface explains the utility of the book:

> There are quite a few who know a bit of samskrita and would very much desire to speak and converse in this great language. But they lack expression. Right words and right construction of sentences fail them and often they have to indulge in some verbal acrobatics. The answer to this predicament can only be to have on hand sets of suitable readymade sentences. That would at one stroke give confidence and knowledge to match one's expressions with one's ideas and emotions.... The sentences presented here have been selected on the criterion of their utility and applicability in day-to-day life. (*Samskrita-vyavahara-sahasri* 2000, III)

Topics covered include:

Meeting Friends
Students
Examination
Film
Women
Office
Health
Telephone
Commerce
Weather
Dissatisfaction
Greetings

The student can learn to say things like:

- Hello! How are you?
- Where do you work?
- I was merely joking, friend.
- When will this bus leave?
- The examination has been postponed.

- Next month we will buy a washing machine.
- Where did you buy this saree?
- How is your health?
- Sorry, wrong number.
- We have to pay money for the milk.
- Please lower the volume of the T.V.
- Will you switch on the fan?
- You are lying.
- Too many mosquitoes.
- Who listens to me here?

The back of the phrasebook contains a section called "Samskrit: A Spoken Language." There we read that the purpose of Samskrita Bharati is to take the language "from the manuscripts to the masses." It exhorts readers to "SPEAK SAMSKRIT!" This is achievable in just ten days. Courses are fun and immersive, involving "songs, stories, word games, oral drills and situational conversations." In this way, "People from different religions and communities, young and old" can learn to speak Samskrit (Sanskrit) with confidence. This includes "doctors, lawyers, engineers, chartered accountants and management consultants." Sanskrit can be a vehicle for national unity (Hastings 2008, 25). But one scholar suggests that this is not another Hebrew revival in the making:

> While small committed groups have successfully kept spoken Sanskrit alive over the centuries, and are keeping it alive today, given the sociopolitical situation in India, making Sanskrit into a truly national language like Hebrew in Israel is nothing more than a dream of a very small number of lovers of Sanskrit. (Deshpande 2011, 228)

For its part the Indian government gives occasional support to Sanskrit projects, depending on the leadership. In the fall of 2015, the Central Board of Secondary Education asked all schools to observe a non-mandatory Sanskrit Week, the purpose of which was "revitalizing the use of simple Sanskrit in the youth." The administrative directive argued that "it is important to familiarise oneself with Sanskrit if one has to understand the growth of Indian civilisation and culture." Possible activities include *kavita rachna* (poetry writing), *Sanskrit Shloka Antyakshari* (competition of Sanskrit verse recitation), *Yuva Sansad* (youth parliament) on Indian languages, and the screening of Sanskrit films. The proposal met with opposition, especially in Tamil-speaking areas. Some objected to the imposition of a language associated with Brahmins, the top caste, arguing that the week should focus instead on the region's own sanctified language, Classical Tamil. This is part of a long-running ideological debate in Indian society (*The Hindu*, August 26, 2015).

My Sweet Lord

Globalization entails the accelerating diffusion and collision of ideas, images, languages, musical styles, and much else, across both geographical space and cyberspace. It is a time of mobility – and unpredictability. The borders between the religious and the technological, the sacred and the profane, the mystical and the commercial, seem to get scrambled. For instance, the Welsh composer Sir Karl Jenkins is said to write "sacred music for secular people" (Jenkins 2015, 107). His *Dies Irae* ("The Day of Wrath") pairs a canonical Latin text with a pounding drum rhythm. It was used as the soundtrack for a deodorant commercial that has been viewed some sixty million times on YouTube (though the footage of dozens of bikini-clad women romping through the forest may account for some of its popularity).

In this postmodern/Californian period of history, the traditional boundaries of religion seem to break down, giving way to new forms of experimentation. Perhaps more than the other languages, Sanskrit has been called upon as a precious linguistic resource in diverse artistic projects. We will discuss three interlinked examples: George Harrison, Philip Glass, and John Tavener. All three exemplified various forms of border-crossing throughout their lives and careers, exploring different musical traditions, converting to new religions, hovering in the zone between music, religion, and language. Harrison and Glass both collaborated with famed sitar master and world music superstar Ravi Shankar. Tavener and Harrison overlapped in the 1960s. The Beatles Apple Record label put out two of Tavener's records: *The Whale* (which Ringo Starr actually played on) and *Celtic Requiem*.

George Harrison, the guitarist for the Beatles, met Ravi Shankar in 1965, inaugurating a lifelong engagement with Indian musical and spiritual practices. He traveled to India and took up the sitar, which he played (poorly) on the song "Norwegian Wood," igniting the so-called Sitar Explosion of the 1960s. Harrison would eventually become quite involved in various Hindu-based movements: first Transcendental Meditation (TM), then the International Society for Krishna Consciousness (ISKCON), popularly known as the Hare Krishnas. Harrison's attraction to the sonic dimension of Hinduism came through in a number of songs he wrote for the Beatles, perhaps most evidently in "Within You Without You," the longest track on the epochal *Sergeant Pepper's Lonely Hearts Club Band* album.

In 1969 Harrison recorded chants with devotees from the Radha Krishna Temple in London, predicting that it would be "the first Sanskrit song in the top ten" (Greene 2006, 143). The "Hare Krishna Mantra" sold 70,000 records on the first day of its release and quickly rose to number one on the pop chart. It was a hit in Germany, France, Sweden, Yugoslavia, and Australia, and elsewhere around the world – in a way, a remarkable expression of Sanskrit's continuing vehicularity. In 1970 Harrison helped record the Govinda prayer with members of the London Philharmonic Orchestra and assorted other musicians. The recording was often played in Hare Krishna temples.

After the dissolution of the Beatles, Harrison released *All Things Must Pass*, a three-record set of songs he had been caching away during his time with the Beatles. Widely hailed as a masterpiece, the album is infused with Hindu themes, including human suffering, the illusory nature of reality, and the longing for release and union with God. "My Sweet Lord" was the international megahit on the album. It was supposed to be "a Western pop equivalent of a mantra, which repeats over and over again the holy names." The ending folds in a Sanskrit prayer:

gurur brahma, gurur Vishnu, gurur deva maheshwara
gurur sakshat, parabrahma, tasmai shri gurave namah

[I offer homage to my guru who is as great as the creator Brahma, the maintainer Vishnu, the destroyer Shiva, and who is the very energy of God.]

Harrison's purpose was ecumenical: "I wanted to show that 'Hallelujah' and 'Hare Krishna' are quite the same thing" (quoted in Greene 2006, 181). The song became a megahit, selling thirty thousand copies a day. It was played so often on the radio that John Lennon, who was famously skeptical about religion, quipped: "Every time I put the radio on, it's 'Oh, My Lord,' I'm beginning to think there *must* be a God" (quoted in Greene 2006, 183). Harrison would later collaborate with Shankar on an album called *Chants of India*. The lyrics were entirely in Sanskrit, and the original album cover has the word *Chants* in faux Devanagari. All of these projects by Harrison and his collaborators seem to be borderline phenomena, somewhere between art and faith, spirituality and commerce.

The American composer Philip Glass also worked with Shankar. He, too, would journey to India and incorporate Hindu (and Buddhist) ideas, though not instruments, into some of his works. One of the most important pieces in Glass's early career was the opera *Satyagraha*, based on the life of Mahatma Gandhi, with a libretto entirely in Sanskrit. The story focuses on the formative period when Gandhi was living in South Africa. It includes three non-speaking parts for Leo Tolstoy, Rabindranath Tagore, and Martin Luther King, Jr., who are meant to represent the past, present, and future of Gandhi and his notion of *satyagraha*, a Sanskrit term meaning "truth force." The libretto, prepared by Constance DeJong, consists exclusively of passages culled from the Bhagavad Gita. Glass decided that the sacred text should be kept in Sanskrit. He gave several different reasons for this bold artistic decision. In *Music by Philip Glass*, he wrote:

> I like the idea of *further* separating the vocal text from the action. In this way, without an understandable text to contend with, the listener could let the words go altogether. The weight of 'meaning' would then be thrown onto the music, the designs, and the stage action. (Glass 1987, 101)

In an interview Glass explained: "I felt to hear the words sung [in translation] de-mystified the experience" (quoted in Hutcheon and Hutcheon 2011, 722). Second, with performances envisioned for Holland (where the opera had its international premiere), Germany, and the United States (where it opened at Artpark in Lewiston, New York, before moving to Brooklyn), "Sanskrit could serve as a kind of international language for the opera" – an interesting twist on Sanskrit's historic value as a lingua franca. At the same time, as Glass noted, it is customary for operas to be presented in their original language – Italian, German, French, Russian, etc. – so, in a sense, the use of Sanskrit is not all that radical. In any event, Glass insisted that a translation of the text be included in the program notes wherever the opera is performed.

A third reason for Glass was Sanskrit's aesthetic scale of value: "One of the most irresistible reasons to me for using Sanskrit was the sound of the language itself. I knew … how beautiful a vocal language it really is.

Neither Dutch nor German nor English could compare to it" (Glass 1987, 101–103). A special phonetic transliteration was devised for the singers, for example:

> ENGLISH:
> Hold pleasure and pain, profit and loss,
> victory and defeat to be the same: then
> brace yourself for the fight. So will you
> bring no evil on yourself.
>
> TRANSLITERATION:
> sukha-duḥke same kṛtvā
> lābh'ālābhau jay'ājayau,
> tato yuddhāya yujyasava:
> n'airvaṁ pāpam avāpsyasi
>
> PHONETIC:
> sŭ-khu dŭ-khā su-mā krit-va
> la-bha-la-bhau jī-a-jī-yau
> tu-to yŭ-dha-yu yŭ-jyus-vu:
> nā-vum pa-pum u-vap-syu-se.
>
> (DeJong and Glass 1983, 40)

What, then, is the nature of *Satyagraha*: Opera? Myth? Ritual? It seems to fall somewhere in between these categories.

The linguistic repertoire or toolkit of an individual reflects the routes taken – and not taken – in their life (Blommaert and Backus 2011, 22). To understand the place of Sanskrit in the works of composer Sir John Tavener (1944– 2013), it is necessary to know something of his personal life trajectory. Tavener grew up as a Presbyterian, was drawn to Catholicism, converted to Orthodoxy, and seems to have ended up as a Christian universalist – committed to the Orthodox faith but open to other traditions like Hinduism and Islam. In terms of his artistic vision, Tavener began his career as a kind of *enfant terrible* in British classical music circles. After his conversion to Orthodoxy, he became a strident critic of Western art music and composed in an almost ecclesiastical vein. He was often lumped together with the Estonian composer Arvo Pärt and the Polish Henryk Górecki as exponents of a musical style sometimes known as holy minimalism – a label he dismissed as "a facetious journalistic caption" (1999, 102). Tavener passed away as a knighted long-haired pilgrim-composer.

Tavener came to feel that the Western musical tradition had led to a spiritual dead-end. Classical music, with its concert halls and orchestras and artificial musical forms (sonata, fugue, etc.), was fatally cut off from the nourishing roots of authentic religious tradition. The whole thing led nowhere. He condemned much of twentieth-century classical music as alienating and an "over-sophisticated contrivance" (Tavener 1999, 99). Tavener's own religious and artistic motto could have been *ad fontes* ("to the sources"). He once proclaimed that concert halls should be blown up and music brought back to sacred precincts (*there*) where it belongs. This meant returning to sacred texts, to chant, to the Word:

> if it can't be sung, then it ceases to be music. It certainly ceases to be sacred music. Sacred music must be able to be in some way sung, because from a Christian point of view the Word must be heard. It is at the service of the Word, as in all great traditions. (Tavener 1999, 47)

Returning to the soul-nourishing Word meant returning to sacred languages. Tavener's compositions were almost invariably vocal in nature, incorporating an array of modern and classical languages: Latin, Greek, Arabic, Sanskrit, and Aramaic, in addition to Italian, German, and English.

In his later years, Tavener adopted a universalist outlook, believing that, beneath the divergent exteriors of the major world religions, there was a single glowing divine core. He would certainly have agreed with George Harrison that "Hallelujah" and "Hare Krishna" were ultimately one. In several compositions Tavener expressed this religious ideology through the combination of sacred languages drawn from East and West. We saw that in *The Veil of the Temple*, which he considered his greatest work.

One of Tavener's last compositions is called *Gnosis*, a term that means something like spiritual knowledge or transformative insight. The work contains "little bits in Arabic, little bits in Sanskrit, little bits in Latin and little bits in Greek." The words are as follows:

Sat	Being
Chit	Consciousness
ānanda	Bliss
Jesu	Jesus
Lā illāha illā llāh	There is no god but God

The first three terms are Sanskrit, *Jesu* is Latin, and the final phrase is Arabic. It is not "a poem, as such, but a series of mystical utterances that

I felt were best expressed in music" (quoted in Palmer 2015, 436). It is critical to this piece, as for the other ones discussed in this section, that the original sacred languages (on the left) are used, and not simply the English translation (on the right). Even in a secular context (*Gnosis* was first performed at the BBC Proms), it is as if the sacred words have a kind of magical or numinous potency, not unlike the examples of Pali and Hebrew discussed earlier in the book.

Because we can assume that the audiences for high-profile postmodern composers like Tavener, Glass, and Jenkins do *not* understand Latin, let alone Sanskrit or Aramaic, textual aids are required. These include concert programs, magazine interviews, phonetic cheat-sheets for the singers, CD liner notes, opera house supertitles, and composer and fan websites. On one level, these are not that different from liturgical supports like the Coptic Reader computer application or the bilingual Hebrew–English *Mishkan T'filah* prayerbook. Whether in the church or the concert hall, sacred languages typically require assistance from local vernaculars.

(Almost) Anything Goes

During the postmodern or "Californian" period of history – a confusing time of globalization, secularization, commercialism, and neotraditionalism – sacred languages are pushed and pulled in different directions. They are valuable symbolic resources used for creating, as well as collapsing, borders. Neotraditionalists call on these ancient revered languages to enhance the borderlines separating their community from everyone else. At the same time, artists turn to sanctified languages to help them test, or even erase, traditional boundaries. In both cases it is often just the *idea* of the language that is paramount, as opposed to any actual contents. The case of Sanskrit exemplifies these conflicting impulses.

In the face of challenges, real or imagined, emanating from the West, some Hindu neotraditionalists look back in history to a supposed golden age when Sanskrit was widely admired, taught, and even spoken by ordinary people throughout India. Promoting conversational Sanskrit is the way to return the nation to its former glory, to become what it is supposed to be. In taking this approach, the profile of Sanskrit is altered from an elite sacerdotal language to an instrument of political unification (Hastings 2003, 512).

The nationalist rhetoric of these Sanskrit devotees is usually overlooked by those in the West for whom the language is a symbol of tolerant interfaith enrichment. From ordinary practitioners of yoga to concert composers like John Tavener, Sanskrit is not at all associated with "institutional violence and the preservation of hierarchy" (Sawhney 2009, 5). For them Sanskrit seems to epitomize religious universalism – the idea that behind the external trappings of the different world religions is a reassuring oneness. In a way, this point of view hearkens back to the heyday of the "Sanskrit cosmopolis," when Sanskrit spread throughout South and Southeast Asia, serving as a cross-cultural vehicle of learning and literature.

It is no surprise that the arts often test religious orthodoxies. Beckham's tattoos, the Contemporary Museum of Calligraphy in Moscow, and Tavener's *The Veil of the Temple* are very different phenomena, but what they have in common is the fact that they combine sacred languages that are normally kept separate by traditional religious borderlines: Church Slavonic and Sanskrit, Hebrew and Latin and Chinese. *The Armed Man*, Karl Jenkins's phenomenally popular piece (discussed in Chapter 5), starts with the text of the Catholic Latin Mass but incorporates the Muslim call to prayer in Classical Arabic as well as verses from the Hindu epic *Mahabharata* in English. These artistic projects mix and match sacred languages in novel ways, creating alternative spaces, sounds, and rituals. Do they augur the rise of a global religious consciousness, a spiritual globality? It is too early to tell.

For now, consider the following scene: Not far from the Contemporary Museum of Calligraphy, a group of Hare Krishna devotees snakes its way down Sokolniki Street. Some passers-by seem amused, others annoyed. Some ignore the spectacle and walk on by, others stop and take photos or videos, while a few even join in. We know that the oral dimension is really primary when it comes to Sanskrit, and the exuberant chanting of these devotees reflects that priority. Moreover, in the course of its history, Sanskrit has been written in a number of different scripts. These devotees carry banners with the *mahamantra* transliterated into Cyrillic – a notable crossing from one scriptworld into another. (See Figure 8.1.).

The world seems to be getting smaller. Things are becoming more interconnected. Religion in some ways is merging with consumerism and pop culture. After George Harrison's efforts, the chanting of this classic Sanskrit mantra became a global phenomenon. "Sometimes in earnest, sometimes in jest, the chanting of 'Hare Krishna' spread around the world" (Greene 2006, 147).

Figure 8.1 Members of the International Society for Krishna Consciousness (ISKCON) chanting with banners of the "Hare Krishna" mantra, Moscow.

The look of the devotees, their dancing, and their chanting seem out of place on this particular street, literally in the shadow of the Temple of the Resurrection of Christ. This rather unusual pre-revolutionary church was built in the Russian-modern style. Painted light green with multiple black onion domes topped by gold crosses, it stands out against the nearby high-rise buildings. Over the entrance there is a painting of Christ with a caption in ornate Church Slavonic lettering that reads, "I am the Light. Believe in the Light that you may become Sons of Light." Inside the walls are appliquéd with more Slavonic inscriptions. It is hard to imagine the sounds of Sanskrit ever emanating from *this* temple.

References

Aklujkar, Ashok. 1996. "The Early History of Sanskrit as Supreme Language." In *Ideology and Status of Sanskrit: Contributions to the History of the Sanskrit Language*, edited by Jan E. M. Houben, 59–85. Leiden and New York: E. J. Brill.

Bhate, Saroja. 1996. "Position of Sanskrit in Public Education and Scientific Research in Modern India." In *Ideology and Status of Sanskrit: Contributions to the History of the Sanskrit Language*, edited by Jan E. M. Houben, 383–400. Leiden and New York: E. J. Brill.

Bhatia, Tej K., and William C. Ritchie. 2013. "Bilingualism and Multilingualism in South Asia." In *The Handbook of Bilingualism and Multilingualism*, edited by Tej K. Bhatia and William C. Ritchie, 843–869. Second edition. Oxford: Wiley Blackwell.

Blommaert, Jan, and Ad Backus. 2011. "Repertoires Revisited: 'Knowing Language' in Superdiversity." *Working Papers in Urban Language and Literacies* 67: 2–26.

Chew, Phyllis Ghim-Lian. 2009. *Emergent Lingua Francas and World Orders: The Politics and Place of English as a World Language.* New York: Routledge.

Contemporary Museum of Calligraphy. 2016. Accessed May 30, 2016. http://www.calligraphy-museum.com/en

DeJong, Constance, and Philip Glass. 1983. *Satyagraha. M. K. Gandhi in South Africa 1893–1914: The Historical Material and Libretto comprising the Opera's Book.* New York: Tanam Press.

Deshpande, Madhav M. 1996. "Contextualizing the Eternal Language: Features of Priestly Sanskrit." In *Ideology and Status of Sanskrit: Contributions to the History of the Sanskrit Language*, edited by Jan E. M. Houben, 401–436. Leiden and New York: E. J. Brill.

Deshpande, Madhav V. 2011. "Efforts to Vernacularize Sanskrit: Degree of Success and Failure." In *Handbook of Language and Ethnic Identity.* Vol. 2: *The Success–Failure Continuum in Language and Ethnic Identity Efforts*, edited by Joshua A. Fishman and Ofelia García, 218–229. Oxford: Oxford University Press.

Gellner, Ernest. 1995. "Fundamentalism as a Comprehensive System: Soviet Marxism and Islamic Fundamentalism Compared." In *Fundamentalisms Comprehended*, edited by Martin E. Marty and R. Scott Appleby, 277–287. Chicago: University of Chicago Press.

Ghuman, Nalini. 2014. *Resonances of the Raj: India in the English Musical Imagination, 1897–1947.* New York: Oxford University Press.

Glass, Philip, and Robert T. Jones. 1987. *Music by Philip Glass.* New York: Harper & Row.

Greene, Joshua A. 2006. *Here Comes the Sun: The Spiritual and Musical Journey of George Harrison.* Hoboken, NJ: John Wiley & Sons.

Hastings, Adi. 2003. "Simplifying Sanskrit." *Pragmatics* 13 (4): 499–513.

Hastings, Adi. 2008. "Licked by the Mother Tongue: Imagining Everyday Sanskrit at Home and in the World." *Journal of Linguistic Anthropology* 18 (1): 24–45. DOI:10.1111/j.1548-1395.2008.00002.x

Hock, Hans Henrich. 1992. "A Note on English and Modern Sanskrit." *World Englishes* 11 (2/3): 163–171. DOI: 10.1111/j.1467-971X.1992.tb00061.x

Hutcheon, Linda, and Hutcheon, Michael. 2011. "Philip Glass's *Satyagraha*: Para-Colonial Para-Opera." *University of Toronto Quarterly* 80 (3): 718–730. DOI: 10.3138/utq.80.3.718

Jenkins, Karl, with Sam Jackson. 2015. *Still with the Music: My Autobiography*. London: Elliott and Thompson.

Malhotra, Rajiv. 2016. *The Battle for Sanskrit: Is Sanskrit Political or Sacred, Oppressive or Liberating, Dead or Alive?* New Delhi: HarperCollins.

Nussbaum, Martha Craven. 2007. *The Clash Within: Democracy, Religious Violence, and India's Future*. Cambridge, MA: Belknap Press of Harvard University Press.

Palmer, Andrew. 2015. *Encounters with British Composers*. Woodbridge, UK, and Rochester, NY: Boydell Press.

Paranjape, Makarand R. 2009. *Altered Destinations: Self, Society, and Nation in India*. New Delhi: Anthem Press.

Patton, Laurie L. 2007. "The Cat in the Courtyard: The Performance of Sanskrit and the Religious Experience of Women." In *Women's Lives, Women's Rituals in the Hindu Tradition*, edited by Tracy Pintchman, 19–34. Oxford and New York: Oxford University Press.

Poggi, Colette. 2012. *Le Sanskrit, souffle et lumière: Voyage au coeur de la langue sacrée de l'Inde*. Paris: Almora.

Pollock, Sheldon. 2006. *The Language of the Gods in the World of Men: Sanskrit, Culture, and Power in Premodern India*. Berkeley: University of California Press.

Ramaswamy, Sumathi. 1999. "Sanskrit for the Nation." *Modern Asian Studies* 33 (2): 339–381. DOI: 10.1017/S0026749X99003273

Sampad and Vijay. 2002. *The Wonder that is Sanskrit*. Pondicherry (India): Sri Aurobindo Society, in association with Ahmedabad: Mapin Publishing.

Samskrita Bharati. 2013. Accessed August 1, 2016. https://www.youtube.com/user/samskritasocial/about

Samskrita-vyavahara-sahasri: A Collection of One Thousand Sentences. 2000. Delhi: Saṃskṛtabhāratī.

Sawhney, Simona. 2009. *The Modernity of Sanskrit*. Minneapolis: University of Minnesota Press.

Sharot, Stephen. 2011. *Comparative Perspectives on Judaisms and Jewish Identities*. Detroit: Wayne State University Press.

Smith, Jonathan Z. 1987. *To Take Place: Toward Theory in Ritual*. Chicago and London: University of Chicago Press.

Sneddon, James. 2003. *The Indonesian Language: Its History and Role in Modern Society*. Sydney: University of New South Wales.

Tavener, John. 1999. *The Music of Silence: A Composer's Testament*. Edited by Brian Keeble. London and New York: Faber and Faber.

Tavener, John. 2002. "The Veil of the Temple (All Night Vigil)." Programme Note. Accessed August 1, 2016. http://www.musicsalesclassical.com/composer/work/1567/14207

Tripathi, Radha. 1995. "Contemporary Sanskrit Writing." *Indian Horizons* 44 (4): 180–186.
Turner, Bryan S. 2011. *Religion and Modern Society. Citizenship, Secularisation and the State*. Cambridge and New York: Cambridge University Press.
The Veil of the Temple. 2004. Compact disc, liner notes. Sony BMG Music Entertainment.
Wilke, Annette, and Oliver Moebus. 2011. *Sound and Communication: An Aesthetic Cultural History of Sanskrit Hinduism*. Berlin and New York: De Gruyter.

Further Reading

Altglas, Véronique. 2014. *From Yoga to Kabbalah: Religious Exoticism and the Logics of Bricolage*. Oxford and New York: Oxford University Press. A theoretically sophisticated analysis of some religious trends in the era of globalization, including the place of Sanskrit and Hebrew.
Arnold, Jonathan. 2014. *Sacred Music in Secular Society*. Farnham: Ashgate. A thoughtful discussion concerning the interconnections between sacred and secular music, including the work of Tavener.
Houben, Jan E. M., ed. 1996. *Ideology and Status of Sanskrit: Contributions to the History of the Sanskrit Language*. Leiden and New York: E. J. Brill. An authoritative collection of essays covering a range of topics and time periods.
Poggi, Colette. 2012. *Le Sanskrit, souffle et lumière: Voyage au coeur de la langue sacrée de l'Inde*. Paris: Almora. An attractive, richly illustrated treatment emphasizing the mythology, symbolism, and iconography of Sanskrit.

Chapter 9

Conclusion

In the preceding chapters we have attempted to present a broad conspectual account of some of the world's main sacred languages: their types and sub-types; their historical origins and vicissitudes; their affiliated social groups and ideological debates; their books, discourses, rituals, venues, teaching methods, and artistic applications. By now it should be clear that, for the religious adherents who maintain them, these supposedly dead languages have a continuing relevance. Some devotees, for example, believe that the "extraordinarily logical nature of Sanskrit … leads to a strong similarity between it and modern programming languages" (Chandra 2014, 98). Whatever we make of such claims, sanctified languages such as Hebrew, Latin, Pali, and Classical Arabic may be usefully imagined as "codes" that help run some of the world's oldest and largest religions – special symbol systems for storing theological information and executing ritual actions. Let us play with this notion as a way of recapitulating some of the topics discussed in this book and bringing it to a close.

Codices

The word *code* comes from *codex* (plural *codices*), meaning a book or manuscript. Sacred languages are closely bound up with authoritative books – the Bhagavad Gita, Qur'an, Avesta, Tipitika, Zohar, *Missale Romanum*. They are fixed, bookish languages, passed on not *in vivo*, in the hubbub of family life, but *in vitro*, by means of schools and clerical organizations. Since they are not mother tongues, sacred languages have something of an artificial quality to them. Sanskrit, as noted above, has been compared to computer programming languages. Others have likened it to a linguistic Lego© kit, with precise interconnecting parts that can be composed and decomposed in endless variation (Poggi 2012, 27). Sanskrit may be at the extreme end of the spectrum, yet the artificial, Esperanto-like nature of Pali and Church Slavonic has also been noted.

Code-Switching

No matter how exalted, sacred languages "remain additional languages for narrow, specific purposes, and they remain such generation after generation, without becoming mother tongues" (Fishman 1991, 360). Consequently, they are necessarily found in bilingual or multilingual situations. Sanctified languages never live on their own, but are always guided and accompanied by spoken vernaculars (which may, as a result, take on some of the sacred language's glory and become "co-sanctified"). In the premodern era, sacred languages subsisted in a linguistic division of labor sociolinguists call diglossia. Just as wine and water have their respective qualities and purposes, sacred languages were positioned as H(igh) varieties over against sundry L(ow) varieties. Everyday languages like Yiddish and Ladino were subordinate to the "holy tongue" of Hebrew. Latin was set over against the national vernaculars of Europe – French, Irish, Hungarian, and so on. Ge'ez was atop Amharic. However, the forces of modernity, including democracy, secularism, and mass literacy, overturned this arrangement in many places, gradually restricting sacred languages to the liturgical sphere, though in some cases giving way there as well. The closest we can get to diglossia today is in certain parts of the Islamic world. There, we can readily observe what sociolinguists call code-switching, as when a mosque sermon will alternate between quotations from the Qur'an, which are in formal Classical Arabic (H), and user-friendly explanations couched in the colloquial Egyptian Arabic (L) (Bassiouney 2013). As discussed in Chapter 3, the pope's alternation between the fixed Angelus prayer in Latin and his more informal remarks in Italian (including wishing the crowd a good lunch) represents a vestigial form of diglossia. A kind of code-switching is also evident when ordinary believers draw upon their linguistic repertoire and interject snippets of their sacred language into everyday conversation in the form of greetings, benedictions, pious exclamations, or scriptural quotations.

Codifications

A code can be a systematic collection of laws or principles. Some religious communities use sacred languages to store information in the form of scriptures, historical chronicles, and legal compendia (e.g., the Latin-language *Codex Iuris Canonici*). The world's historic sanctified languages continue to provide much of the technical vocabulary for explaining the mysteries of divinity and the meaning of life.

> We say words over our misfortunes to alleviate our pain, explain illness by speaking of karma or divine punishment, make schemas for the origin of the world and for the causes of things, and write tomes to build elaborate explanatory universes. (Paden 2016, 132)

Even in vernacular sermons, Pali terms are vital for explaining the Buddhist Dharma. Latin quotations from Augustine and Aquinas still figure in the latest efforts in Catholic theology.

Secret Codes

A code can also be something secret or esoteric. We see this facet of sacred languages especially in the area of alphabet mysticism. This is a religious discourse in which letters are vested with a mystical meaning and power based on their sound, shape, numerical value, or place in alphabetical order. The more a language is considered revelatory, the more likely we will find evidence of alphabetic speculation. Not surprisingly, then, the boldest versions are found with Hebrew and Arabic. We see a more moderate form in connection with Church Slavonic, the letters of which are sometimes said to possess divine significance and to safeguard authentic Christian wisdom, while this mode of thinking is largely absent from the Latin tradition.

Codes of Conduct

Codes are not just informational in nature; they can be behavioral as well ("ethical code"). A religion is a system of behaviors and practices that seek to tap into unseen superhuman power for the purpose of overcoming human limitations, either in the short or long term. There are liturgical practices, like the Latin Mass or Coptic Divine Liturgy, which are multimodal affairs celebrating themes of salvation history and typically performed by clergies on certain days in consecrated places. Thaumaturgical practices, such as *paritta* chanting in Theravada Buddhism or scanning a Zohar chart sold by the Kabbalah Centre, are supposed to bring about immediate real-world boons. Yoga (with its Sanskrit terms and mantras) and other somatological disciplines are meant to lead to physical wellbeing and spiritual enlightenment. Artists working on the edges of religious systems, such as George Harrison, Karl Jenkins, John Tavener, and Marc Chagall, regularly drew on sacred languages for their creative projects.

Decoding

The study of scriptures written in sacred languages like Classical Arabic, Ge'ez, or Hebrew is sometimes a matter of decoding, that is, deciphering the script and sounding out the words in a proper and felicitous manner, without necessarily grasping the contents. In some cases, devotees may memorize and recite huge portions of their scriptures, even though they may not be able to understand what is being memorized or recited. This is not just an occurrence with ordinary believers, but applies in some cases to Theravada Buddhist monks, Hindu priests, and other clerics.

Insider Codes

Sacred languages are markers and makers of communal identity. They may function as visual or verbal codes that separate insiders from outsiders. The Coptic alphabet provides a distinctive logo for the Coptic Orthodox Church. Real or faux Devanagari signals a Hindu or Indian affiliation. The Arabic alphabet is a proud visual symbol for Muslims all around the world – a fact that jihadists, who claim to represent the faith, capitalize on when designing their flags, websites, and regalia. The square Hebrew script is an icon of Jewishness – a fact that is manipulated in provocative ways on kitschy bumper stickers and product labels. The code may also be verbal, as with the Slavonicized jargon of Orthodox churchgoers in Russia or the "Simple Sanskrit" advocated by those seeking to recapture a golden age in India.

Legacy Codes?

A priestly language such as Sanskrit, Latin, Church Slavonic, or Avestan reinforces social hierarchy and may lead to resentment among ordinary religionists. There may be efforts to knock the unintelligible sacred language off its pedestal, so to speak, and promote a community language like Gujarati or Russian in its stead. Well aware of such concerns, the bishops at the Second Vatican Council attempted to chart a *via media* (middle way), making room for mother tongues alongside Latin in the Mass – but once the door was opened to vernaculars *de jure*, the elite priestly code ended up being quickly dispatched *de facto*. In other traditions there have been ameliorative approaches aimed at reducing the intelligibility gap, including projection screens in the sanctuary, bilingual prayerbooks, proposals for stylistic simplification, and so on. Are these viable solutions? Or are sacred languages the equivalent of legacy codes, obsolete pieces of software that have come to hinder the functioning of contemporary religious systems?

As was discussed in Chapter 2, the sociologist Bryan Turner suggests that we are transitioning from an age of revelation to age of information:

> There is always a tension between religious messages that are received by prophets and holy people as revelations and the process by which these messages are converted into texts. Over time these divine messages tend to get encoded into languages that we now regard as dead and hence the whole panoply of interpreters (saints, prophets and priests) became the intermediaries who make the ineffable effable. Literacy becomes a key issue in matters of religious authority. Historically, a literate religious elite has confronted an illiterate laity.... In a democratic environment, the very idea that some truths are ineffable contradicts the ethos of modern society in which everybody claims a right to understand.... The elite's control of ineffable knowledge is compromised and the whole idea of hierarchically organised wisdom evaporates. (2011, 194–195)

Will Sanskrit become the equivalent of Sumerian and Latin like the museum-bound Etruscan? Sacred languages are not all the same. We might hypothesize that languages of primary revelation, including Hebrew and Classical Arabic (and, in its own way, Pali), will be the most likely to survive this transition into the information age. That is because these holy tongues are said to exist in a monocoque relationship with revelation – the linguistic form and the contents are one entity and cannot be easily separated. To be sure, Hebrew has been reduced in the liturgical life of certain Jewish denominations, but it is impossible to imagine it being ousted from the religion altogether. On the other hand, languages of secondary revelation ("holiness one time removed") may have a harder time surviving the information-age upheaval. Latin has already been overthrown within Catholicism, though it continues to be used as the Vatican's linguistic gold standard and there are indicators of a minor comeback elsewhere. The status of Church Slavonic has been debated for the past century. Its place in Russia may seem secure right now, but it has slipped in Bulgaria and Serbia. For its part, Ge'ez has lost ground to the vernacular Amharic. In these cases – notably, all within Christianity – the sanctified language and the contents of revelation are more easily disconnected. Yet, is it possible that the tools of the information age could actually be bent to the service of revelation?

On several occasions we have observed how new technologies are used to maintain and teach sanctified languages. Projection screens, like the supertitles commonly seen in opera houses, are now used in some worship spaces for practitioners to better follow the ritual. Online videos show priests how to chant Coptic hymns or perform the Tridentine Latin Mass. Thick prayerbooks are now accessible in a pocket-sized device. (See Figure 9.1.) Even the most recent Church Slavonic controversy unfolded largely online. By way of conclusion, let us consider one final example.

Unicode

Computer and communication technologies, especially the Internet, are key drivers and symbols of the current phase of globalization. They increase the intensity, ubiquity, and velocity with which words flow and coagulate, gather and disperse, around the world. They have transformed the linguasphere. Unicode is an essential part of the Internet's technological infrastructure. The "perceived normalcy of the fact that people across the world can write and communicate in their languages in different scripts via the Internet" is due in large part to Unicode (Kamusella 2012, 63).

Unicode is a system for encoding text. It grew out of an early 1990s project hatched by a group of employees from Xerox, Apple, and several other high-tech companies concerned with internationalization. It is now under the purview of the Unicode Consortium, a nonprofit organization located in Silicon Valley (California). Members include corporations such

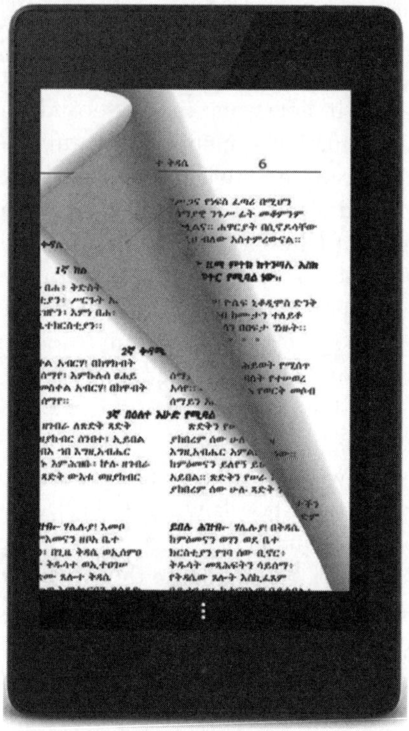

Figure 9.1 Ge'ez-Amharic Orthodox Liturgy smartphone application. Reproduced wih kind permission of Ethiopianapps.

as Google, Adobe, Microsoft, and Oracle, as well as institutions like the Sultanate of Oman and the Government of India. Unicode has become the industry standard and an integral part of the "plumbing" of the Internet, being an integral part of programming languages like HTML, XML, Python, Java, and C+. Seventy percent of the Web's 10,000 most visited sites use Unicode (John 2013).

The goal of the Unicode project is to supersede the various conflicting ways of encoding characters (alphabets, scripts, writing systems) with a single, consistent, universal template. Basically, what Unicode produces and oversees is the Universal Character Set (UCS), a vast table into which are slotted individual letters, ideographs, symbols, punctuation marks, and geometric shapes. Version 9.0 has 128,172 characters and includes everything from ancient *kanji* to contemporary *emoji*.

The Unicode project is complicated and, not surprisingly, controversial. It is complicated because of the number and complexity of the world's writing systems. Take Arabic, for example. Most of the letters assume a different shape depending on their position in a word – initial, medial, or final. Vowel markings are put on top or below the letters. And, of course, there is also the issue of directionality. Arabic is written right to left, whereas the Latin alphabet goes left to right. So, encoding complicated ancient ornate scripts like Arabic or Coptic or Devanagari is not easy from a technological standpoint. Various blogs and websites provide a steady stream of commentary and criticism.

Unicode is also controversial. On the one hand, it seems to squeeze the diversity of the world's writing systems into a singular, standardizing template supported by powerful American corporations. The elaborate mystical speculations about the Hebrew, Arabic, or Slavonic scripts, for instance, are replaced by matter-of-fact designations. The Hebrew letter aleph becomes U+05D0. On the other hand, Unicode is generous in scope and "is designed to meet the needs of diverse user communities within each language, serving business, educational, liturgical and scientific users, and covering the needs of both modern and historical texts" (Unicode Consortium 2016, 14). Rather remarkably, it encompasses all of the scripts discussed in this book. Along with the major players on the world stage (Latin, Arabic, Cyrillic, and Devanagari), it includes Coptic, Avestan, Hebrew, Ge'ez, and Church Slavonic, as well as the various regional scripts, such as Khmer and Thai, used to write Pali.

Unicode is a paradox. It is a system "representing a totality of human languages, *in their difference*, in a single matrix" (Lennon 2010, 172). It is an example of both globalization and globality, a blending and a consciousness of different cultures and traditions around the world. And yet the technology enables different religious communities to preserve and propagate their particular sacred language (e.g., Simmons 2011–2012, "Unicode Slavonic Font Manifesto").

Technologies change rapidly, of course, and it is impossible to predict the shape of things to come. Ear buds (or even implants) may offer practitioners instantaneous vernacular translation of any sacred language. Holographic bilingual texts may be beamed onto any any surface. But even to mention these possibilities is to risk describing a technology that is already outdated, like the pneumatic tubes and quaint devices of older science fiction literature. Futurology seems foolhardy. Nevertheless, we might venture this point: being fixed, highly codified, quasi-artificial languages that already enjoy a kind of virtual existence in books and institutions, sacred languages may in fact be able to survive the transition from the age of revelation to the age of information, sacred space to cyberspace.

For now, they continue to be part of the linguasphere and to occupy important niches in the world's religious and cultural landscape.

References

Bassiouney, Reem. 2013. "The Social Motivation of Code-Switching in Mosque Sermons in Egypt." *International Journal of the Sociology of Language* 220: 49–66.

Chandra, Vikram. 2014. *Geek Sublime: The Beauty of Code, the Code of Beauty.* Minneapolis, MN: Graywolf Press.

Fishman, Joshua A. 1991. *Reversing Language Shift: Theoretical and Empirical Foundations of Assistance to Threatened Languages.* Clevedon and Philadelphia: Multilingual Matters.

John, Nicholas A. 2013. "The Construction of the Multilingual Internet: Unicode, Hebrew, and Globalization." *Journal of Computer-Mediated Communication* 18: 321–338.

Kamusella, Tomasz. 2012. "The Global Regime of Language Recognition." *International Journal for the Sociology of Language* 218: 59–86.

Lennon, Brian. 2010. *In Babel's Shadow: Multilingual Literatures, Monolingual States.* Minneapolis and London: University of Minnesota Press.

Paden, William E. 2016. *New Patterns for Comparative Religion. Passages to an Evolutionary Perspective.* London and New York: Bloomsbury Academic.

Poggi, Colette. 2012. *Le Sanskrit, souffle et lumière: Voyage au coeur de la langue sacrée de l'Inde.* Paris: Almora.

Simmons, Nikita. 2011–2012. "Unicode Slavonic Font Manifesto." Accessed August 20, 2016. http://www.synaxis.info/azbuka/ponomar/manifesto/manifesto.html

Turner, Bryan S. 2011. *Religion and Modern Society: Citizenship, Secularisation and the State.* Cambridge and New York: Cambridge University Press.

Unicode Consortium. 2016. *The Unicode Standard, Version 9.0 – Core Specification.* Mountain View, CA: Unicode Consortium. Accessed August 6, 2016. http://www.unicode.org/versions/Unicode9.0.0/UnicodeStandard-9.0.pdf

Index